REV. ADRIAN DE VISSER

Journey of Grace:
Finding Emotional Healing in a Broken World
by Adrian De Visser

Cover design by Martijn van Tilborgh

Published by Kudu Publishing

Print ISBN: 9781938624940
eBook ISBN: 9781938624933

Journey of Grace is also available on Amazon Kindle, Barnes & Noble Nook and Apple iBooks.

Praise for *Journey of Grace*

"This is a deep and personally engaging read, resulting in self-discovery and healing. Life is full of hurt and brokenness, but Rev. De Visser leads us into God's redeeming love. The book is filled with the kind of stories that encourage and inspire the reader to a better future that Christ makes possible for us."

Dr. Joel C. Hunter
Senior Pastor, Northland - A Church Distributed
Orlando, Florida

"This book could be the very thing that helps set you free from the pain of the past and the inner hurt that haunts you. My friend and colleague, Adrian De Visser, shares from his own personal experience in looking at the need for deep inner healing. He blends his own journey of pain with sound studies in psychology and a keen understanding of scripture to present this powerful message that could transform your life. With wisdom and grace, Adrian addresses our greatest pains and struggles and offers a profound way forward through the grace of Christ. His knowledge and experience in Asia and living and working within shame-based cultures gives this work further impact. I urge you to read his story, soak in the scripture and rest in the hope that Jesus has to offer."

Joseph W. Handley, Jr.
President, Asian Access

"So very often we are tempted to minister to people with deep emotional needs with a quick 'God Will Heal You' type of prayer and leave it alone. In this book, Adrian communicates the deep need for extreme care in this type of ministry. His careful explanation and complete scriptural support makes this book extremely valuable to any pastor or minister that finds themselves in a position of council. Although a very complex issue, Adrian breaks it down to an understandable need and gives such hope to those locked up in hurt. I highly recommend this to all."

Brian Thomas
Pastor of NorthStar Christian Center
Columbia, South Carolina

"The 10 steps of recovery that Rev. De Visser teaches in his book will bring hope and courage to all who seek emotional healing. This book is filled with wisdom from his many years of counseling. His words are biblically sound, and his directions are true. I encourage both professionals and laymen to add this resource to their recovery needs."

Kim Paul Storm, Ph.D.
co-author, Boxes of Secrets: Workbook and Journal

"Rev. Adrian De Visser has spent a lifetime bringing grace to an entire region of the world. While his ministry goes beyond Sri Lanka (and Asia) to the whole world, with *A Journey of Grace* he shares an accumulated wisdom that will help all. By going deep into the reasons for our brokenness that we may know, but often mask, Rev. De Visser shares not only the description of our pain and separation, but also the prescription. In this book you will find the hope you need for understanding and overcoming the emotional struggles that keep you from the assurance of hope in Christ's healing work."

Vernon Rainwater
Pastor, Northland Church
Orlando, Florida

"This is a book that I have known to be in the making over many years, even as it reflects the life lessons and discipleship of my friend and colleague Adrian. The truths, principles and applications you will find in these pages have been fashioned through Adrian's own challenges and experiences, which have only prompted his journey of emotional health and healing that continues even today. Much of this book has been tested and refined through a variety of teaching situations. What I trust you will find through it all is the comfort and grace that Adrian seeks to impart, only because of the comfort he has so abundantly received from the God of all comfort."

Richard Brohier
Associate Pastor, Kardinia Church
Geelong, Australia

Contents

Foreword

THERE HAS BEEN A fresh interest recently, more than ever before in the history of the church, in the issue of emotional pain and of the need for healing from such pain. This brings up the question of whether people hurt more now than they did in earlier generations. I think they do!

Many of the support structures that people had, in unhurried communities where people gave time to their members, are rapidly diminishing from society—even in the supposedly community-oriented Majority World.

With the increase of conveniences and affluence, people have more time to think of their personal problems because their lives no longer entail the struggle for survival that they once did.

The rushed pace of life and increasing individualism in society are leaving people with no time to pay the price of commitment to others. The result is that people are discarding friendships when they become inconvenient, which in turn results in deep hurt to the discarded people.

All through history people received hurt from others, as is amply attested in the Scriptures. But today their chances of recovery by normal means are perhaps less than a generation or two ago. Anyone who works closely with people will soon be confronted by the challenge of ministering adequately to emotionally wounded people.

This book seeks to guide people-helpers with tools to help them minister comprehensively to those who are hurting. It will also help anyone struggling to overcome the effects of hurt in his or her life. It is firmly rooted in scripture and has the benefit of being written by one who has ministered to hurting people over a long period of time. I know it will trigger a process of healing in the lives of many hurting people, either through their reading it or through those who minister to them reading it.

Dr. Ajith Fernando
Teaching Director, Youth for Christ, Sri Lanka

Introduction

WELCOME! BEFORE YOU EMBARK on reading this book, I want you to know the reason I spent so much time writing it. Since I will be encouraging you to be open and honest with yourself as you go through this book and the steps of healing, I thought it would be good to share with you my own story.

I am the youngest in a family of six children. Almost immediately after my birth, my father lost his job and our family was reduced from a middle class lifestyle to that of extreme poverty. It was not uncommon for me to hear my extended family members and friends of my parents comment, “This boy is so unlucky—look what has happened to the family since he was born.”

I grew up blaming myself for the loss and the pain I had caused my family.

Compounding this perception, my father rarely talked with me—I always wondered whether his silence was an expression of rejection. I am not certain if this was true, but I certainly believed this was the case.

While my father intentionally or unintentionally communicated rejection, my mother’s response was totally different. She overprotected me and created within me an unhealthy dependency—a dependency that she nurtured for 17 years. It was only when I was 18 years old that I spent my first night outside the home sleeping on my own.

I still remember that experience. It was the strangest night—I was completely lost.

The combination of rejection and overprotection had destroyed my confidence, making my school life a nightmare. I was slow to learn (after all, my mother was not there to tell me what to do). Often, I was at the receiving end of ridicule from both my friends and teachers, and I was regularly in trouble.

The unaffirming Asian culture in which I grew up did not help me either. Every word of criticism and ridicule deeply registered in my brain. Even as I write this, I have to battle my emotions. I was a lonely, hurting, unsuccessful youth, and the future looked bleak.

It was in this environment that I had an encounter with the Lord. This encounter made such a difference, it was as if I had lived all my life up to that point in darkness, and someone suddenly switched the light on! I was happy, I was optimistic about the future and I embarked on a journey of making Jesus known to others. This initial journey led me to join Youth for Christ on December 1, 1979.

After I joined Youth for Christ and started ministering to others, I recognised that the excitement of conversion and serving Him in a full-time capacity was beginning to fade—I was again battling many issues. Doubts began to creep in about my own salvation and change. I believed that in Christ I was transformed, but my life contradicted all I believed. I lived defeated but spoke of victory in Christ. I was afraid to live on my own because my conscience haunted me. To cover this pain, I plunged into more activity. This would help for a moment, but the reality never changed. I was unhappy and defeated, and interpersonal conflicts raged around me.

As feelings of deep insecurity governed me, the joy of serving my Lord was replaced with guilt and compulsive behaviour. Fearing further rejection, I didn't make my struggle known to my friends or my leaders.

Unknown to me or anyone else, God was taking my own pain and was moulding me to be a better person. The reality of this dawned on me when I started reading the book *Healing for Damaged Emotions* by Dr. David Seamands. This book opened to me a new understanding of myself and how to deal with issues that surrounded me.

Having received help and being privileged to help many others deal with their own pain, I felt it was time to write my experience so that others who have suffered like me will benefit. This book is not a story about instant success, but a story of battling with issues and gaining victory by His grace. Please read this book with an open mind and allow God to minister to you.

God used a few deeply committed friends to help me during this period, and I'd like to mention them here and dedicate this book in their honour:

Richard and Dawn, my first Youth for Christ club directors, who cared for me so much that they shifted the evening Bible study to 5:30 a.m. to accommodate me.

Philip and Philo, my first Christian friends, who extended love and accepted me. This was so refreshing and new to me

Tony and Cal gave me a sense of belonging. I have spent many hours chatting with them, and of course eating delicious food prepared by Cal.

Brian and Parames believed in me and gave me the confidence to trust Him and to venture out to do new things.

Ajith and Nelun encouraged me to study and helped me believe that I can do it.

My wife Ophelia and I were married in 1981, beginning a new chapter in my life. During the past 33 years, she has been such a blessing to me. Her patience and her ability to accept me with all of my failures have laid a great foundation for my emotional recovery.

The birth of my children, Prashan and Thilini, opened a new door to unconditionally love two human beings and care for them. Fathering took on a new meaning, and it also enabled me to stop blaming others, to care for them and be the Dad that I should be. Trying my best to be a caring father was extremely therapeutic and enabled me to understand the love of God the Father for me, and it is with this appreciation that I have written this book.

This book did not evolve as a single writing project. Instead, it spanned over 20 years. This was my teaching material, and I enjoyed teaching it and seeing many be blessed. God brought about radical and transformative change in the lives of those who were living in hurt and pain in Sri Lanka and elsewhere in Asia. Seeing the positive impact, I discussed with Manori, a close family friend, the possibility of using the material and bringing it together in a book form. The book in your hands today is the result of that discussion. It has been through many months of revising, editing and then more revising! With each revision, Manori and I saw how God was shaping the material into a cohesive message.

This project started as my teaching material and includes truth I have gleaned from various books that I have studied and absorbed over the years. Wherever possible we have acknowledged the authors and given them credit, but it is also possible that we have overlooked giving credit to some. It is not my intention to do so, and I hope you will be patient and gracious with me if I have missed a citation or crediting of a correct source.

Finally, let me assure you the reader that my recovery was not instant, but the steps toward healing started one day and continues even today. Healing from the pain of your past is possible, and I invite you now to walk with me along this journey.

Rev. Adrian De Visser
Wattala, Sri Lanka
August 2014

Chapter One

The Problem Identified

ANNE WAS MARRIED WITH four children. The family was always in great turmoil, because she wouldn't trust her husband, her children nor any friends. She was intellectually alert, but suspicion dominated her life. She was also prone to sudden weeping, constantly living in self-pity and wondering why the world was so cruel to her.

She had reached her mid-40s, and crisis after crisis had followed her. In desperation she turned to a counsellor who helped her to begin talking about herself and her past—especially her childhood. As she began to probe herself, one of the startling realities she encountered was that her father never expressed his love for her. She suddenly realised that, from her childhood onward, she has been craving appreciation and attention but had never felt that she received it.

In addition to not displaying any love for her, her father would always demand excellence, and no matter what she did, she felt that she could never make him happy. She realised she had a perfectionist father who could never be satisfied and who had deprived her of affirmation or love.

As she began to grapple with and probe her past, she also recalled a traumatic incident in her pre-teen years when she was sexually abused by a priest. The abuse led her to a crisis in her own moral life. She began to experiment sexually and had constant short-term affairs, but none satisfied her. She started feeling suicidal, rejected and very lonely—even though she was married, had children and lived in a busy, noisy house. She was always antagonistic towards others and left a trail of broken interpersonal relationships, always feeling justified that she was the victim and others had been cruel to her.

She never realised that she was part of the problem, instead believing others were the cause and that she was always the victim. She was showing signs of emotional illness but did not realise it.

This is a typical symptom of a person who is deeply hurting, and it deserves our full and immediate attention. In general, illness can be subdivided into one or a combination of the following three categories:

- Physical illness
- Mental illness
- Emotional illness

Physical and mental illness can easily be detected. There are specialised diagnostic methods developed over the centuries for the study of the human body and its various conditions. Following the diagnosis, there is usually a remedy at hand—over the counter medicine, which will relieve your symptoms or cure them altogether, or perhaps more tests and further diagnosis. Whatever the medical professional's verdict, the detection of the illness, the diagnosis and the treatment can be carried out relatively quickly and seamlessly.

But emotional illness is more difficult to detect. It is hidden and is related to attitudes, hurts and response to hurts. Often, the victim is unaware of the problem, unaware that there is an emotional illness within that is preventing her emotional and spiritual growth. At times, others can see the symptoms of the problem—uncontrolled anger, deep depression, unrealistic perfectionism, strings of broken relationships, deep anxiety, compulsive behaviour and disorders, fear of failure and fear of the future being just a few common symptoms.

Anne was tragically unaware of her hurts, and she was convinced that, since people were determined to ruin her, she had to protect and defend herself from this cruel world. This attitude further compounded her problem. She was not only dealing with existing inner hurts but gradually allowing bitterness, anger and resentment to set in and to control her entire being, setting her on a destructive path.

Even though it is obvious to others, the affected person believes the problem is not with her, but rather with everyone who has caused her pain. This perception leads her to crusade even harder for justice and to fight for her rights. Sometimes it makes her withdraw completely from people. As a result, she becomes a very difficult person to love, and people distance themselves from her. She sees this as another rejection, leading to a life lived in constant pain, anger, bitterness and isolation.

UNDERSTANDING BEHAVIOUR PATTERNS

At this point, I think we need to understand the behaviour patterns of hurting people because we often respond to the symptoms and ignore the underlying hurts. As we have already seen, wounded people are not aware of their own problems.

Let me draw your attention to the following symptoms. This can also be used as a starting checklist to identify possible symptoms of deep emotional hurts within yourself or within those whom you wish to help.

- The individual continues in his pain, unaware that he is the main cause of the problem, blaming everyone else in the world.

- People around him handle him with great caution, or treat him like a plague—a person to be avoided.
- A deeply wounded person will have constant interpersonal conflicts and a trail of broken relationships.
- People with deep hurts often fight against perceived injustice. Unfortunately, they do not look for solutions or ways to help others, but they seem to enjoy raising negative issues and being overly critical, causing pain and division as a result.
- Hurting people often move from one group to another, always dissatisfied with each new community they find. They are looking for love, acceptance and permanence, but their own deep hurts stand in the way of forming healthy, nurturing relationships.

In the process of counselling or helping a friend, or if you can see these behavioural signs in yourself, they should raise a red flag, leading you to start probing more deeply. Love calls us to address issues rather than ignore them until they become an avalanche that drowns us.

LOOKING BEYOND THE OBVIOUS

In the 1950s, Dr. Wilder Penfield, a leading neurosurgeon at McGill University in Montreal, Canada, performed brain surgery on epileptic patients under a local anaesthetic. During the course of surgery, he conducted several experiments. In one of the experiments, he electrically stimulated the cerebral cortex of the brain with a small electrode. The patients reported having dream-like experiences that were, in fact, recorded memories from the past, many of which they had forgotten.

As a result of these experiments, Dr. Penfield drew the following conclusions:

1. The brain records all of our experiences.

2. It also records our perception of the feelings associated with these experiences.
3. Through the function of remembering, we can be aware of the present while reliving a past experience.
4. Recordings of many of our experiences remain in the brain even though we are not consciously aware of them. Some may be recalled at any time, while others are buried deep in the subconscious mind and are available through dreams or external stimuli.
5. These past experiences not only influence the present but also the future, shaping, guiding, and sometimes limiting the present, as well as the future.[1]

Penfield's research confirms that memories have a powerful influence on behaviour and attitudes. When we remember the facts surrounding certain events, we also experience the emotions associated with those events. If those emotions include terror, depression, anger and guilt, we may develop crippling emotional problems. Even when we do not consciously remember painful events, we can still feel their effects.

Theodore Dobson writes, "Accumulated hurts may come out as uncontrollable 'fits' of anger, jealousy or depression. Accumulated guilt may be expressed in physical or psychological illness. Phobias—irrational fears of harmless or only ordinarily dangerous things—may be the result of fearful forgotten episodes in a person's history. These kinds of pain are more harmful and destructive than the original pain that caused them, for they are more difficult to deal with."[2]

Father Michael Scanlan goes further and makes a distinction between what he calls surface memories and root memories.

---

1. Wilder Penfield, "Memory Mechanism," *American Medical Association Archives of Neurology and Psychiatry,* Vol. 67, 1952

2. Theodore Dobson, *Inner Healing: God's Great Assurance,* Paulist Press, New York, 1978

By surface memories he means memories that can be called forth into the consciousness of the person. Root memories are more difficult to discover. They are embedded deeply in one's subconscious mind, below the level of one's awareness. Scanlan continues: "Where a root memory is involved there are many disturbing memories built upon one root memory. These memories are a part of an iceberg above the water. They are very destructive."[3]

Scanlan further comments:

> "The burden of pain that all of us carry drains our energy from creative and productive activity and makes us feel unworthy, guilty, hopeless, broken and unforgivable. The burden would be destructive enough if its effects went no further, but such is not the case. These negative feelings, now converted over a period of time into attitudes, begin to develop within us a negative pattern of behaviour, and our past begins to destroy our present. That which is so negative begins to want to destroy itself, and so we develop habits of self-destruction or habits of sin."

Even though a hurting person desires to break away from his past and be different, he is unable to do so because the past controls the future. Satan enters this hurting arena and exploits the situation, making it almost impossible to break away. Yet, that which is impossible for man is possible for God.

John Wimber of Vineyard Ministries said, "Satan takes the pain of the past, controls the present and destroys the future." Even though that was Satan's plan, I have good news for you. By God's grace, you can overcome the hurts, and by His grace you can also become someone who is qualified to help others who are hurting.

---

3. Michael Scanlan T.O.R., *Let the Fire Fall,* Servant Books, Ann Arbor, Michigan, 1986

However, if you do not seek His help, emotional hurts can cripple your walk with God. In my years of helping people overcome personal emotional hurts and to fulfil their potential, I have come across people who lead emotionally and spiritually crippled lives.

One man I worked with believes that everyone who is around him is plotting to destroy him. He pastors a church, he preaches love and grace but he believes that his community is plotting against him. Sometimes an innocent remark such as, "I didn't understand a part of your sermon," is seen as a monumental personal attack and the first signs of a plot against him, and he becomes emotionally troubled.

Satan begins to work in his mind and blows the incident out of proportion (see Ephesians 4:6-12). This pastor constantly thinks about the innocent remark until he has an explosive confrontation with the believer. Even after this, he continues to overtly or covertly attack this individual, sometimes using the pulpit to preach against the person. He justifies this behaviour by saying that he is protecting himself and the ministry. "I am proving that I am right, and they are wrong," he says. This, however, alienates him from the people within his church, which he again sees as a plot against him by someone.

Another young man I know was constantly "feeling hurt" by others. When probed, he would say that they didn't smile at him or say "good morning," or "that person looked very upset, so he must have a problem with me." He was constantly withdrawing from people based on his perception that others didn't accept him. He ministered to people, but because of his emotional hurts he remained distant from them. After a while he would feel that they had rejected him, and then his escape mechanism was to withdraw completely from them. With each new group of people he was assigned to work with he had the same experience. No matter how much we affirmed him, he continued to believe otherwise and to behave in the same destructive cycle.

Another Christian leader I know was constantly in conflict with those he worked with. He always felt very unworthy but was drawn to ministry, and he covered up his sense of unworthiness with arrogance and acting superior to others. He could never appreciate what others did and was always condemning others and finding fault with their work. By picking on petty details that were not perfectly done, he would take away from his colleagues' efforts, often undermining and discouraging them. He found it extremely difficult to work with peers as equals and in a team spirit. He was able to relate to people only as long as he was the head of the organisation, unquestioningly in power.

Perhaps you have seen similar patterns within yourself or your ministry. If that is your experience, then this book is written just for you.

MANIFESTATION OF DEEP HURTS

The accumulated hurts within people will manifest in various forms. I have presented 16 of the most common symptoms I have come across. As you carefully read the symptoms listed below, how many of them truly describe your inner self?

- A judgmental spirit that is harsh and demanding of self and others.
- Inability to receive any compliment or kind deed from another person without being embarrassed or feeling a sense of unworthiness.
- Always seeking love, acceptance and attention. When not received, feels a sense of anger or jealousy at those who receive it.
- Looking at the past, present and future through eyes of self-pity—and worse, not hoping for any better experiences in the future.

- Strong perfectionist attitude, demanding the impossible from self and others.
- Strong pattern of fearing the future and all that it holds.
- Sense of aloneness and abandonment.
- Guilt and compulsive tendency to compete for position and success.
- Constant expectation of spectacular growth or breakthrough to a new spiritual freedom.
- A distorted self-image, resulting in arrogant behaviour or a sense of unworthiness.
- Lack of confidence or the inability even to fulfil very simple functions, and an overwhelming fear to attempt anything new because it may fail.
- Always on the defensive. Will not accept any form of criticism, as criticism is seen as rejection. To accept one's faults is seen as defeat that might result in rejection.
- Constant feeling of unworthiness.
- A string of broken and hurting relationships.
- Critical and unappreciative of others, always expecting and seeing the worst in others.
- Unhealthy attitude toward the opposite sex and slavery to unwholesome sexual thoughts and behaviour.

When I teach on inner healing, one of the most common questions presented by the audience is found below, based on 2 Corinthians 5:17: "Therefore, if anyone is in Christ, he is a new creation; the old has gone, the new has come!" So the question is, "If the old has passed away, and the new has come, how can a believer be troubled by his past emotional pain?"

I believe the work of the Holy Spirit begins first by leading a person to a point of deep conviction of their own sin. This conviction leads a person to trust in the redeeming work of Jesus

Christ on the cross of Calvary. At this moment, he experiences a theological truth called justification.

Justification, in simple language, means Jesus has cleansed you from your sin and given you a new identity. But this is just the beginning of a new walk with God. It is a blessed entry point, but not the end in itself. The Scriptures also tell us that we should "be Holy as the Father is Holy" (1 Peter 1:14-16). This means that, from the point of justification onward, a believer is eagerly and earnestly seeking to be like the Father.

John Wesley said, "God would never have asked a person to be holy if it was impossible for someone to achieve it on planet earth." And this process is called sanctification, the process through which God gives us grace to face our own realities and shortcomings, to deal with them and to overcome them. This grace may be given to deal with inner pain that we have buried in the depths of our heart and never had the courage to deal with. God not only forgives, but also gives us the grace to overcome.

Let me give you another example of this theological reality. A dear friend of mine who serves with me was rejected by his parents when he was a very young boy. He grew up on the streets, turned out to be a violent young man who would beat and rob people and do anything to achieve what he wanted. A series of incidents led him to come to know the Lord, but his violent behaviour did not cease suddenly. But I watched him with amazement as I saw the grace of God enable him to overcome his violent temper and cruel behaviour. Today, he is a minister of the gospel, but he confides in me that he still battles with his anger.

I strongly believe that we are broken people, saved by grace, who are ministering to other broken people. This does not give us the right to triumphalistic preaching but rather to glory in the grace of God and the possibility that anyone can change because of His grace.

When a young man who has saturated his mind with pornographic literature and images and indulged in unhealthy sexual practices turns to Christ, he is justified and forgiven. But, by the grace of God, he needs to deal with the addictions that he carries. Yes, there is victory, but in the journey toward healing, he needs to grapple with his past.

Another woman I know grew up in a home where she was never affirmed, loved or accepted. She experienced a beautiful conversion—she was justified. But even today she struggles in affirming any human being. She means to do it, but does not have the courage to verbalise her feelings with actual words. She is now a mother, and her children constantly complain, "Mom, we know you love us, but we wish you would tell us sometimes."

THE CHURCH AND THE HURTING

The church, through its message of love and acceptance, draws many hurting individuals to its community. The initial response of the members of the church is often, "Great! A sinner has returned to the Father!" But soon, they get tired of the behaviour of the new believer—his attitudes, his constant desire for attention, his enormous capacity to get hurt by other church members, his indulging in self-pity and, of course, his unforgiving attitude.

When he continues to exhibit behaviour patterns inconsistent with accepted biblical norms, the average church leader is at a loss as to how to deal with the individual. Due to the leader's own inability to help the individual, the new believer is termed a rebel, a troublemaker or, worse, an unrepentant sinner.

The hurting individual, for his part, continues to hang on as much as possible (as his fear of rejection makes it hard for him to leave), until he has had enough and then moves to another Christian community. The new community accepts him with open arms, listens to his bad experiences and the cycle is repeated again.

I am not suggesting that you shut the door to such individuals, but we miss a great opportunity to minister to such individuals if we agree with them blindly and do not help them see the real issue that seems to be trailing them. Of course, I must confess that there are many occasions when the individual has been the victim of an unsanctified, emotionally immature and insecure leader who has made life very difficult for them.

The church contributes to deepening this problem by not recognising that this is a person with deep emotional hurts and by coming alongside them to help them face some of the issues that are tormenting them. I have seen the church specialise in a so-called "spiritual" approach by simply saying, "Let's pray about all this." I am in no way belittling the power and importance of prayer in the healing process, but the hurting person has not even come to a point where he recognises that he has a problem. So even prayer is approached from a defensive standpoint. "I am being victimised, others are attacking me, Lord, fight for me," the hurting person prays. And rather than beginning the healing process, we are encouraging the hurting individual to develop a "martyr complex."

Often, because of their willingness to spend time and give of themselves to the church, combined with their skill at taking responsibilities given to them, these hurting individuals are soon brought into church leadership. In this powerful position, the insecure, hurting individual will use his power and position to victimise and hurt others and to prevent others from blossoming into leadership. To me, these leaders are like the older brother in the parable of the Prodigal Son. They are ruthlessly obedient to what they perceive to be God's will, but falter in the process of loving and caring for those around them. They're very Pharisaical in their standards and have completely missed the heart of God.

I have found through experience that hurting individuals are drawn to the church. This is especially true in the context of Asia, where we are beginning to encounter first-generation Christians who may come from unaffirming, dysfunctional homes. Often, they have experienced physical, emotional and sexual abuse. These individuals are drawn to the church because of the message of love and acceptance. The Christian gospel attracts the hurting. We should be aware of this and be ready to deal with them when they are young in the faith.

Our inability to consider this as a priority has resulted in allowing hurting individuals to assimilate into the church, learn pious language, and—in our shame-based culture—hide their hurts and pretend to be "spiritual." Their language reflects a deep walk with God, but their actions are a shallow replica of what God calls us to be.

The good news is that, when they are young and new in the faith, their eagerness and openness to the Lord will enable these people to face their past and to resolve any hurts they are carrying around. They can be helped and supported to begin their journey toward emotional healing, and the church will be strengthened by inheriting godly, loving and gracious leadership. This, to me, is the foundation for the growth of the church. But the reality I see is that we have hurting leaders who are trying to carry the gospel to a hurting community, talking in a language of love, but without the potential to actually exercise that love and grace. It is very sad for me to say this, but at times I see the church being run by insecure individuals who are trying to consolidate their positions of leadership and exercise power and authority rather than exercising love, grace and compassion.

Church leaders who are legalistic, judgmental and rigid will only be repulsive to the hurting world. And rather than drawing people to God, we will alienate them from His love and forgiveness. If our objective is to see people's lives transformed by the power of the gospel, then dealing with our emotional hurts becomes absolutely essential.

PERSONAL REFLECTIONS

Commit your story to paper. Draw the story of your life like a timeline, from your earliest memory to today. Think as far back as you can and identify the happy, sad, angry, fearful events and experiences that you can remember. Highlight some of the most painful episodes that you encountered. This may take you a few hours or be spread over several days.

What you have committed to paper will give you a good indication of your emotional health. This is just the beginning of yet another spiritual journey that you are embarking on.

GROUP WORK

- Share the results of the checklist of 16 symptoms of hurts listed on page 20. Allow this to be the starting point for an open, honest discussion of how your hurts are manifested through your behaviour.
- Encourage your group to open up and share their personal timeline drawings, explaining the events and experiences that have shaped them.
- If someone within the group feels uncomfortable opening up, pair him/her with a close friend.

Chapter Two

Back to the Origins

GETTING HURT IS THE easy part. Overcoming the pain, anger and the residual scars is a much harder task. But for any healing work to begin, we need to start at the beginning. Let's look into the root causes of our hurts, and where our hurts began.

When my son was about three years old, we were playing in the garden. He ran and jumped into a clump of bougainvillea bushes, which were full of thorns. He yelled in pain, and I rushed over and carried him back into the house to clean his wound. The next day, there was a slight swelling in his foot, and I changed his dressing and assured him that everything was OK. But by the third day, the entire foot was swollen, and yellow pus was pouring out of the wound. I knew there was still something inside the wound causing the infection. As my son screamed in pain and fear, I gently pressed on either side of the wound. As I continued to apply pressure, a long, dark thorn finally emerged. I realised that for the past two days I had only been cleaning the surface of the wound but not actually healing it. I took the thorn out, cleaned and dressed the wound, and this time the wound healed completely.

Similarly, in our childhood we encounter emotional trauma and pain, and when left unattended, it gets buried within us.

These emotional hurts remain with us, and every additional painful experience and encounter we face adds a layer of pain over the old, festering, hurting wound.

This cycle continues until we are willing to face the origins of these wounds, grapple with the emotions they created within us and work toward overcoming the deep hurts they have left behind. However, the tragedy of emotional trauma is that many will bury it, hoping that it will go away some day. Others live in denial. Neither of these approaches will solve the problem.

Unresolved, painful issues will cause you to develop an instinctive mechanism to protect yourself from further hurtful experiences. These can later develop into strongholds and habits, which cut us away from or limit our walk with God and our ability to live with others in harmony.

PRE-BIRTH FACTORS

In my ministry I have encountered many who cannot account for their inner feelings, suicidal thoughts, rejection and deep hurts. At first, I was at a loss as to how to help them. But in a few situations, I sat with the parents and discussed with them their child's early development. I have sometimes probed the mother about her emotional health during the pregnancy. I have been amazed, time and time again, by the number of cases in which mothers describe their time of pregnancy as an unhappy one, wanting to abort the child feeling it was an inconvenient time for a pregnancy.

This prompted me to search for a biblical basis for this link between the emotional condition of the pregnant mother and the subsequent impact on the newborn. I also began to search for current and ongoing scientific research into the subject.

The August 15, 1983, issue of *Time* carried a cover story titled, "Babies: What Do They Know? When Do They Know It?" Reporting on hundreds of medical and behavioural experiments being conducted in the United States, France, Austria and other parts of the world, the article described an enormous campaign aimed at solving one of the most fascinating riddles of human life: What do newborn babies know when they emerge into this world? And how do they begin organising and using that knowledge during the first years of life? The basic answer, which is repeatedly being demonstrated in myriad new ways, is that babies know a lot more than most people used to think. They see more, hear more, understand more and are genetically pre-wired to bond with any adult who cares for them.

One of the most important results of these studies is the conclusive proof that, long before an infant can speak, he is thinking and learning and remembering. As this article states, "Intellect is at work long before any language is available as a tool. Babies develop an important ability to recognize categories. This was once thought to require language. ... How can the un-namable be identified? But babies apparently can recognise perceptions without a word."[4] The article goes on to show how children very early learn their own unspoken language of shapes, sounds, colours and smells, as well as a language of responses and relationships with people. They remember an amazing variety of specific things long before they can speak or have words to identify objects or people.

How far back can we push the frontiers of memory? The *Time* article states, "The search for data is being steadily pushed back from childhood to earliest infancy and even birth!"

Dr. Thomas Verny, a Canadian neurologist and psychiatrist, makes a strong case for pre-birth memory in his best-selling book, *The Secret Life of the Unborn Child.* Dr. Verny traces the prenatal development of the child and comes to this conclusion: The first thin slivers of memory track begin streaking across the foetal brain some time in the third trimester, though

---

4. Otto Friedrich, "What do Babies Know?" *Time Magazine,* Time Inc., 15 August 1983

exactly when is hard to pinpoint. Some investigators claim a child can remember from the sixth month on while others argue the brain does not acquire powers of recall until the eighth month. There is, however, no question that the unborn child remembers or that he retains his memories. We can safely deduce that certainly from the sixth month after conception his central nervous system is capable of receiving, processing and encoding messages. Neurological memory is most assuredly present at the beginning of the last trimester, when most babies, if born, can survive with the help of incubators.[5]

Dr. Verny documents his claims with scores of interesting illustrations of both prenatal and very early infant memories. To many of us this sounds far fetched, but it didn't to our grandparents, who accepted prenatal influence as a matter of fact, though they carried it to ridiculous extremes. I can still hear my grandmother suggesting to a neighbour that perhaps the reason a certain little boy down the street had such a long, ugly nose was that his mother had visited the zoo too often and spent too much time watching the elephants! But we are discovering that a lot of those old wives' tales contained a kernel of truth. For example, most primitive peoples are careful to keep expectant mothers away from frightening experiences.

In a carefully controlled study of 2,000 women during pregnancy and birth, Dr. Monika Lukesch, of Constantine University in Frankfurt, Germany, came to the conclusion that *the mother's attitude toward her baby has the greatest single effect on how an infant turns out.* And just as important, Dr. Lukesch found that *the quality of a woman's relationship with her husband rates second and has a decisive effect on the unborn child.*[6]

Dr. Gerhard Rottmann, of the University of Salzburg in Austria, came to much the same conclusion; his research even

5. Thomas Verny, M.D. and John Kelly, *The Secret Life of the Unborn Child,* Dell, 1982

6. Ibid.

showed that the unborn child is capable of very fine emotional distinctions.[7]

This is illustrated by the biblical story in which the Virgin Mary visits her cousin Elizabeth to tell her about the announcement of the angel and the promised Messiah. This causes Elizabeth to exclaim joyously, "Behold, when the sound of your greeting reached my ears, the baby leaped in my womb for joy" (Luke 1:44).

Based on the above information, I want to suggest that some children experience rejection and lack of love even before they are born into this world. This sense of rejection can haunt them throughout their teens and adult life. The tragedy is that the individual may lack any tangible evidence of rejection but yet experience it deeply, because the rejection occurred prior to birth.

1. LACK OF LOVE

God has created us with a capacity to love and a deep desire to be loved. When this is not actualised, it creates an unhealthy and unnatural vacuum that cripples us emotionally. The natural order that God created allows for a newborn baby to be nestled close to the mother's heart as she nurses him. This is not only a need for physical nourishment, but it is the God-ordained time for a deep bonding experience with the first human being we relate to. This security lays the foundation for a child's healthy emotional development. When this is broken, either by the mother's abandonment of the child or by her state of emotional distress, the bonding is never completed. I have watched and counselled many children who could not relate to others because they were deprived of this early, foundational love.

Eric was born into a large family of ten siblings. Their parents were alcoholics, involved in the illicit alcohol trade. There was never a short supply for their own addiction, and

7. Ibid.

their house was the informal pub in their community, where people gathered at all times and the parents were always busy serving the alcoholics.

The mother had no time for the children, they were never sent to school and they wandered the streets looking for love but never receiving it. There were many days that Eric would go to sleep in hunger and would be rudely woken up in the middle of the night by his mother, who would force him and his siblings to eat the frugal meal she had cooked in haste. The children were very young and sleepy, too tired to eat at that time of night, so she would get them to bite on a chili pepper. The children would wake up screaming from the heat and burning on their tongue. Soon, the children learned to eat quickly when woken up in the night.

Eric grew up never knowing what it is to love or to be loved. He accepted the Lord as his Saviour and came into the church. But he was always seen as the oddball who couldn't fit in. He was looking for love, but he was looking for it selfishly, wanting all the attention for himself and needing to be the first and the most prominent in every activity. If someone else was given special prominence, he was deeply hurt. Soon he became disillusioned with this church and moved on to another. He still continues to visit churches looking for the kind of love and acceptance he craves. But, unfortunately, he never stopped and looked inside of himself to discover the truth of his search.

A lack of love causes serious problems in the lives of people. They are hurting, looking for love and attention. Some have taken on destructive behaviour patterns. Don't be misled: Everyone is looking *to be loved and to love.*

2. REJECTION

Sri Lanka is famous for its wild elephants, and it has become a very popular tourist attraction. However, from time to time there are media reports of rogue elephants that have either been shot or captured and moved to a rehabilitation centre. These elephants are lone rangers that often stray into villages or ruin crops in their search for food. They are single male elephants separated from their herd and left to find their own way in the world, and they will not be accepted into another herd unless they come across a rare herd without a male leader. Researchers who have tracked rogue elephants say that they make attempts to join new herds but are attacked and chased away.

Even human beings are looking to belong to somebody. This somebody is initially our parents. As we reach adolescence, we want to belong to a group, and the fear of rejection by our peers often makes us conform to the prescribed behaviour of this group. Everyone is looking to belong to someone, or some community. But in the real world, rejection is a common reality.

In Asia, I have seen several factors contribute to the rejection of a child. Some of these causes are based on a purely superstitious worldview, but they damage the child's emotions permanently.

- The mother conceives, and it is an unplanned pregnancy that ends up being inconvenient, causes financial difficulty and is stressful for the family. The parents resent the unexpected conception, and after the child is born, they will often unconsciously communicate this resentment to the child.
- The child is born into the family, and the astrologer has predicted that the child is born on an unlucky day and will bring bad luck to the family. Some astrologers go to the extent of suggesting that the child is a bad omen and should be given away for adoption, as his presence in the house may mean death for one or both of the parents. I have encountered many parents who have given away their child for adoption, and some have retained the child but with fear and resentment. All difficulties

the family encounters after such a birth are attributed to the child's presence. I have counselled a young man who always believed that he brought misfortune to his family because, from the day he was born, the discussion among the adults was on the extent of bad luck the child had brought to the family.

- In some families, due to various reasons, the love and commitment between the parents gives way to hatred. This resentment toward the spouse is transferred to the newborn child, whose features may closely resemble the spouse. The child grows up never understanding why his father or mother seems to dislike or even hate him, but this unspoken rejection is deeply felt.
- Parenting is a new experience for everyone. Unfortunately in Asia, we don't have much assistance or training on parenting, especially dealing with strong-willed children. The sheer physical exhaustion felt by the inexperienced mother and the ambitious father result in an unspoken disappointment, as they don't see the model child they had hoped for. Further, he is an embarrassment to the family, resulting in the parents resenting the child. The child, for his part, does not understand his selfish behaviour and is at a loss to understand why his parents do not respond to him with deep affection.
- I believe that we live in a shame-based culture, where a child's performance is seen to reflect on the family. A good looking, smart, talented and high-achieving child will become the pride of not only the family, but the entire community in which he is growing up. But a slow learner who is a low achiever is seen as an embarrassment to all. I constantly see parents criticise, nag and scold a slow-achieving child, comparing him to siblings or cousins of the same age. They do this in the hope that the child will suddenly transform into a high achiever.

But my experience tells me that this will only create an opposite reaction in the child. He will begin to feel unworthy, resent the parents and hate himself for being unable to please them.

- In most Asian countries, a girl child does not enjoy a very healthy position within the family or even the community. This is not a recent development, but a negative attitude passed on from generation to generation. The situation may have improved a little with economic development, but religious and cultural realities dictate that a girl child is of less worth than a male. In many Asian societies, a dowry (the wealth—in money, property, jewellery or any other asset—that the bride's family gives to the groom's family) plays a dominant role in a marriage. The inability to provide a big dowry will mean poor prospects of marriage for a daughter. For most Asian parents, this is a deep shame—to have an unmarried daughter for whom they cannot provide a sufficient dowry is a reflection on them as parents. Thus, many parents prefer a male child as he becomes an asset to the family, one day bringing in a dowry from his wife into the family. The girls are aware of this reality, and they see themselves as a burden to their parents. Their self-worth is low, and cultural dictates rob them of the human dignity that is due them. Often, they see themselves as objects that satisfy the lustful desires of men and whose lot is to take any kind of abuse, including domestic violence, from their husbands.

Most children begin to grasp this rejection from their parents as they start to interact with their peers, especially as they begin school. At this stage, either they will internalise the pain of rejection or react in angry and violent rebellion against their parents. Parents are confused by this new behaviour and attribute it to a new phase of growing up that they must suffer through.

In close-knit societies such as those in Asia, rejection hits at the very core of one's being. In fact, the most intense persecution that new believers face in Asia is the rejection from their immediate family and community. Many have not considered the claims of Christ because of this fear of rejection.

I am still battling to help a young man who was totally rejected by his parents as a child. He was abandoned by both his parents when he was about five years old and lived on the mercy of his neighbours and extended family. When he came into our church, he was an emotional wreck. The gospel of love and the friendship extended to him through our youth group opened the door for him to consider the gospel and to accept Christ as his Saviour. He has lived within the church family since that time.

When he was 16 years old, he traced the location of his mother. With great delight, he went to meet her and introduced himself. His mother had built a new life for herself, with a new husband and children. She didn't want to even acknowledge him as her son for fear that her new family would find out about her past. Her only request to him was never to come back looking for her.

He returned to our church that day, weeping uncontrollably. It has been nearly five years, but he has yet to recover from this traumatic rejection. The sad reality is that since then he has built defensive walls around himself and withdrawn from people. He is an artist but never uses his talents for a productive purpose or to create beautiful things.

Having worked with so many who have experienced rejection, the following are some of the main crippling reactions and behaviours that I see:

1. Anger: As the child looks at the world, he seems happy and contented people. They are confident, carefree and capable. He looks at them, compares himself and feels deep anger and resentment toward his family, peers and

the world. Over a period of time, unresolved anger can transform a person into a bitter, unhappy individual. Wherever he goes, he will carry this bitterness, this unresolved anger, which will result in further rejection.

2. Insecurity: Because of the rejection, and because he has not been affirmed as an important member of the family, he sees himself as having little value to his family and even his community. The insecure young man is totally unprepared for the challenges of life. This cruel, competitive world sends a signal to him on a daily basis that he is incapable, resulting in deep depression and completely paralysed emotions.
3. Constant feeling of unworthiness: The emotional paralysis felt by an insecure person gives rise to a strong sense of unworthiness. Some settle for a very passive, docile lifestyle. Others, without dealing with the symptoms, attempt to assert themselves and live a life of constant competition with others. Jealousy is the norm, and compulsive behaviour governs them.
4. Deep depression: I am not a clinical psychologist, but I have dealt with far too many people who are deeply depressed, and I have realised that for some their need is not for medical attention but rather an affirming love. Through the process of rejection, their self-worth has been robbed, and their ability to perform has been further undermined by the cruel remarks and attitudes of people around them. They project the future and see it as dark and hopeless, with no light at the end of the tunnel. I think we can easily understand how they feel.

In my study of Scripture, I have been deeply intrigued by David's life and propensity to get into trouble. This made me take a closer look at David.

In 1 Samuel 16, God is troubled by Saul's behaviour, and He wants to appoint a new leader for his people. Samuel is summoned to anoint the new leader. He enters Jesse's home, directed by God, and he calls Jesse and his sons, looking for the one the Lord would prompt him to anoint. Having considered all the sons and finding that God was not leading him to anoint any one of them, he turns to Jesse and asks him a question (in verse 11):

> "So he asked Jesse, 'Are these all the sons you have?' 'There is still the youngest,' Jesse answered, 'but he is tending the sheep.' Samuel said, 'Send for him; we will not sit down until he arrives.' "

It is obvious to me that, if Jesse considered David to be an important member of the family, he would have invited David also to be present for the anointing ceremony. There are other signs worth noting: Jesse wanted Samuel to go ahead with the ceremony in David's absence, and when asked if he had more sons, said there was *still* the youngest, almost implying that the youngest was not worthy to be considered.

Was this is an oversight by Jesse, or was David not well accepted in his family? I believe it was the latter. Note David's older brother Eliab's statement in 1 Samuel 17:28:

> "Why have you come down here? And with whom did you leave those few sheep in the desert? I know how conceited you are and how wicked your heart is."

This makes me conclude that David was not respected or recognised for his talents nor appreciated in his family for the work he did. And David's response to Eliab in verse 29 is further revealing: "*Now* what have I done?" This may have been a regular situation in which David was made to feel he was always in the wrong. His next words, "Can't I even speak?" (verse 29), lead me to think that perhaps his family made him feel that his opinion was not valued.

If this was the environment in which David grew up, I am not surprised by his moral failures and the other issues he later encountered. Was his attempt to draw Bathsheba into sin an act of sudden provocation, or was it an act of conquering another human being to prove his own worthiness? In 1 Samuel 25, David's response to Nabal's refusal to provide his soldiers with food is to declare war on him and his family. Reading the story now, we can see that David's response was an extreme one, not in proportion to what happened. However, at the time, Nabal's refusal would have seemed like another rejection to David. Rather than being grateful for David's protection, Nabal did not consider him even worthy of providing some food.

The reason I am calling your attention to David's story is to underscore the important fact that a rejected person, when they sense even a hint of rejection, can react with extreme behaviour, often in unhealthy and violent ways.

3. LACK OF ENCOURAGEMENT AND AFFIRMATION

In Sri Lanka and elsewhere in Asia, I find that we do not have an affirming culture. It is also common to hear parents make negative statements, hoping that these words will cause the children to perform better. Some examples that I have heard and seen are:

- The child returns home after the school exam, having obtained 60 points from a total score of 100. The parents ask, "What happened to the other 40?" Or in some cases, when the child has brought a much better grade than they expected, I have heard parents say, "I'm sure your teacher made a mistake." In the mind of the Asian parent, you are pushing the child to do better. But the child is hurting.
- In a family of two boys, if one is doing very well and the other happens to be a slow learner and lives under the shadow of the other sibling, every mistake he makes and

> every attempt to do better will be compared with the other child, with reminders such as, "Look at your brother; you should learn from his example."

This is true even in the Asian church. I have found that, when preaching and teaching in Western cultures, there is a lot of feedback and affirmation. But you hardly hear any words of affirmation in the Asian church. There is a distant and silent admiration, which does not help the individual feel valued or propel him towards growth.

Researchers are turning up new evidence to support the old truth that encouragement brings out the best in people. In one experiment, adults were given ten puzzles to solve. All ten were exactly the same for all the adults. They worked on them, turned them in and were given the results at the end. However, the results were fictitious. Half the puzzle-solvers were told they had done well, getting seven of ten correct. The other half were told they had done poorly, getting seven of ten wrong. Then all were given another ten puzzles. Again, the puzzles were the same for each person. The half who had been told they had done well with the first puzzles did better with the second set. The other half did worse. Criticism, even though it was given falsely, ruined them.[8]

The best possible way to help someone reach their potential is by encouraging them. Most people require outside encouragement to propel them forward, and it is vital to their growth. Physician George Adams found encouragement to be so vital to a person's existence that he called it "oxygen to the soul."

Victor Frankl said, "If you treat people to a vision of themselves, if you apparently overrate them, you make them become what they are capable of becoming. You know, if we take people as they are, we make them worse. If we take them as

8. John C. Maxwell, *Ultimate Leadership: Three Books to Maximize Your Leadership Potential and Empower Your Team,* Thomas Nelson, Inc., 2007

they *should be,* we help them become what they *can be.* If you say this is idealism—overrating man—then I must answer, 'Idealism is the real realism, because you help people actualize themselves.' "[9]

Henry Ford said, "My best friend is the one who brings out the best in me."

Authors C.S. Lewis and J.R.R. Tolkien maintained a close friendship throughout their careers, sharing their love of mythical stories and a desire to create those stories for the public. It was Tolkien who led Lewis to Christianity, and it was Lewis who encouraged Tolkien to keep writing fiction. It is said the literary world would have neither *The Chronicles of Narnia* nor *The Lord of the Rings* if not for the friendship between these two men.[10]

Every parent wants to bring out the best in their children, and every successful parent knows that encouragement is the way to do it.

4. LIES SPOKEN OVER OUR LIVES

I believe that people write the "script" for our lives, and we "act" this out on the "stage" of our lives. Let me explain this statement. When we have words—negative or positive—spoken over our lives by a person we love and respect, we begin to believe these statements and start living out what they say. If we hear words that affirm and encourage us, it will help us do better and attempt greater things. If we constantly hear criticism and belittling statements, we will believe that we are worthless, incapable and unsuccessful in anything we attempt.

---

9. John C. Maxwell, *Developing the Leader Within You,* Thomas Nelson, Inc., 2008

10. John C. Maxwell, *Encouragement Changes Everything,* Thomas Nelson Inc., 2008

This is so true when we consider the outbursts of parents, in their anger and frustration with children. I have heard many parents make these statements:

- "Mark my words, you will never make it in life."
- "You are an unlucky child."
- "It was only after your birth that we began to suffer so much; you must be the cause."
- "Mark my words; you will suffer much in the future."
- "You are a bad omen."

Parents, sometimes in deep desperation, say horrible things in public about their children. This is an outburst of their anger and frustration felt at the moment, but these words can have a devastating and long-lasting impact on the child.

After many years of listening to these statements, I have come to two conclusions:

1. Parents, teachers or even church leaders did not mean what they said but were expressing their frustration or anger felt at the time.
2. They made these statements hoping that the child would wake up to reality and do better or improve.

But the tragedy is that such an outburst deeply wounds a person, and constant repetition makes a person believe the lie. Finally, they not only believe the lie, they also begin to live it out.

This is a common issue I have come across throughout Asia. Not only is it a common problem, Satan has also taken advantage of this and ruined the potential of many men and women. This is seen even in the church, as men and women live out the untruths that were hastily pronounced over them as children.

I believe this is a major problem in our communities today. Some want to fly, and they have the potential to fly, but they have believed a lie that has crippled them.

5. PARENTS WHO ARE HARD TO PLEASE

Parents who have gone through emotional trauma, who themselves are still hurting, are unable to provide an environment of loving acceptance. They mean well, but they unconsciously communicate rejection.

Recently I heard about an incident in which a young girl of six years cleaned her room without being asked to do so—she spent hours cleaning and arranging the room to the best of her ability. Finally, she felt it was good enough to show her mother and called her in. The mother walked in and ridiculed her feeble attempt, pointing out all the dust she had missed, the haphazard way of organising her toys and the poorly-made bed. To the mother, she was showing the child how she could improve. But to the child, her attempt to win the acceptance of her mother had failed.

No matter what they do, or how they do it, some parents show no appreciation of their children's efforts. In addition to not appreciating them, they insult and belittle the child privately, and worse, in public.

In the previous chapter, I have highlighted a few ways in which deep hurts manifest in our lives. Among these are:

- A judgmental spirit that is harsh and demanding on self and others.
- A strong perfectionist attitude, demanding the impossible from self and others.

Parents who have not faced up to their own hurts and needs will unconsciously go on hurting and damaging their children. Parents play the most important role in developing or ruining the personality of a child. Through constant nagging, strong words of judgment or not appreciating the efforts of the child, the parent is communicating to the child that they are dumb and useless.

David Seamands has this insight to share, in his book *Healing Grace*:

> "People remember a single hurtful criticism most vividly, while tending to a string of compliments. And they will feel a positive or a negative statement about what they are much more deeply than one concerning what they did. Thus, it is easy to see why the put downs of being can be so completely shattering to our self-esteem. They hurt us not simply on the outside, for our behaviour; but they pierce right into the inside of us, where the concepts and feelings about ourselves originate.
>
> "If these were simply isolated statements, occasionally uttered by exasperated parents who were normally fair and loving, that would not be so harmful. But when they represent the general attitude and atmosphere of the home, the effects on the self-image can be serious."[11]

6. OVERPROTECTIVE PARENTS

Overprotection is yet another very serious problem in Asia. Children are treated as helpless babies from the day of birth and continue to be treated as helpless babies even into their teens. It is a common observation in Western countries that a child is expected to become independent by the time they reach their late teens. Furthermore, Western cultures encourage children to earn their pocket money through babysitting and other chores around the house.

But this is not a common expectation in Asian culture. In fact, we seem to have gone to the other extreme. Parents provide for the children, and very rarely do they expect the children to earn for themselves and support their studies. In fact, it is a very common trait for the parents to save for their children's future, decide on their marriage partners and even expect them to continue living with them after their marriage.

11. David A. Seamands, *Healing Grace,* Victor Books, 1988

Even though I strongly support the concept of a large extended family, the downside of it is that it has taken away the potential for creative initiative and action by children and teenagers. We see this within the church in Asia, where young people are not encouraged or brought forward into leadership at an early stage but are mollycoddled and often insulated, treated as those who know nothing and can contribute little.

By not providing an environment for the child to become independent through performing even simple acts, but rather setting the stage for greater dependence on them, the parents are communicating a very harmful message to the child: "You are incapable." With time, the child not only believes this, he becomes totally dependent on the parents.

After the initial joy of mollycoddling the baby and creating overdependence, the parents are now wondering why their little boy or girl is so dependent. They begin to complain and compare their child with others. By such acts, they communicate the terrible message: "Son, we love you, but look how stupid and incapable you are." Overprotection may not necessarily be motivated by pure love, but instead can be unconsciously satisfying your own ego by causing others to be dependent on you.

7. DIVORCE AND SEPARATION

The divorce of parents creates an insecure environment for the children. Some children take it very personally and hold themselves responsible for the divorce. They presume that even if it was not their fault, at least they were not able to prevent the divorce. Some children are brought up by a single parent, and this is becoming a very common problem, even in rural areas and villages across Asia today. The loss of one parent in the life of the child brings about insecurity and deep emotional hurts.

Tammy was a young woman in her early 20s when I first met her. She had been through a series of short relationships and was confused and hurting. As we began to talk, she started sharing with me the trauma of her parents' divorce. "I will never forget the night they told my brother and me that they were getting a divorce. We heard them screaming and shouting for hours, and we knew something was wrong. We watched through the keyhole as they yelled and screamed at each other across the living room," she recalled. As she relayed these memories, the tears were streaming down her face. "After they told us about the divorce, I ran to my room and locked the door. I turned off all the lights, lit candles and used flashlights. I went around the room starting up every single music box I had until it was a loud, unclear scream of music. Then came the pictures. Depression was immediate. I started to cut up pictures of my broken family, and some I burned in the light of the candle. My heart was broken. I started to fear for my brother's and my future. Where would we live? Which parent would take us? Would we be separated?"

The pain of this traumatic divorce and separation left a deep impact on Tammy's life. Her mother soon remarried, and Tammy resented this new man in their house—someone she saw as a replacement for her father. She rebelled against all the rules of her home, school and church and began a string of short, unfulfilling relationships. Today, Tammy has found healing and fulfilment, but it was a long and painful journey to overcome the trauma of her parent's divorce.

Divorce is an intensely stressful experience for all children, regardless of age or developmental level, and many children are inadequately prepared for the impending divorce of their parents.

8. LEGALISTIC, GRACELESS HOMES

Legalistic parents are those who have established standards of living that they are not willing to negotiate and that they think are the only standards of life. Children must live or die by these die-hard standards. Some children can easily conform to such rules, but others have a hard time. They comply because they have no other option, but deep down there is resentment, causing permanent damage.

When their standards are not met, legalistic parents also communicate their disapproval through verbal outbursts or "the silent treatment." The rule of thumb in a graceless home is, "We are right; you are wrong." The relationship can be restored, and communication can begin only when the child accepts his failure, attempts to meet the standards and proclaims how sorry he is. Children often hate to accept this scenario but have little choice but to do so.

The home becomes an extremely unhappy place, and the child's freedom is entirely deprived. Here again, the children don't often realise what they are missing until they start making friends and visiting other homes. It is often at this stage that the child reacts in rebellion, and the inner root of hurt begins to go deep into their emotions.

9. SEXUAL ABUSE

Every year a staggering 10,000 girls in Sri Lanka face sexual abuse by their relatives, and they mostly occur in families where the mother has taken up overseas employment, with more than half the rapes committed by fathers, according to a survey in 2010.[12]

An Indian government report issued in 2007 stated that over 53 percent of all Indian children have been subjected to sexual abuse.[13] Globally, over 4.5 million people are estimated

12. Champika Liyanaarachchi, *One World South Asia News Report*. Colombo, Sri Lanka. 2010

13. Ministry of Women and Child Development, *Report on Child Abuse in India,* New Delhi, India, 2007.

to have been sexually exploited, trafficked and enslaved for the commercial sex trade from 2002-2011.[14]

Sexual abuse has become an acute problem within Asian cultures, where the extended family lives in the same premises together. Our church ministers to many sexually abused young girls and boys, providing them with a safe place to live and work toward recovery from the trauma they have experienced. As we work with these children, we have been shocked to find that almost all instances of abuse were perpetrated by a close family member, family friend or neighbour.

Living in a shame-based culture, a family would rather deny a reality than be embarrassed by a sexual scandal. And in a community in which family honour is considered something to be guarded, Asia's children have been sacrificed on the altar of family honour.

In my pastoral counselling with victims of sexual abuse, I find that they grapple with five different emotions:

1. Fear
2. Shame
3. Guilt
4. Anger
5. Enjoyment

There are many reasons sexual memories can be painful. The first is that our sexuality is at the very core of our identity. Our masculinity or femininity is deeply wrapped up with who we are and how we view ourselves. Damage to this area is bound to affect our self-esteem deeply.

The second reason is that sex creates such powerful emotions. It is so strong that God's plan allows several years of growth and development before the onset of puberty. In this

14. UN Women, *UN General Assembly Report: Tracfficking in Women and Girls,* New York, 2012

way, our bodies and emotions become mature enough to handle these powerful feelings. One of the most terrible facts about child molestation is the awakening of such overwhelming emotions at such an early age and under such frightening conditions. It could be compared to what happens when you try to operate a high-voltage electrical appliance through a small extension cord. The wires overheat and eventually burn out. In a similar way, sexual molestation produces an emotional short-circuit which can cause serious emotional and sexual damage.

But perhaps the most important reason these memories are so painful is that sexual feelings can be the most contradictory emotions we humans experience. We need to help counselees understand their own confusion and turmoil over their sexual traumas. What they have undergone can result in their experiencing sex as an incredible combination of desire and dread, pleasure and pain, fascination and fear. In one and the same emotion is a contradictory combination of compulsive longing and guilty contempt. This is why unhealed sexual traumas carried into married life often produce terrible inner conflicts.

A true story, related in Philip Yancey's *What's so Amazing about Grace?* deeply moved me when I first read it. And I would like to share a summarized version of Daisy's story here.

> "Daisy was born into a working-class Chicago family, the eighth child of ten. The father barely earned enough to feed them all, and after he took up drinking, money got much scarcer. Daisy, closing in on her hundredth birthday as I write this, shudders when she talks about those days. Her father was a 'mean drunk,' she says. Daisy used to cower in the corner, sobbing, as he kicked her baby brother and sister across the linoleum floor. She hated him with all her heart.
>
> "One day the father declared that he wanted his wife out of the house by noon. All ten kids crowded around their mother, clinging to her skirt and crying, 'No, don't go!' But

their father did not back down. Holding on to her brothers and sisters for support, Daisy watched through the bay window as her mother walked down the sidewalk, shoulders drooping, a suitcase in each hand, growing smaller and smaller until finally she disappeared from view. Some of the children eventually rejoined their mother, and some went to live with other relatives. It fell to Daisy to stay with her father. She grew up with a hard knot of bitterness inside her, a tumor of hatred over what he had done to the family. All the kids dropped out of school early in order to take jobs or join the Army, and then one by one they moved away to other towns. They got married, started families and tried to put the past behind them. Their father vanished—no one knew where, and no one cared.

"Many years later, to everyone's surprise, the father resurfaced. Drunk and cold, he had wandered into a Salvation Army rescue mission one night. To earn a meal ticket he first had to attend a worship service. When the speaker asked if anyone wanted to accept Jesus, he thought it only polite to go forward along with some of the other drunks. He was more surprised than anybody when the 'sinner's prayer' actually worked. The demons inside him quieted down. He sobered up. He began studying the Bible and praying. For the first time in his life, he felt loved and accepted. He felt clean.

"And now, he told his children, he was looking them up one by one to ask for forgiveness. He couldn't defend anything that had happened. He couldn't make it right. But he was sorry, sorrier than they could possibly imagine. The children, now middle-aged and with families of their own, were initially skeptical. Some doubted his sincerity, expecting him to fall off the wagon at any moment. Others figured he would soon ask for money. Neither happened, and in time the father won them over, all except Daisy.

"Long ago, Daisy had vowed never to speak to her father, 'that man' as she called him. Her father's reappearance rattled her badly, and old memories of his drunken rages came flooding back as she lay in bed at night. 'He can't undo all that just by saying, "I'm sorry," ' Daisy insisted. She wanted no part of him. The father may have given up drinking, but alcohol had damaged his liver beyond repair. He got very sick, and for the last five years of his life he lived with one of his daughters, Daisy's sister. In fact, they lived eight houses down the street from Daisy. Keeping her vow, Daisy never once stopped in to visit her dying father, even though she passed by his house whenever she went grocery shopping or caught a bus.

"Daisy did consent to let her own children visit their grandfather. Nearing the end of his life, the father saw a little girl come to the door and step inside. 'Oh, Daisy, you've come to me at last,' he cried, gathering her in his arms. The adults in the room didn't have the heart to tell him the girl was not Daisy, but her daughter Margaret. He was hallucinating grace.

"All her life, Daisy determined to be unlike her father, and indeed she never touched a drop of alcohol. Yet she ruled her own family with a milder form of the tyranny she had grown up under. She would lie on a couch with a rubber ice pack on her head and scream at the kids to 'shut up!' 'Why did I ever have you stupid kids anyway?' she would yell. 'You've ruined my life!' The Great Depression had hit, and each child was one more mouth to feed. She had six in all, rearing them in the two-bedroom row house she lives in to this day. In such close quarters, they seemed always underfoot. Some nights she gave them all whippings just to make a point; she knew they'd done wrong, even if she hadn't caught them.

"Hard as steel, Daisy never apologised and never forgave. Her daughter Margaret remembers as a child coming in tears to apologise for something she'd done. Daisy responded with a parental catch-22: 'You can't possibly be sorry! If you were really sorry, you wouldn't have done it in the first place.'

"Daisy was hurt, her pain was real, and you would have expected her to be gracious to others—especially to her children—but this was not the case. This is one of the saddest and common episodes I have observed in the ministry. The hurting individual suffers the consequences of the failure of the father or the mother, hates them for what they have put them through, but ends up doing the same, hurting those who are very close to them."[15]

Whatever the origins of your emotional pain, and whatever the degree of pain experienced, I know that the pain is real to you, even today. The good news is that you need not continue to live in pain; there is a path to victory. The path I present in the next few chapters is not a quick fix, but rather a lifelong journey living in His victory. If you are looking for an immediate solution, you will be disappointed. But if you are looking for a life of victory and a life of usefulness, you are at the right place—read on!

PERSONAL REFLECTION

- On a scale of 1 to 10 on an emotional health scale, where do you place yourself?
- Think about the reasons you are there. What are the root causes?
- Understanding this and being able to do this means that you are halfway to dealing with your emotional hurts.

---

15. Philip Yancey, *What's So Amazing About Grace?* Zondervan Publishing, 2002

Chapter Three

Walking Down Memory Lane

I HAVE WORKED WITH many hurting individuals and have always found that a good place to begin the journey toward healing is to first take a walk down "memory lane." By this I mean uncovering and unlocking painful and hurtful memories that may have been long buried or ignored.

Let me share a story that struck a chord with me when I first read it. It's from David Seamands' book, *Healing Grace*:

> "Mitzi was excited. 'It's all beginning to make sense; the pieces are fitting together. At least now I understand where I need help and what I need to be praying about. And there's hope—no, better than that—Harry and I know there's healing ahead, and that's making such a big difference in everything.'
>
> "I couldn't keep from liking this fine young couple, both so attractive and intelligent, obviously deeply in love with one another and strongly committed to the highest ideals of a Christian marriage. But like so many others, they had discovered from the very start that they couldn't seem to keep from hurting and being hurt by each other. As we

counselled together, it became clear that the heart of the problem was Mitzi's hypersensitivity and unrealistic expectations. Some people have been described as 'accidents waiting to happen.' It seemed Mitzi was a deep reservoir of pain waiting to be tapped into. All her life, pastors and teachers had told her to just forget the past, claim victory in Christ and develop new skills for coping with the present and future.

"So Mitzi was surprised when I encouraged her not only to become aware of the painful memories, but to write them down so she could share them with me and her husband. She did this conscientiously and prayerfully.

"Now we both felt the time was ripe, and so had scheduled the in-depth healing prayer session. One by one, Mitzi visualized before the Lord some of her most hurtful and humiliating childhood and teenage experiences. As we prayed, our imaginations were literally 'back there' in time. She was not simply remembering the past. She was reliving and reflecting incidents, often in remarkable detail, as if she were actually there now. Although it was a struggle, Mitzi was forgiving the many people who had hurt her, and in turn, she was receiving God's forgiveness for her long-held resentments against them.

"When, during the prayer time there was a long unexpected pause, I gently suggested that if the Spirit was showing her something new, she should go ahead and share it with the Lord. The tone of her voice became that of a little child as she began her prayer, 'Dear Jesus...' and told Him something she had not remembered for many years. She was about four years old and, together with her family, was visiting her grandmother. Grandma had woven a tiny blanket for her doll. Mitzi was a painfully shy child. It was almost impossible for her to even say 'hello,' 'hi,' or 'thank you' to anyone. When Grandma gave her the blanket, her parents asked, 'Isn't that nice of Grandma to work so hard and make such a pretty blanket for your dolly? Now Mitzi, tell her thank you.' Mitzi whimpered out her childish prayer, 'O Jesus, You know how badly I wanted to say thanks to Grandma, but there was a big lump in my throat, and I just couldn't say it. Dear Jesus, I tried so hard, but it wouldn't come out.'

"Now Mitzi shook with sobs. I tried to comfort her, asked her to imagine herself sitting on Jesus' lap, like the children in the Bible. This gave her the necessary encouragement to go on. The deepest hurt was yet to come. 'My little sister was there and said she wanted the blanket. So Mother and Dad told me if I didn't say thank you, they'd give it to her. And when I couldn't say it, they did. They gave it to Patti! O Jesus, You know how much I wanted to say it. But no one understood, no one cared. It's not fair, it's not fair!'

"As we continued praying, Mitzi saw how much this and other similar experiences had influenced her life. She had allowed deep bitterness to enter her heart. She had carried it against her parents and her sister. Now it had become the pattern of her life. Whenever she sensed injustice or misunderstanding, she became tongue-tied, filled with bitterness and unable to communicate. Thus, she could never resolve problems. In subsequent sessions, we worked together to help her learn new ways of openness with Harry and other people. To this day, Mitzi insists that the time of healing prayer was the turning point of her life."[16]

We human beings have an enormous capacity to bury our pain and live in the present, and we fool ourselves that the past has no connection with the present. Unfortunately, this is not true. A cancer was buried, but it is festering, and it is hurting. It is only by visiting such painful episodes that we even become aware that we have buried these experiences. The tragedy,

---

16. David A. Seamands, *Healing Grace,* Victor Books, 1988

which I see again and again as I meet with people, is that these buried experiences that you may not even know are there control your present actions and behaviour and define who you are.

I saw this during a recent visit to Bangladesh. I had just finished a day-long workshop with a group of local pastors, teaching on the subject of emotional healing. A young pastor came up to me and requested a private meeting, which we scheduled for later that day. He began to share about his conversion, his ministry work and finally he got down to the real reason he had wanted to talk with me. He said, "I have been battling homosexual tendencies from my teenage years, and it's something that really troubles me as I can't understand where it comes from or why I can't overcome it. When you were teaching us today and talking about suppressed memories, I suddenly remembered a painful incident I had buried deep within me. I was sexually abused by a male relative when I was very young. Later, I had no recollection of it—I suppose I had buried this painful incident in my mind. But now I understand why I have been having these homosexual feelings, and I know I have to deal with my past if I am to truly overcome this in my life."

As I prayed with him, I was thankful that this young pastor had begun the process of overcoming his past and walking into the future in victory. His painful memory, though buried for many years, had been attempting to define who he was and to control him. Can I encourage you now to go down your own personal memory lane? Here are a few guidelines as you travel this path:

1. KNOW FOR CERTAIN THAT IT WILL BE PAINFUL, BUT PERMANENT RELIEF WILL FOLLOW.

This will bring back many memories and the emotions that surround the event or events, but it is important for us to face the reality of the pain, rather than bury it. Facing the problem the second time is to deal with the problem. Through the first experience, you became a victim, but the second visit is to deal with the negative emotions that surround the issues.

Often people deal with the symptoms of a problem, but this is extremely shortsighted. When dealing with emotional pain, it is important for us to deal with root causes rather than with symptoms.

2. PRAY AND SEEK THE HOLY SPIRIT'S COUNSEL. HE WILL REVEAL THE BURIED PAIN.

In contrast to the position of ignoring hurts and past failures, the Psalmist sets a great example for us in Psalm 139:1-3 (ESV):

> "Lord you have searched me and known me. You know when I sit down and when I rise up, you discern my thoughts from afar. You search out my path and my lying down and are acquainted with all my ways."

In these three verses, the Psalmist acknowledges the fact that the Lord has searched him and knows him very intimately. He derives comfort from the fact that God is everywhere; that He knows all that pertains to us; that we can never be hidden from His view; that He has known us from the beginning; that as He fashioned and formed us—making us what we are—He knows all our necessities, and can supply them.

This Psalm consists of three parts:

1. A celebration of the omniscience and omnipresence of God as a ground of confidence and hope (verses 1-18).

- The fact that he knows all that there is in the heart (verses 1-6).
- The fact that he is present everywhere (verses 7-12).
- The fact that all in our past life has been known to God; that He has created us and that His eye has been upon us from the beginning of our existence (verses 13-16).

- The fact that His thoughts toward us are precious, and numberless as the sand (verses 17-18).

2. The feelings of the psalmist in relation to the acts of the wicked as a proof that he loved God (verses 19-22).

These reflections seem to have sprung from the Psalmist's contemplation of the divine character and perfections, which lead him to hate all that was opposed to a Being so pure, so benevolent, so holy. On looking into his own heart, in view of what God is, he was conscious that he had no sympathy with the enemies of God. Such was his love for the character of God, and such his confidence in Him that he could have nothing in common with them in their feelings toward God, but wished to be dissociated from them forever.

3. The expression of a desire that, as God saw all the recesses of the human soul, He would search the Psalmist's heart, and would detect any evil He might see there, and deliver him from evil, and lead him in the way which conducted to life eternal (verses 23-24).

Anyone may feel, and must feel, that after all that he knows of himself—after all the effort that he makes to ascertain what is within his heart—there are depths there that his eye cannot penetrate, and that there may be sins of thought and feeling there that he has not detected. But it is only from the consciousness of sincerity, and a true desire to honour God, that one can pray that God would search him, and that he would detect and bring out every form of sin that he may see concealed and lurking in the soul. He who can sincerely offer this prayer is a pious man.[17]

In verse 23, the Psalmist invites God again to search him, and in verse 24 he says, "See if there is any *grievous* way in me." Some translate the word "grievous way" as "offensive" or

---

17. Albert Barnes & James Murphy, *Barnes Notes on the Old and New Testaments – Psalms Vol 1 & 2,* Blackie Publishers, 1870-1872

"hurtful way." David is aware that there may be hurtful memories that are buried within him, causing him to behave in destructive ways. He certainly had many destructive ways, as we learn from his life.

This is the tragedy of buried sin: It controls and governs our behaviour and attitudes. It is only when a believer diligently seeks the truth and the origins of his inner hurts, that the Holy Spirit is able to unravel some of the hidden pain and our responses to the pain.

DEAL WITH ISSUES WHICH GOD WILL HIGHLIGHT

The next steps will help you to deal with the different issues that cripple a person emotionally. At this stage, I would only suggest that you be open to dealing with the issues that God will show you, as you begin to walk down your memory lane. How you can deal with the issues, in practical terms, is covered in the next chapters and steps of the healing process.

Because I know the pain you will experience, I have prayed this prayer for you:

> "God, as my friend begins the journey down memory lane, will You, by Your Spirit, travel with him/her? Give him/her the courage to face the past and the pain that has been consciously or unconsciously buried. Will You bring to memory those painful moments and help my brother/sister by your grace to bring them to closure and to experience the victory that You give those who are willing to face reality and seek Your help. I thank you for Your presence and for the gift of victory, so that he/she can live to his/her maximum potential and serve others in need. In Jesus' name, Amen."

Chapter Four

Jesus Understands Your Pain

ONE OF THE COMMON traits of those with damaged emotions is that the traumatised person wonders whether anyone will ever understand the pain he or she has experienced. This compels some to share their pain very openly, with a heavy dose of self-pity, while others react in just the opposite way: They bottle their pain. Because they have concluded that no one will ever understand or really care, they fear that sharing their hurts will bring further rejection.

It is in this context that I want you to explore with me the following passage, Hebrews 4:14-16:

> "Therefore, since we have a great high priest who has gone through the heavens, Jesus the Son of God, let us hold firmly to the faith we profess. For we do not have a high priest who is unable to sympathize with our weaknesses, but we have one who has been tempted in every way, just as we are—yet was without sin. Let us then approach the throne of grace with confidence, so that we may receive mercy and find grace to help us in our time of need."

Here are some truths I have gleaned from this passage:

- "For we do not have a high priest who is unable to sympathize with our weaknesses."
- "But we have one who has been tempted in every way; just as we are—yet was without sin."

Our high priest not only understands our pain, but also invites us to draw near to the throne of grace:

- "Let us then approach the throne of grace with confidence, so that we may receive mercy and find grace to help us in our time of need."

Jesus knows our human condition. It is not something He has heard about, but something He fully knows; for He, too, was a man. We may approach Him confidently because He knows our weakness.

Our high priest has gone through the entire gamut of human suffering, and so He is able to "sympathise." This word means to "feel" with a person to the point that the hurt and pain are actually felt within one's own heart.

HOW CAN JESUS UNDERSTAND MY PAIN?

He can, because He is both God and man. Philippians 2:5-7 (ASV) says:

> "Have this mind in you, which was also in Christ Jesus: who, existing in the form of God, counted not the being on equality with God a thing to be grasped, but emptied himself, taking the form of a servant, being made in the likeness of men."

The one who was existing in the form of God took on the form of a servant. The word "taking" does not imply an exchange, but rather an addition. The "form of God" could not be relinquished, for God cannot cease to be God; but our Lord could, and did, take on the very form of a lowly servant when He entered human life through the incarnation.

Jesus Christ made Himself of no reputation; that is, He emptied Himself. The word "emptied" means to completely empty. It is the picture of "pouring water out of a glass until it is empty" or of "dumping something until it is all removed."[18]

This picture of being completely empty portrays just how far Christ went in humbling Himself for us. What was it that was poured or emptied out of Jesus Christ when He left heaven and came to earth?

1. Christ did not lay aside His deity when He came to earth. He could not cease to be who He was—God. No person can ever cease to be who he is. A person may take on different traits and behave differently; a person may change his behaviour and looks, but he is the same person in being, nature and essence. Jesus Christ is God; therefore, He is always God—He always possesses the nature of God.
2. Christ laid aside some of His rights as God—laid aside His right to experience the glory and majesty, honour and worship of heaven. In coming to earth as a man, He was to experience anything but His glory and majesty, honour and worship. Men would treat Him far differently than a heavenly being.

   Matthew Henry has a brief, but excellent statement of this fact: "He emptied Himself, divested Himself of the honours and glories of the upper world and His former appearance, to clothe Himself with the rags of human nature."[19]
3. He emptied Himself of the right to act as God, and confined Himself to being a mere human, humbling Himself even to die on the cross.

---

18. William Barclay. *The Letters to the Philippians, Colossians, and Thessalonians.* John Knox Press, Westminister, 2003

19. Matthew Henry. *Matthew Henry's Commentary on the Whole Bible: Complete and Unabridged in 6 Volumes.* Hendrickson Publishers, 1991

Because He confined Himself to act as man on earth, He experienced all of the pain and suffering that we humans experience.

THE PAIN JESUS EXPERIENCED

Jesus experienced pain, rejection and humiliation during his life on earth:

- At birth, King Herod attempted to kill Him (Matthew 2:16).
- He was called an illegitimate child; even Joseph wanted to abandon Him (Matthew 1:18-19).
- He experienced the pain of hunger when He fasted before the commencing his public ministry (Luke 4:2).
- He experienced thirst. So He asked the woman at the well for water (John 4:7).
- His own family could not understand Him (John 7:2-5; Mark 3:21).
- The night before He was crucified the disciples were not even willing to spend the night with Him (Luke 22:40-46).
- His close friend, Judas, betrayed Him (Luke 22:21-22).
- In the hour of need, the Apostles were fighting for positions of honour (Luke 22:24).
- His closest friend denied Him (Mark 14:66-71).
- He was insulted and mocked by the guards (Luke 23:36).
- On the cross, He experienced humiliation and terrible pain (Matthew 27:28-31, 39-46).
- When He was crucified, only Mary, the Apostle John and a few other women were with Him (Matthew 27:55-56).

The extent of the pain that Jesus suffered is borne out in this fictional account in John Stott's *The Cross of Christ*:

"At the end of time, billions of people were scattered on a

great plain before God's throne. Most shrank back from the brilliant light before them. But some groups near the front talked heatedly—not with cringing shame, but with belligerence.

" 'Can God judge us? How can he know about suffering?' snapped a pert young brunette. She ripped open a sleeve to reveal a tattooed number from a Nazi concentration camp. 'We endured terror... beatings... torture... death!'

"In another group a negro boy lowered his collar. 'What about this?' he demanded, showing ugly rope burn. 'Lynched... for no crime but being black!'

"In another crowd, a pregnant schoolgirl with sullen eyes. 'Why should I suffer?' she murmured. 'It wasn't my fault.'

"Far out across the plain there were hundreds of such groups. Each had a complaint against God for the evil and suffering He permitted in His world.

"How lucky God was to live in heaven where all was sweetness and light, where there was no weeping or fear, no hunger or hatred. What did God know of all that man had been forced to endure in this world, for God leads a pretty sheltered life, they said.

"So each of these groups sent forth their leader, chosen because he had suffered the most. A Jew, a Negro, a person from Hiroshima, a horribly deformed arthritic, a thalidomide child. In the centre of the plain, they consulted with each other. At last they were ready to present their case. It was rather clever.

"Before God could be qualified to be their judge, He must endure what they had endured. Their decision was that God should be sentenced to live on earth—as a man!

" 'Let Him be born a Jew. Let the legitimacy of His birth be doubted. Give Him a work so difficult that even His family will think Him out of His mind when He tried to do it. Let

Him be betrayed by His closest friends. Let Him face false charges, be tried by a prejudiced jury and convicted by a cowardly judge. Let Him be tortured. At the last, let Him see what it means to be terribly alone. Then let Him die. Let Him die so that there can be no doubt that He died. Let there be a great host of witnesses to verify it.'

"As each leader announced his portion of the sentence, loud murmurs of approval went up from the throng of people assembled. And when the last had finished pronouncing sentence, there was a long silence. No one uttered another word. No one moved. For suddenly all knew that God had already served His sentence."[20]

Since He understands your pain, why not tell Him how you feel now?

The Roman Catholic Church has an interesting activity during the season of Lent, named the "Way of the Cross," in which 14 stations are marked, commemorating the agony and the pain that Jesus experienced on that final day.

A young boy whom I counselled followed the Way of the Cross, meditating on how much the Lord suffered. When he reached the last stop, which is the death of Christ, he wept so bitterly. While weeping, this is what he said: "Now I understand, now I know that Jesus can understand my pain. Even though I had worshipped Him for many years, I had never realized until this moment that He took such a beating, refused to use His God-powers, but experienced all of human pain to the very end." That was not only a point of revelation for this young man, but it was also a life-changing experience.

Jesus understands how you feel. You can come to Him, just as you are, and express how you feel, knowing well that He not only understands but He invites us to experience His mercy and grace. As Hebrews 4:16 states, "Let us then approach the

---

20. John R. W. Stott. *The Cross of Christ.* Inter Varsity Press. 1986

throne of grace with confidence, so that we may receive mercy and find grace to help us in our time of need."

If it means that He only understands our pain, then we could communicate to Him, but nothing more could be achieved. But in the verse above Paul invites us to approach His throne of grace with confidence, so that we may receive mercy and find grace in our time of need. As you begin to remember the past, it is possible that you might want to live in self-pity. Or it's possible that you have already used your past as a crutch to protect and defend yourself, formulating attitudes or responses to attitudes.

I have dealt with many people who would rather live in self-pity than deal with the issues confronting them. They are more comfortable because this is their established identity. This is a satanic trap. Would you at this point resolve within yourself that you want to be healed, that you want to experience victory? This is your choice. The pain was inflicted, and you had no choice then. But victory is possible; this is your choice now.

PERSONAL REFLECTION

Seek a place of quietness, where you feel secure to express your feelings and emotions aloud. The reason I want you to articulate your thoughts is that I want you to hear what you are saying and know that Jesus understands how you feel.

Express your sorrows, hurts and anger, and do not be afraid, knowing that Jesus understands you.

Let me also appeal to you that you do not live in the past, but take steps from now onward toward securing permanent healing, cleansing of memories and commencing of a new life.

GROUP WORK

This assignment might entail making yourself more vulnerable. Would you be willing to share your pain with someone you trust in the group or a friend you respect?

Chapter Five

His Grace Will Make the Difference

JOHN NEWTON WAS BORN in 1725 in London. His mother, who was a godly woman who taught him to pray as a child, but she died when he was only seven years old. After a few years, at the young age of eleven, his father, who was the captain of a ship, took him to sea for the first time. His seafaring life is well known and included being wrecked, becoming the captain of a slave ship, and a slave himself for two years on an island off the coast of Sierra Leone. While a slave, Newton lit a fire of driftwood on the shore to attract the attention of passing ships. His father's friend, another ship captain who was searching for him, sent a longboat ashore to investigate, and John was rescued.[21]

He was on this ship returning across the Atlantic, when it encountered a great storm that threatened to engulf it. The storm was terrific, and when the ship went plunging down into a trough of the sea, few on board expected her to come up again. The hold was rapidly filling with water. As Newton

21. D. B. Hindmarsh. *John Newton and the English Evangelical Tradition between the Conversions of Wesley and Wilberforce.* Clarendon Press, Oxford. 1996

hurried to his place at the pumps, he said to the captain, "If this will not do, the Lord have mercy upon us!" His own words startled him. "Mercy!" he said to himself in astonishment. "Mercy! Mercy! What mercy can there be for me? This was the first desire I had breathed for mercy for many years!" About six in the evening the hold was free from water, and then came a gleam of hope. "I thought I saw the hand of God displayed in our favour. I began to pray. I could not utter the prayer of faith. I could not draw near to a reconciled God and call him Father. My prayer for mercy was like the cry of the ravens, which yet the Lord does not disdain to hear."

John Newton, this cruel 18th-century captain, who traded men captured in Africa as slaves to the rich in America, after this conversion said:

"I am not what I ought to be,
I am not what I want to be,
I am not what I hope to be,
But by the grace of God, I am not what I was."[22]

This is the wonder of *His* grace.

In the previous chapter, we concluded that Jesus understands our pain and that He desires we draw near to Him to receive mercy and grace. In this step of our journey, we will study this fact in detail and appropriate His grace in our journey toward healing.

We are convinced at this stage that Jesus understands our pain. But right now, our need is to appropriate His grace for personal change. For such a change, it is important that we have a clear understanding of why God invites us to receive His grace.

Grace is a word that is commonly used in the Christian community, but just as often it is also used as a word to communicate

---

22. Stephen W. Smith. *The Lazarus Life: Spiritual Transformation for Ordinary People.* David C. Cook. 2008

something religious that we don't quite understand. The word grace in the scriptures is used in three different contexts:

1. God saves us by grace (Ephesians 2:8). This is the fundamental truth of Christianity.
2. God gives us grace to change us.
3. God gives us grace to bear with pain and difficulties.

In this chapter we want to look at points 1 and 2 above.

WE ARE SAVED BY GRACE

This is best demonstrated in the story of the prodigal son, which is recorded in Luke 15:11-19. The chapter begins with the Pharisees and scribes taking offence at Jesus because He was associating with people of disrepute. Jesus, without defending or explaining His behaviour, begins to tell them three stories (Luke 15:3ff). I want to draw your attention to the third story, to explain what it means to be "saved by grace."

In Luke 15:11-12, Jesus states, "'There was a man who had two sons. The younger one said to his father, "Father, give me my share of the estate." So he divided his property between them.'"

This is written in a Middle Eastern context, in which the inheritance is divided only after the father's death. When the father is alive, this subject is never discussed. When the son demanded his share, to an Eastern mind it would have amounted to saying, "You are as good as dead. I am more interested in my inheritance." It is amazing that the father in this story did not protest but willingly gave the son his inheritance.

Jesus continues, "Not long after that, the younger son got together all he had, set off for a distant country and there squandered his wealth in wild living. After he had spent everything, there was a severe famine in that whole country, and he began to be in need" (Luke 15:13-14).

The younger son squandered the money and wasted his life, then finally came to his senses and said, "How many of my father's hired servants have food to spare, and here I am starving to death!" (Luke 15:17).

The phrase, "He came to his senses," is used to describe someone who has lost his mind, but by some experience he is healed and becomes totally sane. It was only at this stage that the son recognised the damage he had done to the father and to himself. When he recognised this, he decided to go back to his father and tell him, "I am no longer worthy to be called your son; make me like one of your hired men" (Luke 15:19).

The Scriptures don't include this, but as I visualise this story in my mind, I can see the prodigal son stopping several times on his journey back home and asking himself, *How can I go back to my father after all I did to him?* I am also sure he practised what he was going to ask his father, in hopes of being accepted back as a hired servant.

While the son was going through his own agony, the father continued to live in the pain of the loss of his son. As he looked out for his son, suddenly one day he saw him walking toward the house. The father's response is an example of "grace dispensed":

> "So he got up and went to his father. But while he was still a long way off, his father saw him and was filled with compassion for him; he ran to his son, threw his arms around him and kissed him. The son said to him, 'Father, I have sinned against heaven and against you. I am no longer worthy to be called your son.' But the father said to his servants, 'Quick! Bring the best robe and put it on him. Put a ring on his finger and sandals on his feet. Bring the fattened calf and kill it. Let's have a feast and celebrate. For this son of mine was dead and is alive again; he was lost and is found.' So they began to celebrate" (Luke 15:20-24).

In verse 21, the son declares to the father the life he has lived and wrong he has done. In his mind, this disqualifies him from being a worthy son. But as we see in verses 22-24, the father has a completely different perspective, accepting him back as his beloved son and calling for a celebration.

The party begins, and the older son enters the scene (v 25). Of course, he is quite irritated and annoyed that the father should treat his brother, who has squandered his father's money, with such great honour and celebration:

> "But he answered his father, 'Look! All these years I've been slaving for you and never disobeyed your orders. Yet you never gave me even a young goat so I could celebrate with my friends. But when this son of yours who has squandered your property with prostitutes comes home, you kill the fattened calf for him!' " (Luke 15:29-30).

In this parable, Jesus shows us three clear attitudes:

- the sense of unworthiness and repentance (the prodigal son/the sinner)
- the legalistic attitude that requires a payment for sin and is unwilling to accept someone who has sinned (the older brother/the Pharisees)
- the grace that is willing to accept the repentant sinner (the father/God)

The son realised his true position of being unworthy. And he was. But the father treated him as a worthy son. *This is grace.* I think this is eloquently described in the words of Donald Barnhouse, the late pastor and Bible scholar:

> "Love that goes upward is worship,
> Love that goes outward is affection,
> Love that stoops is grace."[23]

Rather than this grace being celebrated and lived out in our churches, a sense of unworthiness has been falsely propagated

---

23. Donald Grey Barnhouse. *Romans, Man's Ruin, vol. 1.* Wm B Eerdmans Publishing Company, Grand Rapids, 1952

in the modern church and equated with "true spirituality." This has resulted in believers having a warped sense of identity.

Instead, my position is that I *was* unworthy, but He has *now* made me *worthy*. This understanding is a basic prerequisite for an intimate walk with God. We have been elevated to a position of sons and daughters. That is who we are *now*. But unfortunately, we live more like servants than sons and daughters.

Please read the following statements and determine for yourself whether you are one of those who celebrates the grace of God and enjoys sonship, or whether your mind has been perverted by legalism and you still come before God as an unworthy servant. These are extracted from David Seamand's *Healing Grace*.

1. The servant is accepted and appreciated on the basis of what he does; the child on the basis of who he is.
2. The servant starts the day anxious and worried, wondering if his work will really please his master; the child rests in the secure love of his family. This is a common problem I see in the church, mainly among people who have been deeply hurt.
3. The servant is accepted because of his workmanship; the son or daughter because of a relationship. I see believers working desperately hard to be accepted by God, but God categorically says, "I have made you worthy by my grace."
4. The servant is accepted because of his productivity and performance; the child belongs because of his position as a person.
5. At the end of the day, the servant has peace of mind only if he is sure he has proven his worth by his work. The next morning his anxiety begins again; the child can be secure all day and know that tomorrow won't change his status.

6. When a servant fails, his whole position is at stake—he might lose his job. When a child fails, he will be grieved because he has hurt his parents, and he will be corrected and disciplined. But he is not afraid of being thrown out.[24]

Please meditate on the following passage:

"I no longer call you servants, because a servant does not know his master's business. Instead, I have called you friends, for everything that I learned from my Father I have made known to you. You did not choose me, but I chose you and appointed you so that you might go and bear fruit—fruit that will last—and so that whatever you ask in my name the Father will give you" (John 15:15-16).

In addition to us being made worthy by His grace, this passage sheds light on our new inheritance and identity. He has elevated us from the position of a slave to being His friend. As a friend, He has revealed to us all that He has heard from the Father. True friends share secrets. God, in his mercy, has called me a friend and shared His mind with me. Praise God!

In verse 16 above, Jesus says, "You did not choose me, but I chose you." Even our selection is not based on anything that we have done, but it is the sovereign will and purpose of God. And He has chosen us so that we should go and bear fruit. This should propel us into ministry with a deep sense of expectancy to be used by God.

Jesus concludes with the promise, "Whatever you ask the father in My name, He may give to you." What an antidote for those who suffer from low self-esteem or a poor understanding of themselves!

Here is another story that demonstrates this concept of grace:

---

24. David A. Seamands, *Healing Grace,* Victor Books, 1988

King Saul and his son Jonathan had died following a battle. When word of the dual tragedy reached David's attention, it grieved him. Knowing that David was now Israel's new king, the members of Saul's family fled for their lives, erroneously thinking that David would treat them like all the other monarchs of Eastern dynasties. The scene portrayed in Scripture is one of pandemonium.

Jonathan, son of Saul, had a son who was lame in both feet. He was five years old when the news about Saul and Jonathan came from Jezreel. His nurse picked him up and fled, but as she hurried to leave, he fell and became crippled. His name was Mephibosheth.

In the haste to escape, Saul's grandson suffered a permanent injury. Not having medical help available, and not knowing where to turn for such assistance, the boy never recovered from the fall. He lived the balance of his life lame in both feet.

> "Years passed, and David established his position as the King of Israel. One day he was thinking of the goodness of the Lord to him, and in the process he remembered Jonathan and asked a question, 'Is there anyone still left of the house of Saul to whom I can show kindness for Jonathan's sake?' " (2 Samuel 4:4).

It's a question of grace, asked by a grateful man. It is quite clear that David was ignorant that his friend had any member of his family surviving, but soon he had news:

> "Now there was a servant of Saul's household named Ziba. They called him to appear before David, and the king said to him, 'Are you Ziba?' 'Your servant,' he replied. The king asked, 'Is there no one still left of the house of Saul to whom I can show God's kindness?' Ziba answered the king, 'There is still a son of Jonathan; he is crippled in both feet.' 'Where is he?' the king asked. Ziba answered, 'He is at the house of Makir son of Ammiel in Lo Debar' " (2 Samuel 9:2-4).

When Mephibosheth was brought before the King, he was perhaps trembling with fear. All his life he was told to conceal his identity. The man he feared most was the King of Israel, and now he was facing him.

> "When Mephibosheth son of Jonathan, the son of Saul, came to David, he bowed down to pay him honor. David said, 'Mephibosheth!' 'Your servant,' he replied" (2 Samuel 9:6).

With deep fear, he was anticipating the king to call in the torturers and have him killed, but on the contrary he heard something that he couldn't believe:

> " 'Don't be afraid,' David said to him, 'for I will surely show you kindness for the sake of your father Jonathan. I will restore to you all the land that belonged to your grandfather Saul, and you will always eat at my table' " (2 Samuel 9:7).

David wanted to show kindness to Mephibosheth, not because he deserved it, but rather because of his Father. Mephibosheth could not believe what he heard, and his response indicated it.

> "Mephibosheth bowed down and said, 'What is your servant, that you should notice a dead dog like me?' " (2 Samuel 9:8)

Mephibosheth's humility is painful. It was perhaps in part the result of his helpless lameness and the other misfortunes of his life. The King continued, "I will restore all your land, but I will do more. You will eat with my family—you will be a part of my family." Undeserving, but yet unconditionally loved. This is grace.

GRACE FOR CHANGE

In my dealing with people who have been deeply hurt, I have found that, rather than live in the liberation that Christ offers, they live in a "performance" mode. This gets compounded in our Asian culture, which has no understanding of grace. In both Hinduism and Buddhism, you work out your own salvation, and you appease your gods with offerings, vows and sacrifices so that they do your bidding. In this context, grace goes against the very grain of their religious worldview.

Unfortunately, this thinking is carried into the church, resulting in people working hard to be "accepted" by God. Perhaps you are deeply wounded, and you look at the future through the eyes of pessimism. I have great news for you: He not only accepts us by grace, He gives us grace to change.

I want to take you through an interesting passage of Scripture that offers hope in the midst of the deep pain that you may have experienced:

> "After that, He appeared to more than five hundred of the brothers at the same time, most of whom are still living, though some have fallen asleep. Then He appeared to James, then to all the apostles, and last of all He appeared to me also, as to one abnormally born. For I am the least of the apostles and do not even deserve to be called an apostle, because I persecuted the church of God. But by the grace of God I am what I am, and His grace to me was not without effect. No, I worked harder than all of them—yet not I, but the grace of God that was with me" (1 Corinthians 15:6-10).

Paul writes candidly of his own poor track record. After listing the gallery of the "greats" to whom the risen Lord appeared (Peter, James and the apostles), he states, "Last of all He appeared to me." This is not false humility, but a historical fact. Paul refers to himself as "one untimely born." You may be shocked to know the Greek term refers to one born before the full period of gestation, one who was aborted, literally, "the dead foetus." It means one who was totally devoid of spiritual life.[25]

25. Sir William Robertson Nicoll (Ed.) *The Expositor's Bible.* Funk & Wagnells. 1900

Paul also sees himself as the least of the Apostles, having been one who persecuted the church. But he does not continue to live in self-pity. Even though his past was horrible, he proudly claims, *"But by the grace of God I am what I am, and His grace to me was not without effect."*

THE GRACE OF GOD CAN BRING ABOUT A MARVELOUS CHANGE

In my experience in dealing with people with deep wounds, I have come to a point of categorizing them as follows:

Those who embrace God's grace and look for change. They are positive, they are proactive and they become marvelous "trophies" of God's grace.

> Roy was only nine years old when his father died. Two years later, his mother threw him out of the house saying, "I can't feed you or look after you." From that time, he had no home, no one to love and no one to teach him right from wrong. Hardened by these experiences, he took to a life of crime. He was imprisoned many times, but these periods of incarceration only hardened him further.
>
> One day, walking the streets, he saw a Christian pastor preaching to a small crowd. He was so annoyed by the preacher's emphasis on a loving God that he walked up to the preacher, beat him up and dismissed the crowd. No one dared to challenge him, for he was known as a ruthless criminal. The next day, the preacher saw Roy in the street, ran up to him, hugged him and then ran away again. Roy was so confused that he thought to himself, *I beat this guy, and this morning he comes and hugs me.* He had never been hugged by anybody, and this led to a series of events that resulted in him entering into salvation. Today he pastors a church and is the father of three girls whom he deeply loves and cares for. Saved from a former life of crime, today he introduces Jesus to people, and the story of change continues.

Those who are deeply wounded and live in perpetual self-pity. Their self-pity has overcome their desire to gain victory. They use their self-pity as a crutch to continue to gain sympathy from those around them. For them, the attention received at that moment is far more important than gaining permanent victory. The pain has almost become their identity, and they would rather live with the pain than deal with it.

This is the story of Sharon. She was a young girl who had an encounter with the Lord. She was intelligent, had a great mind and wanted to do better in life. Her siblings were very different, settling down to do any mediocre work, with no ambition to improve their life circumstances. They always made fun of her and looked down on her ambitions to improve her life. Almost weekly she would storm into my office, sobbing and saying, "God is unfair. I want to be somebody, but God placed me in a family that wants me to be nobody." Her high ambitions and the reality in her home caused her to be filled with self-pity. With time, I saw the glow and the smile fade away, and self-pity begin to dominate her life.

Those who blatantly refuse to change. Often this is because they are determined to punish those who have hurt them. They are aware that grace is available for change and for a new life, but they know that change comes by being willing to forgive those who have caused you pain. Their commitment to punish those who have hurt them is greater than their need to be free from the past and receive healing.

Rohan was a young boy who was employed by a Christian organisation and turned out to be an excellent carpenter. He earned well, and there was a dramatic change in his own lifestyle. But soon arrogance caught up with him, and he was dismissed from his workplace. He could have continued as a carpenter and earned his money, but he decided to beg in front of the organisation's office.

> When he was asked why he gave up carpentry to begin a life of begging, his response was, "I want the leaders in this organisation to suffer. I will make them suffer. Every time they see me begging, that will trouble them and cause them grief."

Having worked in a youth organization for many years, I have heard many young people publicly proclaim, "My parents caused me grief; I will teach them a lesson by a lifestyle that will dishonour them."

It is amazing for me to note that in all three situations above, the grace of God is available for change. But it is an individual's choice to appropriate the grace for change. I have joyfully watched people change and sadly watched people continue in their pain. At this point, you may be asking, *How do I take God's grace and allow it to change and heal me?* Let's look at a verse of Scripture that explains this concept:

> "But those who hope in the Lord will renew their strength. They will soar on wings like eagles; they will run and not grow weary, they will walk and not be faint" (Isaiah 40:31).

I find it interesting here that the word "renew" can also be translated as "exchange." Since Jesus has also suffered extreme pain, rejection and agony, He has the capacity to not only understand us, but also to give us grace. This grace is divine ability to deal with your pain, to overcome it and to be victorious.

However, the tragedy is that Christians think that, because you're well informed and are aware of your own problem, you can change on your own. This is contrary to biblical teaching. I do not change. His grace changes me. You may not witness this initially, but with time, those around you and you will see the difference.

So let me invite you to a life of intimacy with God. There are no shortcuts for change. It happens as you seek His face, sit at

His feet, allow Him to comfort you and redirect you in life. Let me urge you to spend quality time with the One who loves you and the One who has the capacity to change your thinking and to redirect your life into one of meaningful service to God and others.

Chapter Six

The Lord Is Sovereign

One of the most refreshing truths I have learned over the years is the fact that God is sovereign. The sovereignty of God is a theological term that refers to the unlimited power of God, who has complete control over the affairs of nature and history. This includes even my personal history.

In biblical history, we see that God allows some men and women to experience deep personal pain and trauma. I do not know the reason why. In some instances, such as the story of Job, God allowed Job to go through a series of painful experiences because He had confidence in him.

> "The Lord said to Satan, 'Where have you come from?' Satan answered the Lord, 'From roaming throughout the earth, going back and forth on it.' Then the Lord said to Satan, 'Have you considered my servant Job? There is no one on earth like him; he is blameless and upright, a man who fears God and shuns evil.' 'Does Job fear God for nothing?' Satan replied. 'Have You not put a hedge around him and his household and everything he has? You have blessed the work of his hands so that his flocks and herds are spread throughout the land. But now stretch out Your hand and

strike everything he has, and he will surely curse You to your face.' The Lord said to Satan, 'Very well, then, everything he has is in your power, but on the man himself do not lay a finger' " (Job 1:7-12).

When reading this passage, I am always struck by the extent of the pride and delight God takes in Job. The pain Job experienced had nothing to do with the wrath of God, but rather the confidence of God in His child.

I am quite disturbed by the "health and wealth" gospel that identifies suffering as God's wrath toward a person or as punishment for hidden sin. Those who believe this preach that prosperity is the favour of God, and any suffering, painful experience or sickness is interpreted as a rejection by God.

For a hurting person who has been rejected and deeply wounded by others, this seeming rejection by God during difficult circumstances or illnesses can completely rob them of their faith in Him. It also robs them of the opportunity to understand and come to God as their loving Father. This often leads to bitterness against people and the supreme Creator.

As you read this, I would like you to stop and prayerfully consider whether you too have been thinking that the pain you have experienced is because God is punishing you or because He has rejected you. If so, I urge you to read through the passage of scripture from Job above and to ask yourself whether it is possible that your own painful experience was because God is confident in you and is preparing you for great exploits.

I am in no position to explain why there is so much pain and suffering in this world. I can only conclude that pain and suffering was not part of God's plan when he created man. It is only the result of the fall of man. The wilful disobedience of man resulted in the human calamities that we face today.

But here again we see the loving kindness (Hebrew, *hesed*) of God, which didn't allow man to continue in his pain and suffering. God sacrificed His own Son to re-establish the covenant relationship that reconciles us with God, pays the penalty for the sin of mankind and establishes His kingdom on earth. This kingdom is to be characterised by love, justice and fair play. This, to me, is not a kingdom lost but a kingdom re-established. The intent of this book is to highlight emotional pain and to deal with it so that we can each live our kingdom purpose.

I believe that, in some difficult situations, God uses the trauma and the pain to draw us to Himself, and also to prepare us to serve others effectively. Romans 8:28 highlights this concept: "And we know that in all things God works for the good of those who love him, who have been called according to his purpose."

This verse may cause many of you to wonder how a loving God could have allowed you to go through so much pain and trauma. Often, I am asked, "Why did God allow this to happen to me? Couldn't he have stopped it or protected me?" I do not have an answer to this question, but I can tell you that there is sufficient biblical evidence to suggest that God will use your pain for His glory and to make you an empathetic person who can feel for and serve others—but only if you will allow Him to do so. This is a choice that will help you confront the pain of your past and live today with a greater purpose.

Let's look at a few stories from the Bible to highlight how God, in His sovereign purpose, used pain in the lives of people for a greater cause.

1. JOSEPH

Reading the amazing story of Joseph in Genesis 37-50, we discover that Joseph was the youngest in the family, that he was favoured by his father and that from a young age he had a close walk with God. He enjoyed visions of the future that he eagerly shared with his father and his brothers. These visions indicated that some day even his older brothers would be serving him.

The combination of being the father's favourite and the evidence of God's favour drove the brothers to jealousy, and they schemed to kill him. Even at this juncture, God intervened through one of the brothers and saved him from death but still allowed him to be sold into slavery in Egypt. All this happened because God had a greater purpose for Joseph.

In Egypt, young Joseph enjoyed the favour of Potipher, but again, because of the sinful actions of Potipher's wife, an innocent Joseph ended up in prison. At this stage, when he was unfairly judged and punished, God was orchestrating His purpose to use Joseph to save the life of millions. It was because of his prison experience that Joseph had a direct encounter with the king that resulted in him being appointed as the prime minister in Egypt.

There is no doubt that Joseph suffered great emotional pain and trauma, but it was for a greater purpose. God allowed Joseph to suffer at the hands of his jealous brothers because He had a greater purpose for him in life.

What attracts me most in this story is Joseph's ability to forgive his brothers, when he says, " 'You intended to harm me, but God intended it for good to accomplish what is now being done, the saving of many lives. So then, don't be afraid. I will provide for you and your children.' And he reassured them and spoke kindly to them' " (Genesis 50:20-21).

Even in the midst of pain, Joseph's ability to say these words to his brothers comes out of a deep walk with God. Joseph believed that God is sovereign and would fulfil His purpose. This is the difference between a man who believes in the sovereignty of God and one who does not.

2. MOSES

Moses was born, and there was a cruel verdict that all Hebrew male newborns must be killed. Moses' parents attempted to hide him, and they did so for a few months. But soon it became obvious that the baby could not be hidden for much longer. In sheer desperation, the mother made a reed basket and floated the child into the river to an unknown future.

I'm sure the parting was very painful, but I am amazed that God's divine intervention allowed, at that very moment, for Pharaoh's daughter to come to the river and discover Moses. The Scriptures tell us that her heart was moved with compassion, and she adopted Moses to be her own son. I'm sure she was aware that this was a child of a slave father and mother.

Moses was now in the palace. But within him there was a compassion for his people. In his haste, he killed a man and paid a heavy price by being driven into the wilderness. I'm sure in the wilderness Moses must have kept asking the question, *Why God? Why?* Perhaps you too are asking this same question.

Reading through Exodus, we see the events in Moses' life unfold, each event leading to another until God uses Moses to deliver the people of Israel and lead them to the Promised Land.

God took Moses to the palace to be trained as a commanding officer. And God took Moses to the wilderness to teach him dependence. And God brought him out of the wilderness to deliver the people of Israel. There was much pain, but there was a greater purpose. Moses had a great responsibility, and great was also his testing.

3. PAUL

After Paul's conversion, he was set apart as the apostle to the Gentiles, and he was faithful to this task. In Acts 16:6, Paul attempted to enter the region of Phrygia and Galatia, and Scripture says, "Having being forbidden by the Holy Spirit to speak the word in Asia..." At this stage he attempted to enter Bithynia and the Scripture tells us that "the spirit of Jesus did not allow them." And then he had a vision in which a man pleaded with him to come to Macedonia.

The reason I presented all these details is to establish the fact that Paul was obeying God's command along every step of his journey. The very next day, he travelled to Macedonia. His obedience was rewarded, and a girl was delivered of an evil spirit (see Acts 16:16-18). The Apostles were then falsely accused, beaten and imprisoned (see Acts 16:19-25). They were perplexed by the beating and the false accusation, but they continued to believe that God is sovereign. They were even singing, in the midst of the pain and confusion (see Acts 16:25). Only someone who believes in the sovereignty of God can sing and praise Him in the midst of suffering.

At this stage, yet another unexpected event took place. There was an earthquake, and the jailor was about to kill himself because he feared the prisoners had escaped. Paul responded again as a man who believed in the sovereignty of God (see Acts 16:28). The jailor and his family were converted, and Paul sailed to Thessalonica.

It is amazing for me to note what took place subsequently. The church of Philippi was established, and the Scriptures show that they financially supported Paul twice in his trips to Thessalonica (see Philippians 4:16), once to Corinth (2 Corinthians 11:9) and long afterward, when he was a prisoner in Rome (see Philippians 4:9,14,18). The church of Philippi not only supported him financially, there is evidence to suggest that it was this church that took the gospel to the West, and the Western churches, in later years, took it to the rest of the world.

When the events in Macedonia were unfolding, it must have been very confusing for Paul. I am sure he asked the question, *Why, Lord?* many times—when he was unjustly accused, when he was being beaten, when he was imprisoned. But for us today, we can see how God used all that suffering to give birth to the church of Philippi and the multitude of churches in the West and the rest of the world.

I am persuaded that your suffering at this point, even though it is so painful, may be the foundation on which greater good is built. Let me also present a very difficult concept that I believe will enable you to deal with your pain. God is not governed by time, as we are. We humans refer to things as in the past, the present or the future. But because God is not governed by time, everything for Him is in the present. The implication of this is that He witnessed your pain but never abandoned you.

We see this truth being played out through circumstances in which God brought individuals to intervene and protect you and me as we went through difficult and traumatic experiences. In the case of Joseph, there was the older brother who prevented him from being killed. In the case of Moses, He brought Pharaoh's daughter. In the case of Paul, there was Lydia and her family.

The Bible tells us that Satan is a liar and that he wants to kill and destroy (see John 10:10). He even tried to kill Jesus soon after He was born (see Matthew 2:13). This was the intention of the evil one even in your own life—to destroy you. But the fact that you are alive and reading this book today tells me that God has intervened in your life. You are battered and bruised, but not destroyed. You are alive for a greater purpose.

There are many who believe that the will of God is always very fulfilling and satisfying and requires no pain or sacrifice—almost like a fairy tale with a happy ending. When difficulties arise, they think God has abandoned them or that it's the judgment of God. Is this Christianity or a fairy tale? When Jesus left the glory of Heaven and took on the reality of dying on a cross, it was an extremely painful and shameful experience, but the final purpose of God was fulfilled.

Paul says we are called not only to believe but to suffer for him (see Philippians 1:20). I think that the church has, to a certain extent, taken away this reality and replaced it with a "soft" gospel, one that is devoid of pain and suffering.

In Colossians, Paul says that he completes the sufferings of Christ on the cross (see 1:24). This does not mean that the sufferings of Christ were incomplete, nor that the work of atonement was incomplete on the cross, but rather that Paul recognises that taking the message of salvation to others will involve an element of suffering.

Your suffering was not in vain. It will make you a better person. You will understand the hurts and pain of others far more effectively, and God will use your pain in the process of sanctification. This is not our home. We are in preparation for our home in heaven. The pain we endure here is temporal, but an eternal crown awaits us. So let's persevere in the midst of all the pain, because of the assurance that we can conquer it.

Your response to your past pain, from this perspective, will enable you to minister effectively, with empathy. Your refusal to see your past from the perspective of eternity will cause you to be a bitter and angry person. Today you have a choice. You can view your past from two angles:

- You can think, *I suffered a lot, and some people hurt me,* and allow yourself to wallow in your hurt and pain. This, of course, will give rise to self-pity and anger.
- You can begin to understand that God allowed some suffering and that He is using the very pain—or will use it—for your good and for His glory.

What will you choose? Your happiness, freedom and the fulfilment of God's purpose through the painful episodes in your life can happen today! It all depends on your choice. Someone hurt you, and you suffered greatly. But you can reverse that order and bless people so they can be blessed, rather than continuing the cycle of pain. You can be an agent of change!

PERSONAL REFLECTION

In previous chapters, I have encouraged you to go back and walk down memory lane, looking at your past painful experiences and recalling each painful incident. I would now like you to take that walk again, but this time, look for the people and situations through which God intervened in your life to prevent your physical death or your complete emotional destruction. Identify these people by name.

First, I urge you to look at this list of names and to thank your loving Father for each one of these people whom He brought into your life at the right time and right place.

Second, I encourage you to write, call or meet up with these individuals and to thank them personally for the way in which they carried out God's purpose in your life.

By doing this, you will be able to recognise the interventions of God in your life in the past, be thankful and awed by how He has never abandoned or forsaken you. And you will also become more aware of God's continued interventions in your life today. Trust me, this will be a very therapeutic step for you.

Chapter Seven

God Loves You

IN THE PREVIOUS CHAPTERS we highlighted the desire to love and to be loved as one of the key needs a human being has. Every human being has the potential to love and a great desire to be loved.

But it is possible that you never experienced genuine love and that you are still hurting because of it. In my opinion, the first place to correct this is to establish a right theology on which you can base your present and your future—the truth that God loves you.

LOVE: EXPRESSED AT CREATION

The very first two chapters of the Bible depict a loving Father who creates a beautiful world for His children. It tells us how God, lovingly and with great care and purpose, added element after element until all of nature was complete. And He created this world with such great care to be used and enjoyed by His final creation—man and woman. He made man and woman in His own image (see Genesis 1:27). He then invited them to multiply, subdue the world and rule it.

To my Asian mind, this is a typical story of a father who deeply loves and cares for his children. He provides for them, arranges a marriage and creates an environment in which they can be happy. The unfortunate theological reality is that we have developed our theology based on the fall of man. We have majored on redemptive theology but abandoned a "creative theology." Creative theology suggests that God is a gracious God, who created this beautiful world so that His children can enjoy it.

LOVE: EXPRESSED ON THE CROSS

Your heavenly Father never intended pain and harm, but it was brought upon the world by the wilful disobedience of man (see Romans 6:23). It is against this backdrop of human rebellion against God that God promised a Saviour to redeem mankind: "And I will put enmity between you and the woman, and between your offspring and hers; he will crush your head, and you will strike his heel" (Genesis 3:15).

The Bible suggests that there is no greater love than a person laying down his life for others. This is what God did for you—not when you were "good," but He loved you even while you were living in sin.

This is further supported by Romans 5:8: "But God demonstrates His own love for us in this: While we were still sinners, Christ died for us." In His love, He created a world for you. In His love, He sent His Son to die for you. And in His love, He has prepared a home with Him for you in the future (see John 14:1-4). You may have been deprived of all human love, but you can be confident that God has never deprived you of His love.

The failure to recognise the *agapé* love of God and to be fulfilled by this love often leads us to look for love elsewhere and to feel unloved and rejected when we don't receive the love we expect from those around us.

The following are three real-life stories highlighting the response of three very different people to the lack of love in their lives. In each case, their response was extremely destructive—to themselves or to others. I am highlighting this fact so that you can evaluate your life in the light of these stories. You may be able to identify similar destructive patterns, which may have been a response to the lack of love felt in your own life.

SUPPRESSING EMOTIONS

David was a successful young man, the kind of person whom others envied because he "had it all." He had started a successful business, was happily married with a young family, volunteered in many community activities and was a leader in his church.

I came to know David as he helped us out on a project, and soon we would discuss issues as mundane as the latest cricket scores or sometimes deep, theological subjects. I found David to be intelligent, engaged and eager to learn and serve the Lord. But as I spent more time with him, I began to see that David was also grappling with some difficult issues in his personal life. The David that we saw from the outside didn't seem to be the same David inside. After a few days, our discussions turned from the issues of the world to David's own personal struggles.

At first I found it so hard to believe as David started sharing about what a failure he was in life. I invited David to meet me regularly since I didn't want our conversations to end with the project we were working on. As we talked over many weeks, I learned that David had grown up as an only child to a wealthy, older couple. His parents loved him, I'm sure, but they failed to communicate this to him.

He shared with me story after story of his childhood—stories of his parents ignoring him, of them constantly belittling his efforts and pushing him to do better and the many times his father showed he was disappointed in his only child. David had hidden these stories in his heart, and as he talked it was like a dam had burst and everything was gushing out.

In his mid-40s David was coming face to face with the hurts of his past and all the pain he had buried for years that now had to be faced and acknowledged. I'm sure this kind of experience is not limited to David. There are many who did not receive adequate love and support from their parents and continue to live defeated lives.

DOING ANYTHING TO EXPERIENCE LOVE

As a young child, Ayesha was deprived of love from her mother and stepfather. She was also brutally raped by her stepfather on many occasions. The compound effect took a major toll on the life of this child. By the time she was in her teens she was desperately looking for someone to love her. Her desire for love was misunderstood by her male peers who took advantage of this to have meaningless sexual flings with her. This drove her into further desperation. She was longing to be loved but never found this love.

Later, in a counselling session, when this subject was brought up, with tears flowing down her face she admitted that she would do anything even for just one moment of feeling loved. The story of this child ends in tragedy. She is still on a hopeless quest for love but has not found it yet.

PERFORMING SO THEY WILL BE LOVED

Sean is a young man whose father committed suicide when he was very young. His mother was plagued by many other family problems, and she wasn't able to demonstrate love or to give the time and attention the children needed. He grew up believing he needed to do things to be accepted.

Today, as a young adult, he goes out of his way to help anyone but will never allow anyone to help him or to treat him with generosity. In his eyes he is not worthy, but he must continue to perform for acceptance. Almost all his relationships are based on him serving them. He is unable to relax, to enjoy a friendship or even a conversation. For him to feel good, he needs to be doing something for others.

Having selflessly served others, he also expects them to be grateful and to always express that gratitude. When gratitude is not expressed, he goes into a rage but never communicates the cause of his anger, preferring to walk away from that relationship. When someone does express gratitude, he waves away the words of appreciation, almost as if they are not necessary. So people around him are extremely confused, wondering what caused him to be angry with them.

In a fallen world, there are many who will fall into this pattern of desperately seeking love. In their journey and quest for love there is a good possibility they will receive more hurt because they have a warped understanding of love and the modes of communicating this love.

Humans may have failed you, and it's possible that you are still hurting, but God assures you that His love is of greater depth and acceptance than any human love.

> "I no longer call you servants, because a servant does not know his master's business. Instead, I have called you friends, for everything that I learned from My Father I have made known to you" (John 15:15).

This shows that God has not only accepted us but is also extending his friendship to us. In the Old Testament only Abraham (2 Chronicles 27; Isaiah 41:8) and Moses (Exodus 33:11) were given this privilege. Here, Jesus is extending the same privilege to us. The realisation that God has extended His right hand of friendship to me is very sobering and refreshing—sobering, because this friendship is offered to me by the omnipotent Lord, who is seated on the throne; refreshing, because even though humans may not have extended love to me, God in His amazing love has accepted me as a friend.

Friends enjoy intimacy. Friends share secrets. Friends look out for each other. Friends stand by each other in times of need. Friends celebrate their victories. Friends mourn when the other falls. That is our privilege, and this is something that I believe Satan does not want you to understand and celebrate, because if you do so, your walk with God and your relationship with all human beings will change so dramatically.

I have previously shared the statement by John Wimber: "Satan takes the pain of the past, controls the present and destroys the future." This is one classic example of how he does it—he takes the hurt of our lack of love and confuses our mind to view God in the same manner. This robs our potential to do great exploits for the Lord in the present and the future. Understanding this will help you to see God in new ways and to respond to His love. This is a vital part of the healing process, and we focus on this in Chapter 10: "Seeing God in New Ways."

UNDERSTAND YOUR POSITION IN CHRIST

I have laboured to this point to present the love of God for us, which goes contrary to human thinking—especially to one who has been deprived of true love. Since it's so important for us to know the true love of God, I have presented Scripture to help you understand three vital components of this message:

- You are accepted by God.
- You are secure in him.
- You are significant to him.

Please read the following verses very carefully and speak them out loud to yourself so that you can hear these words being spoken into your life.

I AM ACCEPTED BY GOD

I am a child of God:

"Yet to all who received him, to those who believed in his name, he gave the right to become children of God" (John 1:12).

I am a friend of Christ:

"I no longer call you servants, because a servant does not know his master's business. Instead, I have called you friends, for everything that I learned from My Father I have made known to you" (John 15:15-16).

I have been justified:

"Therefore, since we have been justified through faith, we have peace with God through our Lord Jesus Christ" (Romans 5:1).

I have been bought with a price—I belong to God:

"You were bought at a price. Therefore honour God with your body" (1 Corinthians 6:20).

I am a saint:

"Paul, an apostle of Christ Jesus by the will of God, to the saints in Ephesus, the faithful in Christ Jesus" (Ephesians 1:1).

I have been adopted as God's child:

"He predestined us to be adopted as His sons through Jesus Christ, in accordance with His pleasure and will" (Ephesians 1:5-6).

I have direct access to the Holy Spirit:

"For through Him we both have access to the Father by one Spirit" (Ephesians 2:18).

I have been redeemed and forgiven of all my sins:

"... in whom we have redemption, the forgiveness of sins" (Colossians 1:14).

I am complete in Christ:

"And you have been given fullness in Christ, who is the head over every power and authority" (Colossians 2:10-11).

I AM SECURE

I am free from condemnation:

"Therefore, there is now no condemnation for those who are in Christ Jesus, because through Christ Jesus the law of the Spirit of life set me free from the law of sin and death. I am assured that all things work together for good" (Romans 8:1-2).

And we know that in all things God works for the good of those who love him, who have been called according to His purpose" (Romans 8:28).

I am free from any condemning charges against me:

"What, then, shall we say in response to this? If God is for us, who can be against us? He who did not spare His own Son, but gave Him up for us all—how will He not also, along with Him, graciously give us all things? Who will bring any charge against those whom God has chosen? It is God who justifies. Who is he that condemns? Christ Jesus, who died—more than that, who was raised to life—is at the right hand of God and is also interceding for us" (Romans 8:31-34).

I cannot be separated from the love of God:

"Who shall separate us from the love of Christ? Shall trouble or hardship or persecution or famine or nakedness or danger or sword?" (Romans 8:35).

I have been established, anointed and sealed by God:

"Now it is God who makes both us and you stand firm in Christ. He anointed us, set His seal of ownership on us, and put His Spirit in our hearts as a deposit, guaranteeing what is to come" (2 Corinthians 1:20-22).

I am hidden with Christ in God:

"For you died, and your life is now hidden with Christ in God" (Colossians 3:3).

I am a citizen of heaven:

"But our citizenship is in heaven. And we eagerly await a Savior from there, the Lord Jesus Christ" (Philippians 3:20).

I have not been given a spirit of fear but of power, love, and a sound mind:

"For God did not give us a spirit of timidity, but a spirit of power, of love and of self-discipline" (2 Timothy 1:7).

I can find grace and mercy in time of need:

"Let us then approach the throne of grace with confidence, so that we may receive mercy and find grace to help us in our time of need" (Hebrews 4:16).

I am born of God, and the evil one cannot touch me:

"We know that anyone born of God does not continue to sin; the One who was born of God keeps them safe, and the evil one cannot harm them" (1 John 5:18).

I AM SIGNIFICANT

I am the salt and the light of the Earth:

"You are the salt of the earth. But if the salt loses its saltiness, how can it be made salty again? It is no longer good for anything, except to be thrown out and trampled by men" (Matthew 5:13).

I am the branch of the true vine, a channel of His life:

"I am the true vine, and My Father is the gardener. He cuts off every branch in Me that bears no fruit, while every branch that does bear fruit He prunes so that it will be even more fruitful. You are already clean because of the word I have spoken to you. Remain in Me, and I will remain in you. No branch can bear fruit by itself; it must remain in the vine. Neither can you bear fruit unless you remain in Me. I am the vine; you are the branches. If a man remains in me and I in him, he will bear much fruit; apart from Me you can do nothing" (John 15:1-5).

I have been chosen and appointed to bear fruit:

"You did not choose Me, but I chose you and appointed you so that you might go and bear fruit—fruit that will last—and so that whatever you ask in My name the Father will give you" (John 15:16).

I am a personal witness of Christ:

"But you will receive power when the Holy Spirit comes on you; and you will be My witnesses in Jerusalem, and in all Judea and Samaria, and to the ends of the earth" (Acts 1:8).

I am God's temple:

"Don't you know that you yourselves are God's temple and that God's Spirit lives in you?" (1 Corinthians 3:16).

I am a minister of reconciliation:

"Therefore, if anyone is in Christ, he is a new creation; the old has gone, the new has come! All this is from God, who reconciled us to Himself through Christ and gave us the ministry of reconciliation: that God was reconciling the world to Himself in Christ, not counting men's sins against them. And He has committed to us the message of reconciliation. We are therefore Christ's ambassadors, as though God were making His appeal through us. We implore you on Christ's behalf: Be reconciled to God" (2 Corinthians 5:17-20).

I am God's co-worker:

"As God's co-workers we urge you not to receive God's grace in vain (2 Corinthians 6:1).

I am seated with Christ in the heavenly realm:

"And God raised us up with Christ and seated us with Him in the heavenly realms in Christ Jesus" (Ephesians 2:6).

I am God's workmanship:

"For we are God's workmanship, created in Christ Jesus to do good works, which God prepared in advance for us to do" Ephesians 2:10).

I can approach God with freedom and confidence:

"In Him and through faith in Him we may approach God with freedom and confidence" (Ephesians 3:12).

I can do all things through Christ who strengthens me:

I can do everything through Him who gives me strength (Philippians 4:13).

I have incorporated at the conclusion of this chapter the Bell Illustration, which reinforces these scriptures in a very visually appealing and striking manner. I have been unable to trace the origins of this illustration, but it is one that I find effective in conveying who we are in the sight of God.

BELIEVE AND ENJOY THE LOVE OF GOD

It is possible that you are one of those who has never experienced true love. Satan would want you to continue in the same framework and to be an angry and bitter person. The day that you understand that the omnipotent God loves you unconditionally, you will become an awesome weapon in the hands of a mighty God.

I believe these steps below will contribute to developing a vital relationship with God. So my advice to you is that you continue this as a regular exercise until it becomes a part of what you believe and how you live.

1. Let me reiterate the key message I have been trying to communicate through this chapter: *Do not doubt the personal aspect of God's love.*
2. Whenever you encounter a difficulty in life, the first attack will be in this area. Satan's voice and your subjective

feeling will be, *God does not love me.* When this happens, confront the subjective lie and replace it with the biblical reality that God loves you (see scriptures above). Difficulties in life do not mean God has withdrawn His love, but it means that God is working out His purposes in your life. Even the evil done by others to you can be used by God for your good and for His glory.

3. Know the fact that God's love is not based on your subjective feelings, but find freedom in the truth that He loves you unconditionally.
4. Constantly seek the presence of God and bask in his love. He has been waiting to shower you with His love; you have a lot of catching up to do!
5. Say goodbye to self-pity, this is your worst enemy. Memorise Romans 8:28.
6. Read the Psalms regularly. The authors of the Psalms were men who experienced the full gamut of emotions. They expressed their pain to God but consoled themselves by meditating on the character of God. This presented them with a new understanding of God's love.
7. Give yourself to loving others. It's by loving others that you really actualise your potential to love and understand the love of God for yourself.
8. Develop an accountable relationship with someone who truly loves God and you. Share with him or her your struggles and let them minister to you.

THE BELL
I KNOW WHO I AM.
I am God's child (John 1:12).
I am Christ's friend (John 15:15).
I am united with the Lord (I Cor. 6:17).
I am bought with a price (I Cor. 6:19-20).
I am a saint (set apart for God) (Eph. 1:1).
I am a personal witness of Christ (Acts 1:8).
I am the salt & light of the earth (Matt. 5:13-14).
I am a member of the body of Christ (I Cor. 12:27).
I am free forever from condemnation (Rom. 8: 1-2).
I am a citizen of Heaven. I am significant (Phil.3:20).
I am free from any charge against me (Rom. 8:31-34).
I am a minister of reconciliation for God (2 Cor. 5:17-21).
I have access to God through the Holy Spirit (Eph. 2:18).
I am seated with Christ in the heavenly realms (Eph. 2:6).
I cannot be separated from the love of God (Rom. 8:35- 39).
I am established, anointed, sealed by God (2 Cor. 1:21-22).
I am assured all things work together for good (Rom. 8:28).
I have been chosen and appointed to bear fruit (John 15:16).
I may approach God with freedom and confidence (Eph. 3:12).
I can do all things through Christ who strengthens me (Phil. 4:13).
I am the branch of the true vine, a channel of His life (John 15:1-5).
I am God's temple (I Cor. 3:16). I am complete in Christ (Col. 2:10).
I am hidden with Christ in God (Col. 3:3). I have been justified (Rom. 5:1).
I am God's co-worker (I Cor. 3:9; 2 Cor. 6:1). I am God's workmanship (Eph. 2:10).
I am confident that the good works God has begun in me will be perfected (Phil. 1:5).
I have been redeemed and forgiven (Col. 1:14). I have been adopted as God's child (Eph. 1:5).

I belong to God.
Do you know
who you
are?

Keep this bell ringing...

"The Lord bless you and keep you; the Lord make His face shine upon you and be gracious to you; the Lord turn His face toward you and give you peace" (Numbers 6:24-26).

Chapter Eight

Forgive Those Who Hurt You

THE PROCESS OF HEALING is extremely complicated, and yet it is well within our reach. In my experience in working with those who have been deeply hurt, I categorise them into four groups:

Group A are those who recognize that they have a problem and are willing to take steps to move toward a better life. They are proactive, willing to forgive those who have hurt them and willing to change—and they *do change*. Their hearts have been touched by God

Group B are those who use the pain of their past as a crutch. This pain and their present way of living have become their identity. They are engrossed in themselves and are afraid to take steps for the future because, if they begin to deal with their issues, they will eventually lose their identity.

Group C is another group that is wrapped up in self-pity. They have lived all their lives blaming others and are never willing to do anything toward change in their lives. They enjoy the attention they attract through their self-pitying lifestyles, little realizing that each time they relate their painful stories in the hope of gaining sympathy from an audience, they are reopening the wounds and reliving the pain of their past.

Group D are basically not interested in finding a solution. Their one consuming passion is revenge and retribution. Their hearts are filled with anger, and their sole focus is to get even with those who inflicted pain or, for that matter, anyone who stumbles onto their path. Their desire to hit back is far greater than their desire to be healed. In fact, they are so consumed by their anger and bitterness that they often do not even realize they need to seek healing.

Even though each of these groups seems very different in how they are coping with their hurts from the past, the one common theme among them is how they deal with both receiving and giving forgiveness.

To receive and give forgiveness may be alien concepts to you. Perhaps you have heard these words, but their significance may not have dawned on you.

Nelson Mandela taught the world a lesson in forgiveness, after emerging from prison after 27 years and being elected president of South Africa, he asked his jailer to join him on the inaugural platform. He then appointed Archbishop Desmond Tutu to head an official government panel with a daunting name: the Truth and Reconciliation Commission (TRC). Mandela sought to defuse the natural pattern of revenge that he had seen in so many countries where one oppressed race or tribe took control from another.

For the next two-and-a-half years, South Africans listened to reports of atrocities coming out of the TRC hearings. The rules were simple: if a white policeman or army officer voluntarily faced his accusers, confessed his crime and fully acknowledged his guilt, he could not be tried and punished for that crime. Hard-liners grumbled about the obvious injustice of letting criminals go free, but Mandela insisted that the country needed healing even more than it needed justice.

At one hearing, a policeman named van de Broek recounted an incident when he and other officers shot an eighteen-year-old boy and burned the body, turning it on the fire like a piece of barbecue meat in order to destroy the evidence. Eight years later van de Broek returned to the same house and seized the boy's father. The wife was forced to watch as policemen bound her husband on a woodpile, poured gasoline over his body, and ignited it.

The courtroom grew hushed as the elderly woman who had lost first her son and then her husband was given a chance to respond. "What do you want from Mr. van de Broek?" the judge asked. She said she wanted van de Broek to go to the place where they burned her husband's body and gather up the dust so she could give him a decent burial. His head down, the policeman nodded agreement.

Then she added a further request, "Mr. van de Broek took all my family away from me, and I still have a lot of love to give. Twice a month, I would like for him to come to the ghetto and spend a day with me so I can be a mother to him. And I would like Mr. van de Broek to know that he is forgiven by God, and that I forgive him too. I would like to embrace him so he can know my forgiveness is real."

Spontaneously, some in the courtroom began singing "Amazing Grace" as the elderly woman made her way to the witness stand, but van de Broek did not hear the hymn. He had fainted, overwhelmed.[26]

This, to me, is forgiveness—the willingness to let go of the anger toward the person who has caused so much pain and, more importantly, to love the person as if they never hurt or failed you.

This was the model that was set before us by the Lord Himself. Three years of sacrificial ministry for people—caring,

---

26. Philip Yancey, *Rumours of Another World: What on Earth are we Missing?* Zondervan, 2003

healing, feeding and loving them—resulted in a betrayal and an unjust trial in which even the chief judge had to admit that he found nothing wrong with Him. But under pressure from the crowd, the same judge condemned Jesus to death by washing his hands and claiming that he was not responsible for the act. Jesus was handed over to murderous soldiers who treated Him as an object of ridicule, tortured Him for hours and, the next day, forced Him to carry a cross on a rugged, uphill road.

When Jesus reached His destination, He was stripped of His clothes in public humiliation, and then they nailed Him to a cross. Those who were amused by His pain and humiliation began to mock Him, including one of the convicts who was crucified alongside Him. Amid this extreme pain, humiliation and loneliness, He cried out to the Father, saying, "Father, forgive them, for they know not what they do" (Luke 23:34, ESV).

This same Jesus, prior to His crucifixion, taught us the necessity of forgiving and the grave emotional and spiritual consequences if we do not forgive.

> "Then Peter came up and said to Him, 'Lord, how often will my brother sin against me, and I forgive him? As many as seven times?' Jesus said to him, 'I do not say to you seven times, but seventy times seven. Therefore, the kingdom of heaven may be compared to a king who wished to settle accounts with his servants. When he began to settle, one was brought to him who owed him ten thousand talents. And since he could not pay, his master ordered him to be sold, with his wife and children and all that he had, and payment to be made. So the servant fell on his knees, imploring him, "Have patience with me, and I will pay you everything." And out of pity for him, the master of that servant released him and forgave him the debt. But when that same servant went out, he found one of

his fellow servants who owed him a hundred denarii, and seizing him, he began to choke him, saying, "Pay what you owe." So his fellow servant fell down and pleaded with him, "Have patience with me, and I will pay you." He refused and went and put him in prison until he should pay the debt. When his fellow servants saw what had taken place, they were greatly distressed, and they went and reported to their master all that had taken place. Then his master summoned him and said to him, "You wicked servant! I forgave you all that debt because you pleaded with me. And should not you have had mercy on your fellow servant, as I had mercy on you?" And in anger his master delivered him to the jailers, until he should pay all his debt. So also my heavenly Father will do to every one of you if you do not forgive your brother from your heart' " (Matthew 18:21-35, ESV).

This is not an isolated teaching, but a concept that Jesus repeatedly taught the people gathered around Him.

"Pray then like this: 'Our Father in heaven, hallowed be Your name. Your kingdom come, Your will be done, on earth as it is in heaven. Give us this day our daily bread, and forgive us our debts, as we also have forgiven our debtors. And lead us not into temptation, but deliver us from evil.' For if you forgive others their trespasses, your heavenly Father will also forgive you, but if you do not forgive others their trespasses, neither will your Father forgive your trespasses" (Matthew 6:9-15, ESV).

This is what we all know as the Lord's Prayer. Having taught us how to pray to our Father, Jesus immediately highlights the truth that, if we do not forgive, we will not in turn receive forgiveness.

The Scriptures use seven different words—three Hebrew and four Greek—to express the idea of forgiveness. The most frequently used Greek word means "to release" the other person and self, "to hurl away," to throw it away, "to free oneself" from being entangled.[27]

The inability to forgive results in resentment. Resentment literally means "to feel again." Resentment clings to the past, relives it over and over again, picking each fresh scab so that the wound never heals. I often compare the inability or unwillingness to forgive to a free man who walks into a jail, locks himself in and throws away the key—then begins to complain that he has lost his freedom.

I have counselled many hurting people who share with me that often, when they are alone and emotionally low, they find themselves unconsciously reliving the hurtful incidents of their past. They can spend minutes or even hours reliving each aspect of an incident, sometimes speaking out loud and being fully engaged as if the incident is happening again in the present. They also share that often this process starts with one painful memory, but will then trigger other, related memories. After some time, the person returns to reality—suddenly realising that, although they are feeling extreme pain, anger and hurt, the person who hurt them is not even present. But they have once again fully experienced the deep emotional, spiritual and physical impact of the hurtful incident.

I began to ask myself why so many hurting people experience this symptom of slipping back to that one, traumatic experience. And then I realised that this is what Paul was cautioning the Christians in Ephesus: "Be angry and do not sin; do not let the sun go down on your anger, and give no opportunity to the devil" (Ephesians 4:26-27, ESV).

I believe that when we hold on to our anger, it's very easy for us to give an opening for the evil one to dominate and control our thinking, impacting our present and our future based on

27. *International Standard Bible Encyclopedia,* Electronic Database, Biblesoft, 1996

anger from the past. I am also concerned that many Christians have not experienced the full potential of the joy of the gospel because of their inability to forgive and to enjoy the peace of the Lord. Many believers, traumatized by their own pain and an unforgiving attitude, live a life of perpetual anger, reliving the pain from their past and snapping at those around them. When I see an irritable believer who talks of love, joy and peace but exhibits sharp, biting anger, I know there is a hurting person who has not resolved his past issues.

One day after a seminar, as I was walking toward the back of the room talking to participants, I noticed a middle-aged lady I knew seated by herself in the back row. I walked up to her and casually asked, "Why are you alone?" Her reaction was immediate and extreme. She jumped out of her seat and almost shouted at me, "What do you mean? The Lord is with me!" I was speechless and embarrassed by her reaction. For a few minutes, I couldn't understand why she had reacted so violently to a simple question about why she was seated alone as others mingled together in small groups around her.

A few minutes later, I realised that my question had triggered a lot of concealed anger within this person. I knew that as a young woman she had fallen in love with a man whom her parents considered unsuitable, and they opposed her marriage. She gave up the relationship with deep anger and resentment but in outward submission to her parents.

As I drove home from the seminar, I began to realise that my simple, unthinking question had connected to her past pain and triggered a disproportionate response to my question. I was deeply saddened and also concerned at how she was adding a spiritual patina to cover her pain. As the years passed, she gradually isolated herself completely from people, living inside a shuttered house, and whenever I or other concerned friends attempted to visit her, she would say that she was in "a time of prayer" and could not be disturbed.

Recently, her mother passed away, and she refused to even attend the funeral. Her reason for this was that "I cannot be away from the Lord for even a minute." She was a vibrant believer in her young days but today has become a recluse who has no contact with anyone. I can trace this change in her back to the time when she was forced to end her relationship with the man she loved. I believe that the anger at being forced into this decision never truly left her. She clung to this anger, allowing it to dominate her mind and to define who she was.

We forgive not merely to fulfil a higher law, but we also do it for ourselves. The first and often the only person who is healed by the act of forgiveness is the person who does the forgiving. When we genuinely forgive, we set a prisoner free and then discover that the prisoner was ourselves. This is a liberating and exhilarating experience, one that cannot be described but can only be experienced.

Corrie ten Boom, author of *The Hiding Place*, writes of an incident in Munich after the end of World War II:

> "It was at a church service in Munich that I saw him, a former S.S. man who had stood guard at the shower room door in the processing center at Ravensbruck. He was the first of our actual jailers that I had seen since that time. And suddenly it was all there—the roomful of mocking men, the heaps of clothing, Betsie's pain-blanched face.
>
> "He came up to me as the church was emptying, beaming and bowing. 'How grateful I am for your message, Fraulein,' he said. 'To think that, as you say, He has washed my sins away!' His hand was thrust out to shake mine. And I, who had preached so often to the people in Bloemendaal the need to forgive, kept my hand at my side.
>
> "Even as the angry, vengeful thoughts boiled through me, I saw the sin of them. Jesus Christ had died for this man; was I going to ask for more? Lord Jesus, I prayed, forgive me and help me to forgive him. I tried to smile, I struggled

to raise my hand. I could not. I felt nothing, not the slightest spark of warmth or charity. And so again I breathed a silent prayer. 'Jesus,' I prayed, 'I cannot forgive him. Give me your forgiveness.'

"As I took his hand, the most incredible thing happened. From my shoulder along my arm and through my hand a current seemed to pass from me to him, while into my heart sprang a love for this stranger that almost overwhelmed me. And so I discovered that it is not on our forgiveness any more than on our goodness that the world's healing hinges but on His. When He tells us to love our enemies, He gives, along with the command, the love itself."[28]

I hope that now you have come to a point of understanding the essential role played by forgiveness in your healing process. There can be no healing without forgiveness.

It is both easy and extremely difficult to forgive. It's easy because you are fulfilling a command of God, and as a believer you have no option but to submit and obey the will of God. But it is difficult because your physical and emotional pain is wrapped up in your anger. Personally, I would rather be satisfied with revenge than take the step of forgiving. To forgive might seem like adding insult to injury. Someone has caused me pain, and now I am being asked to let him get away scot-free. To forgive goes against the logic of human justice and fair play.

But that is the power of the gospel. The gospel does not focus on justice because if that were the case, Jesus need not have died on the cross of Calvary. If He had insisted on justice, then you and I would remain condemned and doomed forever. His willingness to forgive while we were yet sinners (Romans 5:8) gave us hope, forgiveness and the possibility of eternal life.

Living in a sinful, broken world, the power of forgiveness will illuminate that we are the children of the Lord who operate on

---

28. Corrie Ten Boom, *The Hiding Place,* Bantam Books, 1974

a higher plane not based on the laws of justice and retribution. You have no option but to forgive. May I appeal to you to visit that one painful memory, or it may be a string of painful memories. I can guarantee that as you recall those painful memories, you will experience physical and emotional hurt. But transcend that hurt, and proclaim verbally that you forgive the person who caused you that pain. Speak the words that will release you from the bondage of unforgiveness.

For some of you, this one act will not be the end. Satan will bring back the memory of pain and may even whisper to you that it is not justice and fair play to let go. But remember that he only wants to enslave you to a life of deep sorrow. Every time he brings back these memories, publicly profess that you have forgiven the person who wronged you and that the hurtful incident no longer has any power over you. You will be surprised at the joy and the peace that you will experience.

Let me also encourage you at this stage to share with a friend this process you are going through, and I advise you to ask them to hold you accountable to this new life of forgiveness. Know that your victory is complete.

PERSONAL REFLECTIONS

- Read Genesis 45-50. While reading this passage, put yourself in Joseph's sandals. Highlight all the injustice he experienced from his family, his employers and his friends.
- Once you have done this, read through the passage carefully to list out how Joseph responded to each of those incidents of injustice, cruelty and betrayal.
- I am persuaded that if Joseph had not taken the path of forgiveness, he would have lived as a bitter, angry man, and he would not have been used by God to save his people from the famine.

Chapter Nine

Deal With the Strongholds

In the previous chapter, we looked at how our past experiences remain embedded in our hearts and minds. Our hurtful memories remain vivid, and it is possible for us to continue feeding on them, almost enjoying the hurts and allowing ourselves to live in self-pity. This is very dangerous because our enemy, Satan, will take the opportunity and exploit it to his advantage to keep us in deep bondage and to make our ministry ineffective.

Satan takes the hurts of the past, or the background of the individual, to control the present and to destroy the future God intends. But this is unnecessary suffering for a child of God.

THE ORIGINS OF STRONGHOLDS

In Sri Lanka, one of the most popular tourist destinations is an elephant orphanage where baby elephants wounded or abandoned in the jungle are rescued and brought for care and rehabilitation. These baby elephants have the potential to grow to be big animals weighing over five tons, and the caregivers at the orphanage know that, before they grow to their maximum size, it is essential to bring them under some form of control.

Often, this is achieved by making the elephant believe and accept a lie. The baby elephant is tied to a strong pillar using an iron chain. The young elephant attempts to break the chain, not once but many times, without any success. After several attempts, the elephant accepts the reality that it is impossible to break the chain. "It's stronger than I am," concludes the baby elephant.

In a few years, this baby elephant is a huge animal weighing thousands of kilos. He is still tied with the same iron chain to the same pillar, but his strength is now so immense that a slight twist of his leg could uproot the pillar. But he will not attempt to break the chain as he still believes that it is stronger than him. A stronghold based on a lie has been built in his mind.

In the same way, this is how a stronghold is built in the minds of humans:

> "The weapons we fight with are not the weapons of the world. On the contrary, they have divine power to demolish strongholds. We demolish arguments and every pretension that sets itself up against the knowledge of God, and we take captive every thought to make it obedient to Christ" (2 Corinthians 10:4-5).

Paul highlights the word "strongholds" in this passage (verse 4), and then in verse 5 he presents the possibility of us demolishing these strongholds. The strongholds he is talking about are arguments and every pretension that sets itself up against the knowledge of God.

It is also interesting to note that he says in this same verse, "We take captive every thought to make it obedient to Christ," using a metaphor of a military fortification. My conclusion, based on the evidence of this passage, is that the strongholds Paul is talking abut are those built in the minds of human beings.

Consider this diagram:

- Continuous emotional pain can give rise to unhealthy attitudes. Our attitudes are a reaction or a defence mechanism to avoid or deaden the pain experienced.
- Attitudes, over a period of time, will give rise to a lifestyle or behaviour patterns (some of these attitudes and behaviour patterns can be very sinful).
- Behaviour patterns (attitudes) over time can be become strongholds in the life of a believer.

Peter was only three years old when his father left them. He can hardly remember his father or his abrupt departure from the family, but he can well remember the day his mother too left him in the care of his grandmother, telling him that she was going away to find work. She never returned, but for many months he waited at the door each evening, hoping that this would be the day when she came home.

It was almost a year later that his grandmother casually informed him that his mother was remarried and living in another village with her new husband. The anger Peter felt at this betrayal was instant, and the pain was like a knife cutting into him. But he kept these feelings buried deep inside, withdrawing from everyone around him. This deep anger was exploited by the evil one to establish a stronghold in his mind.

In his late teens, Peter came to know the Lord through one of our church programmes. As he was being discipled in his new walk with the Lord, he was helped to confront and deal with these deep feelings of betrayal, the pain of rejection and the loss of his parents' love.

But unfortunately, he was not willing to deal with the attitudes that he had developed over the years to protect himself from more pain. I came to understand that he had a very low-self worth and confidence in himself, and he believed that everyone he met would reject him too. He would often create situations that would cause people to turn away from him. This was a scenario he preferred so that he would not draw close to them and possibly be hurt by them. This was a deeply established stronghold.

I saw Peter as a young man with immense potential, a creative person who had an artistic eye and the skilled hands to turn anything into a work of beauty. He also loved the Lord and had a genuine desire to learn more about Him and to serve Him.

But I also watched as he reacted sharply to the slightest criticism, withdrew from people whom he perceived as having rejected him and his sudden outbursts of anger. He could also go for days without speaking to anyone. These behaviour patterns isolated him from other young people and from effectively ministering to others.

In counseling people who have experienced deep emotional hurts, I have come to conclude that strongholds are *real issues* in the lives of people who have *suffered much* in the past.

Sandra was a young girl who came into our teenage girls centre as a young teen. From a very young age, she had been sexually abused by her stepfather and his friends. But what I found most startling was that she had developed a belief that her value was based only on the sexual favours she granted men. She continued to devalue herself and only saw herself valued when she was fulfilling the lustful desires of men. This became her lifestyle and a stronghold.

Today she is working toward mental and physical rehabilitation, but her experiences have grown into a stronghold, and her personality is wrapped up in these experiences. She is slowly learning that these strongholds can be broken and that she needs to value herself based on what God says about her.

Not only Sandra, but we all need to believe what God says about us, and we need to replace the lies people have spoken into our lives—and our own faulty view of ourselves—with His truths.

I would urge you to pay very close attention to the concept of strongholds. They can begin from what seems merely a harmful suggestion or thought. You may be surprised to discover that the evil one can make suggestions to you, which may be extremely disastrous if you believe, accept and fulfil them.

Robert was a successful pastor and leading evangelist who built a large church with hundreds of church plants in his country. One day while preaching, the thought entered his mind that his wife was no longer good enough for him. He believed it, he accepted it and he began to nurse the thought. Before long, his family life was a mess. Everything his wife did was wrong, and soon the marriage ended in divorce. But it didn't stop here. He went from one marriage to another. He lost his ministry and credibility in the process, and he was completely ruined.

When he came to his senses, similar to the experience of the prodigal son, he realised that his fall began when the thought entered his mind that his wife was not good enough. He entertained the thought from the evil one, believed it unquestioningly, accepted it and acted on it. It is interesting how Satan can feed thoughts into the mind of a believer that can then grow to be a stronghold that will destroy a person. Here is a biblical illustration of this truth:

> "From that time Jesus began to show his disciples that He must go to Jerusalem and suffer many things from the elders and chief priests and scribes, and be killed, and on the

> third day be raised. And Peter took Him aside and began to rebuke Him, saying, 'Far be it from You, Lord! This shall never happen to You.' But He turned and said to Peter, 'Get behind Me, Satan! You are a hindrance to Me. For you are not setting your mind on the things of God but on the things of man' " (Matthew 16:21-23, ESV).

In verse 21 Jesus begins to show His disciples that He must suffer many things, be killed and be raised on the third day. Peter's immediate response is to take Jesus aside and rebuke Him. In the Jewish context, and in a rabbi-disciple relationship, it would be very improper to question, let alone rebuke, your rabbi. And yet Peter goes even further by saying, "Far be it Lord, this shall never happen to You."

Jesus responds by saying, "Get behind me, Satan, you are a hindrance to Me." Satan attempts to hinder Jesus' mission through Peter, and Jesus recognises this and does not allow it to go any further. Reading the entirety of Matthew 16, I'm surprised that it's in this same chapter that Peter acknowledges Jesus is the Messiah and Jesus entrusts Peter with the authority to lead the church:

> " 'But what about you?' he asked. 'Who do you say I am?' Simon Peter answered, 'You are the Messiah, the Son of the living God.' Jesus replied, 'Blessed are you, Simon son of Jonah, for this was not revealed to you by man, but by My Father in heaven. And I tell you that you are Peter, and on this rock I will build My church, and the gates of Hades will not overcome it.' "

It's worth noting that, at one point Peter speaks the inspired words illuminated by God, and in the next moment he is speaking words that come from the pit of hell! Should this not encourage us to be more cautious with our thoughts? I believe this is the reason in Psalms 119:9 we are told: "How can a young person stay on the path of purity? By living according to your word."

There is an assumption within the Christian community that because we've accepted the Lord Jesus Christ as our Saviour, satanic influences and thinking do not invade our lives. The above passage certainly dispels this myth. A close study of the Scriptures will reveal that all references about Satan and his activity—and the warnings about him—are given to believers and not to unbelievers.

- In Ephesians, Paul warns the "saints in Ephesus" that "our struggle is not against flesh and blood, but against the rulers, against the authorities, against the powers of this dark world and against the spiritual forces of evil in the heavenly realms" (6:12).
- Peter, addressing "God's elect," says in 1 Peter 5: 8-9, "Be alert and of sober mind. Your enemy the devil prowls around like a roaring lion looking for someone to devour. Resist him, standing firm in the faith, because you know that the family of believers throughout the world is undergoing the same kind of sufferings."

This assumption—that Christians have automatic protection—has led many people to drop their guard and become unaware that thoughts from the pit of hell have invaded their thinking. If allowed to take root, these thoughts will soon bring about disastrous behaviour. A stronghold is not built in our minds overnight. It happens over a period of time, sometimes months, sometimes years. I have also come across instances in which a stronghold has been built even prior to birth:

- As part of many of the animistic religious practices in Asia, parents offer children to different deities for protection and wellbeing. Many of these deities are demonic, and once a child has been handed over to them for protection, the deity owns the child's soul. I personally believe that this child needs to be redeemed through an act of faith.
- The circumstances in which a child is conceived and born can affect the emotional wellbeing of a child (see Chapter

2). I have counselled many who have grappled with suicidal tendencies, and as we probed their past, and I spoke to their mothers, I sometimes found that they had tried unsuccessfully to abort these children. There seems to be a clear link between the emotional pain of the mother that has been transferred to the child during the pregnancy, and this can later develop into a stronghold.

But no matter what the origins or how powerful the stronghold in your life, believe today that it can be broken!

> "The weapons we fight with are not the weapons of the world. On the contrary, they have divine power to demolish strongholds. We demolish arguments and every pretension that sets itself up against the knowledge of God, and we take captive every thought to make it obedient to Christ" (2 Corinthians 10:4-5).

Let me present to you six simple yet powerful blows you can deliver to shatter these strongholds in your life.

BLOW 1: IDENTIFY THE STRONGHOLDS THAT ARE CONTROLLING YOUR LIFE.

Every stronghold originates from a painful incident, and a lie based on this incident that the evil one brings to mind. These lies come not from God but from our own childhood or traumatic experiences in which we have experienced pain and rejection, and which Satan magnifies in our minds even now. I am surprised how many believers continue to believe these tragic untruths.

How can you identify a stronghold in your life? A stronghold is an attitude and a behaviour that controls you—it overpowers you, often when you least expect it. It is a compulsive behaviour and an attitude that is clearly contrary to the teaching of Scripture (others may have pointed this out to you already).

I have seen that the level of the stronghold can vary from person to person. With some, it is patently obvious when you spend a few minutes with them. Others have learned the art of managing, hiding and covering up the stronghold. Both are equally dangerous because if you don't deal with the stronghold, the final outcome will be spiritual disaster.

As you seek to identify the strongholds, you will first need to look at the behaviour patterns. It is only as you keep going deeper to the root of these behaviours that you will confront the original lie.

THE LIE	THE RESULTS
I am not worthy.	This leads a person to an improper understanding of God's love and grace, and he is unable to enjoy the freedom that comes to a believer through grace. He believes he is unworthy, compares himself to everyone he meets, behaves in a defeated manner, allows negative thoughts to control him, brings gloom and doom statements into every conversation, and, as a result, is ineffective in social relationships and in ministry.
God does not love me personally and for who I am.	This lie leaves a person unable to understand his own relationship with God. He approaches God with a sense of doubt, unable to appropriate the blessings and promises of Scripture. He does not see God as someone who has loved him from even before his conception, but rather as someone who sits in judgment over him. Rather than live in the secure love of God, he constantly performs for His acceptance. He lives with a servant's mentality.
God will never bless me.	He lives a very defeated life. He continues to rationalise in his thinking that he's not worthy or good enough. *I don't believe God can bless me,* he thinks. *I need to survive with the minimum blessings and be grateful for that, rather than believe that God can bless me and use me.*

THE LIE	THE RESULTS
I am an unlucky person.	Often this is influenced by a pagan religious worldview, which is very common in our Asian cultures. Even though the person has become a believer, his worldview has not been affected. He believes he is born again, but his worldview tells him that he is an unlucky person. He was born at the wrong time, wrong place and in the wrong circumstances. I encounter many Christians who strongly believe this lie, but have been able to cover it up with faulty spiritual virtues, such as an excessive modesty that does not allow room for any affirmation or enjoyment of God's blessings.
I will lose the good things in my life. They cannot last.	This person talks of faith but has allowed fear and anxiety to control him. He will imagine the wildest possible scenarios of how things can go wrong. I have grappled with this issue as I have worked with people who have struggled with this issue themselves. I always reach the conclusion that a crippling fear was transferred from a parent or an influential adult in this person's childhood who plagued the child with fearful thoughts and attitudes toward life. This transferred fear becomes a stronghold.
Lies spoken over your life	This is very common in our Asian cultures. Parents, in angry outbursts or sometimes as an effort to push the child to improve, will make negative statements that they themselves may not even believe. For example, statements like this are often heard in Asian families: "You will never succeed," "You're a curse on this family," "You have brought bad luck to us." When these statements are repeated over time, the child begins to believe them, and a stronghold is developed.
I am not good enough, and I must strive to be better.	This is seen in a drive to achieve self-attained perfection.

THE LIE	THE RESULTS
Sexual obsessions	Very often, these sexual obsessions begin to develop in the life of teens, and in some cases they are a response to abuse in childhood. It is at this stage that a child can develop a healthy attitude toward the opposite sex and to marriage, or they can develop a very unhealthy attitude that cripples their relationships. In an Asian shame-based culture, these inner struggles are never exposed or discussed with a concerned adult who can help. The tragedy is that the problem deepens as they grow, until one day it emerges in unacceptable, harmful sexual behaviour. This behaviour is met with disapproval and rejection in our society, which further opens the door to a life of immorality as this person no longer has anything to lose. The greatest tragedy is that this person goes on hurting others, abusing another generation that will follow in his own footsteps, thereby re-creating this vicious cycle.
God is not satisfied with me.	I have seen that this lie often originates from an upbringing in which a child never receives affirmation or recognition from his parents. Constant nagging, regular lectures on what he is doing wrong and continuous negative feedback result in a belief that everything he does has to be perfect in order to win approval. This makes him a difficult person to live and work with, as he has high expectations of others, demanding perfection in everything. As a believer, this is transferred to his relationship with God, and he works hard to gain God's approval by his performance—being active in ministry, running a perfect programme or sometimes even in giving. But because he is trying to win God's approval, rather than accept God's love given in grace, he continues to feel less than a child of God.

THE LIE	THE RESULTS
Fear that others will do better than you or be more successful than you	This lie originates from a very insecure upbringing in which there has been little affirmation, but rather ridicule, belittling and constant comparison with others, whether siblings, cousins or neighbourhood children. Over the years this develops into a constant threat of someone entering one's sphere who may be better. This fear is reflected in regular interpersonal conflicts and petty acts of jealousy.

BLOW 2: PRAY AND BREAK THE AUTHORITY AND THE POWER OF THE STRONGHOLD.

Once you have identified the stronghold in your life, you need to break its authority. The demolishing of strongholds can be an instant act, or it may take time. The only way you will know this is by the complete victory that you have won over the stronghold. I have seen some who walked out of a stronghold, and it never controlled them again—a perfect and complete victory. Others have struggled for some time with overcoming their stronghold.

Let's read again the passage from 2 Corinthians 10:4-5:

> "The weapons we fight with are not the weapons of the world. On the contrary, they have divine power to demolish strongholds. We demolish arguments and every pretension that sets itself up against the knowledge of God, and we take captive every thought to make it obedient to Christ."

God has provided us with weapons we can use to break the power of the stronghold. We take advantage of this, and through an act of faith, break these strongholds that have been established.

I would encourage you to seek a mature believer whom you trust and share freely about your stronghold and the pain you are struggling with. Pray with him/her. This confidence and the willingness to trust someone opens the door for you to be accountable to this person in the future. This is a healthy Christian practice. Thank God for the victory Jesus has won over every stronghold (read Colossians 2:13-15).

BLOW 3: SATURATE YOUR MIND WITH GOD'S WORD.

Saturating your mind with Scripture and hiding in your heart His word is essential. It will become the doorkeeper that prevents the evil one from polluting your mind with unsanctified thinking.

> "I appeal to you, therefore, brothers, by the mercies of God, to present your bodies as a living sacrifice, holy and acceptable to God, which is your spiritual worship. Do not be conformed to this world, but be transformed by the renewal of your mind, that by testing you may discern what is the will of God, what is good and acceptable and perfect" (Romans 12:1-2).

In verse 2, Paul urges us to "be transformed." The word used here is *metamorphoo* in Greek. This is the same word from which we get the English word "metamorphosis," which is best described through the illustration of a caterpillar becoming a beautiful butterfly.

The butterfly's life begins as an egg that the female lays on the underside of a leaf, and the larva, or caterpillar, hatches from the egg about six days after being laid. These tiny creatures are ravenous and quickly begin to eat away at every leaf in sight, ending up almost two inches long at the end of this cycle.

By spinning silk and forming a cocoon, the caterpillar makes a little shell in which it can form a chrysalis. The caterpillar finds a leaf to hang upside down from and begins to cover itself with either two leaves wrapped in silken threads or a cocoon made entirely of silk. The pupa, or chrysalis, is what the caterpillar is called while it is changing into a butterfly. Once inside this protective space, the chrysalis forms and amazing changes occur. This stage lasts an average of twelve days, at the end of which a beautiful butterfly emerges.

I am persuaded that the renewal of our mind is the key to spiritual victory over strongholds. The lie that we believed over the years now has to be replaced with the truth from God's word. And as we allow our mind to dwell on this truth, we need to start living it in our lives. As we begin to replace the lie with God's truth in our lives, this will be reflected in our behaviour patterns.

BLOW 4: ALWAYS BE ALERT

Being constantly vigilant of the possibility of a mental onslaught from the evil one will help a believer to discern which thoughts originate from the pit of hell.

I find the example of Jesus, when he was tempted (Luke 4: 3-13) yet proactively use Scripture to confront the lies of Satan, to be a powerful model. It is unbelievable to me that the modern church adopts every conceivable strategy but has not adopted the principle of hiding God's word in the heart of the believer and using it proactively to counteract the lies of the evil one.

May I encourage you to memorise passages of Scripture that confront the lies of your stronghold and respond to every suggestion of the evil one with these words.

BLOW 5: LEARN, UNDERSTAND AND ACCEPT RIGHT THEOLOGY.

I know and believe that the victory over strongholds has already been won. We now need to appropriate this victory into our lives and celebrate it each day with the life we live. Please read Romans 6:2-14. Here are some important truths that emerge from this passage:

- **We are dead to sin:** Paul writes "we died to sin, how can we live in it any longer?" (verse 2). The tense he uses here is the aorist tense, which signifies that "we died in the past, and we are continuing to die to sin in the present." In verse 4, Paul uses the words "we were buried with Him in baptism," and he links us to Jesus' resurrection by saying, "we too might walk in the newness of life" (ESV). We have died with Christ, and we enjoy the potential of newness of life in Christ.
- **We are set free from sin:** In verse 5, Paul repeats himself by saying that we're united with Jesus in His death and assuring us that we will be united with Him in His resurrection. And he concludes his argument by saying "so that we would no longer be enslaved to sin." The power of sin and its enslavement has been broken. He supports this argument (in verse 7) by saying that "anyone who has died has been set free from sin."
- **We are alive in Christ:** In verse 8 Paul continues by saying that "if we have died with Christ, we believe that we will also live with Him." He continues the argument by saying, "For we know that since Christ was raised from the dead, He cannot die again; death no longer has mastery over Him. The death He died, He died to sin once for all; but the life He lives, He lives to God" (verse 9-10).
- **Sin is no longer your master:** In verse 11 he concludes his argument by saying, "So you also must consider yourself dead to sin and alive to God in Christ Jesus." By continuous celebration of the truth that we are dead to sin and alive to Christ and by continuously harnessing the power of the resurrection that is within us, we will destroy the power of sin and strongholds that evil has built. That is why he concludes in verse 12 by saying, "Let not sin reign in your mortal body so that you obey its evil desires."

BLOW 6: PUT ON YOUR ARMOUR.

Take on the armour of God for daily living (see Ephesians 6:10-18). Satan will do all that is within his power to tempt you again, destroy your confidence in the Lord and make you believe the lie you can never overcome the stronghold.

You have already overcome your stronghold, so rejoice!

> "But the Lord is faithful, and He will strengthen and protect you from the evil one" (2 Thessalonians 3:3).

In our shame-based culture in Asia, the legalism that exists even within the church has prevented people from being honest about their own personal struggles and strongholds. Let me suggest that you are not alone in this struggle.

Do not let this mislead you. Let me encourage you to seek God. He understands our struggles. He's the Father who forgave the prodigal son. He's the Lord who told the woman who was about to be stoned by the Pharisees, "Neither do I condemn you; go and sin no more." He was the model of a gracious father who stood before Zacchaeus and invited himself to his home, rather than condemning him.

And He is the Lord who invites you with the following words:

> "If we claim to be without sin, we deceive ourselves, and the truth is not in us. If we confess our sins, *He is faithful and just and will forgive us our sins and purify us from all unrighteousness"* (1 John 1:8-9).

Chapter Ten

Seeing God in New Ways

"WHAT COMES INTO OUR minds when we think about God is the most important thing about us," A.W. Tozer wrote. "Worship is pure or base as the worshiper entertains high or low thoughts of God. For this reason, the gravest question before the church is always God Himself, and the most portentous fact about any man is not what he at a given time may say or do, but what he in his deep heart conceives God to be like. We tend by a secret law of the soul to move toward our mental image of God."[29]

We determine our particular image of God based on our personal experiences and our upbringing.

Amali is a young woman in our church who is extremely dedicated to walking with God. She loves Him, and it's obvious to all those around her that she has an intimate walk with Him. But talking to her one day, it soon became obvious to me that she was totally disillusioned in her walk with God. As I began to press on to find out why she was so defeated

29. A. W. Tozer. *The Knowledge of the Holy.* Harper & Row, New York. 1961

in her mind, she revealed to me that she felt that God was "far away" and "too perfect for her to even be in contact with Him." She felt that she could not please Him by anything that she could do, no matter how hard she tried.

Troubled by her theology, I began to probe her relationship with her own father. It was as if I had opened a can of worms! She began to explain how difficult it was to please him, that he was a perfectionist who demanded more than perfection from his own children. As she began to unload her past experiences with her father, I watched the tears streaming down her face, and she desperately said, "I wanted to please him, but I could never be perfect enough for him."

At the end of this talk, I challenged Amali to go to the Scriptures and develop her own biblical understanding of God the Father. I gave her some passages of Scripture that she should begin with and encouraged her to formulate her own personal image of God based on biblical truth. A few weeks later I met her again, and I was amazed by the transformation and her own confession that she was beginning to understand how in the past she had seen God through the eyes of her relationship with her father.

Our images of God are not always the same as what the Scriptures tell us about God but can be determined and developed by our relationships with our parents and the religious leaders who instructed us in our childhood. Images are not abstract ideas; they are pictures. That is why they are so powerful. They are a combination of thoughts and feelings.

Long before we were old enough to think in words, we thought in pictures or images. These images are loaded with emotion. From our early days of life, we began storing memories of our emotional experiences. Images of our mother's face when she was distressed or when she was pleased, or of our father's face when he was angry or when he was laughing—all these are stored in our memory. These images became linked with the comfort we felt or with the increased fear we felt in interacting with these important faces and voices.

All of our experiences, from our earliest days, have been stored in our minds, some of them as emotionally-laden images. These images of parents or other early caretakers form the basic foundation of our expectations in relationships with all other people, including God.

Our images of God, therefore, may not be the same as our doctrinal affirmations about God. We may affirm that we believe in a God of love and grace, but our images of God may be of an abusive bully. And this image is likely to have a more powerful impact on our emotions and behaviour than our doctrinal statements about God because our images of God are rooted in early, formative experiences.

When we examine our private images of God and discover significant distortions, we may feel horrified at the thought that we could harbour such negative images of God. Viewing God in negative ways may seem unacceptable and frightening. In spite of our fears, however, I believe it is critical that we explore our personal images of God.

Here are some of the common distortions of God's image, which I have come across:

1. GOD IS UNPREDICTABLE.

Once I was counselling a young boy who would not do anything that he thought would "upset" God. He felt he must do his devotions, he must pray, he must witness; and it seemed almost a compulsive, programmed behaviour.

Spending time with him, it became obvious that he was very fearful of God, and he was always trying to make sure that God would not explode and punish him with sicknesses or take away his presence. He was very insecure in his relationship with God. As I began to watch him, it was obvious that, although he believed in a God of love, mercy and acceptance, he approached God as if he was prone to emotional outbursts based on the boy's behaviour.

I was deeply concerned about this boy and his walk with the Lord. Exploring his relationships with his family, his mother was described as a perfectionist, and the father was described as an unpredictable person who could be smiling one moment and suddenly explode in anger the next. Everybody in the home walked on eggshells, and everyone related to the father through fear, because they didn't want to accidentally trigger an angry outburst.

2. GOD IS UNAPPROACHABLE.

God is seen as someone who is at the very top, in a position that we find hard to reach.

You say to yourself, *I'm going to work hard to reach God now. I want to be close to Him, and I want to please Him.* So you start doing things that you think will please God. But you find that God is always at the same distance, too far to reach, no matter what you do. There is an inner voice that always says, *This is not good enough.*

3. GOD IS EMOTIONALLY DISTANT.

Theologically he believes that God is interested in him, but a sense of unworthiness and the environment of unworthiness in which he may have grown up tell him he's foolish to believe that God is interested in him.

God is so big, so powerful, how can He be interested in someone as insignificant as me? he asks. He can rattle off passages of Scripture or even preach a sermon about God's love, but deep down his own unworthiness denies him of a loving relationship with God.

4. GOD HAS HIS FAVOURITES.

This concept again breeds within our families, our schools and even our churches. Very unconsciously, parents may pick their favourite children, who are petted, pampered and loved more than the others. The other children have no say in it but observe the unfair treatment of the favourite in contrast to them.

This same wrong placement of value is perpetuated in our school system, where teachers pick their favourites based on their academic capabilities, family connections or the charismatic personality or the outward appearance of the student. This is inescapable in a fallen world, but unfortunately it's practiced even in our churches.

Those who have had the privilege of being the favourite have developed a certain sense of security based on the acceptance they received from their parents or teachers.

Others who were not so fortunate have struggled with feelings of rejection and unworthiness and may have a low self-worth. They have come to know the Lord, but they are unable to shake off the dust of their former thinking. They know that God does not play favourites, but they relate to God with the thought that they are not his favourite.

This root cause brings about many wrong behaviour patterns. They may ask someone who they see as a "favourite" of God to pray for them—it's as if their own prayers will not be validated by God. They may ask the "favourites" to bless them and their families during life's happy occasions. They will even shift their membership from one church to another, based on their warped understanding that God has a special "favourite" in the new church.

The worst impact is on their personal walk with God. Deep down, they want to do something for the Lord, be accepted by the Lord and be validated in the work they do. But the sense of understanding that God has favourites, and that they are not one of them, robs the joy and confidence to plod on.

5. GOD IS ONLY A JUDGE.

The Bible talks of God as a judge. There is much teaching on the final judgment. But there is also sufficient teaching to show us that God is a loving father. The Scriptures also tell us that Christ was judged on the cross for our sins and has already paid the penalty for our sins. This does not mean that we are excused to live a life of sin, but the Scriptures show us that we are forgiven, and we have an advocate in the person of Jesus Christ, who intercedes on our behalf (1 John 2:1-2).

But in the church we have many children of God who see Him as a judge and not a loving father, as someone who keeps a big book where all their sins are written, and that His retribution will one day follow. This warped thinking is heightened when they go through a difficult time in their life, whether sickness or other difficult circumstances. Their first response and their theological basis for explaining the difficulty is to say, “This is punishment for some wrong that I have done.”

I am sure there are many other distorted images of God that you have also come across and can add to this list.

Some of our images of God are conditioned by the religious leaders who teach us in our formative years or the culture of the church or organization that we grew up in. An emotionally hurting preacher or Sunday school teacher will always project an image of God based on his or her experiences. Very often, this is how legalism becomes part of our understanding of God. The preacher, over the years, has conditioned the minds of people, perhaps unknowingly, to believe that God is more interested in certain standards of behaviour than in a personal relationship with a believer.

Legalism has robbed the joy of many people and many churches because legalism expects a believer to conform to a code of behaviour in order to be accepted by God or the legalistic community. Violation of this code is seen as falling from grace and is often judged by absolute rejection of the "fallen" believer by the so-called "spiritual" community. An alcoholic is looked down upon as though he's beyond redemption. A girl who sells her body for a living is called names, and any association with her is seen as questionable. And someone associating with "people of the world," those with a different lifestyle, is seen as worldly or ungodly.

Insecure men and women can use legalism to control others through fear, guilt and persuasive arguments. In this process they truly miss out on the understanding of a gracious God, and their right to enjoy freedom in Christ has also been robbed because of their obsession with conforming to a set of rules and codes of conduct.

This culture of legalism has not helped emotionally hurting people to experience the true freedom that is ours as children of God.

Ashan was a young man I know who grew up in a home where any discussion about the opposite sex was always treated as a secretive, adult topic to be covered only in whispers by the older generation. Growing up in this home, Ashan understood that any relationship with the opposite sex is frowned upon as inappropriate and something to be kept for a future, unknown and unspecified time. But as he became a teenager and came to an age of sexual reasoning, he became curious to know what happens in the adult world and was drawn to what seemed like forbidden territory.

As Ashan retells his story, he began to talk about girls and sex with peers. They would discuss this hidden subject secretively and often come to conclusions that were distorted, unhealthy and without a perspective of an experienced adult. Soon he was addicted to pornography, avidly reading books or watching pirated movies on DVD. One of his friends had access to unsupervised internet at home and would download adult movies for Ashan and other friends.

At home, Ashan faced a family who had a "holier than thou" attitude, and he was not able to share these struggles. So he began to lead a dual life, trapped in this lie.

The Christian community also adds to the dilemma faced by boys like Ashan. When this topic is mentioned (which is extremely rare), it is preached as a "hellfire, brimstone and judgement" sermon. This results in further condemnation of the young man. He is struggling with issues but has no freedom in the home to talk, no freedom in the church, and so he develops a dual lifestyle that continues into adulthood.

Legalism led him to begin living this dual life. And now legalism has trapped him in this lifestyle, making him feel dirty and unworthy of even coming before the throne of grace.

I believe that we must confront sin, but it must be preached from a perspective of grace that gives the sinner hope and does not leave him with a sense of guilt and rejection. The one and only holy person who walked on this earth never went around condemning sinners, nor did He condone their sin, but always gave them hope. No wonder sinners were attracted to Him. This is the grace that hurting people within and outside our churches are looking for—they are already condemned; they are looking for hope. Legalism is the death knell of hope.

HEALING OUR DISTORTED IMAGES OF GOD

Distorted images are wounds that need time and attention in order to heal. This does not happen automatically just because you make a commitment to Christ. Distortions are often deeply rooted in early life experiences. Hence, healing deeply may mean healing slowly. It also means healing will take place when we are able to replace the distorted images with a more biblically sound image of God and His character.

It is important to remind ourselves that God is on our side in this process. He desires for us to have a closer walk with Him. He is interested in us having a right view of Him because we are called to represent Him to the nations.

According to Scripture, God is love and wants us to experience this love in practical ways. God has gone to great lengths to reveal Himself and His love to us. In addition, according to Scripture, God is a healing God who is personally invested in replacing our distorted images with images rooted in grace and truth.

We cannot fix our distorted images of God by a single act of courage or dedication. Some of us have tried this approach, but we are soon forced to recognise our powerlessness over deeply rooted images. What we can do is risk asking God to reveal His grace to us personally, to heal our distorted images and to give us the capacity to take in His divine love.

From my experiences working with many people, coming alongside them as they grapple with their own distorted images of God, I suggest to you the following steps of healing in this area:

1. EXPLORE YOUR PRIVATE IMAGES OF GOD.

Be very honest with yourself, and put down on paper your images of God. How do you see him? Do you fear Him? Or do you love Him? We might, for example, ask ourselves:

- What are my worst fears about God?
- When I find myself avoiding God, what thoughts and feelings about God are causing me to pull away?
- How do I think God sees me?
- What do I think God expects of me?
- What pictures come to mind when I think about God?

- What do my behaviour and feelings tell me about how I see God?

This kind of exploration can be painful, but it is the kind of truth-telling that leads to healing.

Caution: if you have been raised in an evangelical Christian community, you will have the "correct" answers to these questions. But the "correct" answers may not be how you really feel. Put down in writing how you really feel. Don't allow your answers to make you feel condemned as unspiritual, but recognise that this is an essential part of creating a new, right image of God. Know that God delights in your honesty more than your hypocrisy.

2. BEGIN TO TALK ABOUT YOUR PRIVATE IMAGES OF GOD.

This may feel like a risky thing to do. We may need permission and support to express our more disturbing images of God. A trusted friend, a pastor, a support group or a therapist can be helpful in providing both the permission and the safe place that is needed for exploring these painful images.

Telling the truth, even to just one other person, is an important step in breaking the power of distorted images. Healing happens when you are among people you can trust and where you feel safe, so identify those with whom you can confide and discuss this issue. Be assured that it is better to express your distorted images of God, rather than conform to the spiritual atmosphere in your church.

It's also true that, because our distorted images of God were formed in relationships, it will be in the context of relationships that the distortions will be healed. We cannot do this alone. We need to experience God's love from other people. Investing in relationships that allow us to experience grace over and over again will make it possible for us to learn to trust, to attach and to begin to form the right images of God as a nurturing and compassionate Father.

This growing capacity to trust and to attach to other humans will impact our level of trust and attachment with God. New, nurturing images will be able to compete with our earlier images. Support groups, counselling and friendships can all help provide such healing experiences.

These relationships will have limits. People will never be perfect, but "good enough" experiences of love and grace from others, over a long period of time, can at least partially repair the damage done by early losses.

3. EXPLORE THE POSSIBLE ORIGINS OF THESE IMAGES.

It might be helpful to examine what role God played in your family as you were growing up and to look at any similarities between your descriptions of God and your descriptions of your parents and other important people in your early life.

This separating one from the other is, for many of us, a grieving process. It involves acknowledging early life experiences for what they were, feeling the loss of what should have been, protesting the unfairness of these experiences and awakening unfulfilled longings.

Our distorted images of God may tell us something about the losses and traumas we experienced early in life. Identifying these experiences and grieving about them are an important part of the healing process. Seeing the connection between our experiences with early caretakers and our images of God sets in motion a process of separating one from the other. This is how we begin to realise that God is not the same as the humans who have, in one way or another, failed or hurt us.

The same is true if the source of your distorted images of God lies not within your family but within the Christian community. If you attended a shame-based church during your formative years, it is very likely that this reinforced any dysfunction from your family. Again, the goal of exploring the origins of distorted images is not to assign blame. The goal is to start sorting out who is God and who is not God.

That sounds easy enough, but it's not nearly as easy as it sounds. As we explore the origins of our distorted images of God we are in the process of letting go of idolatrous attachments to people (parents, religious leaders and other important people) who are not God, in order to establish a deep, lasting and intimate attachment to the living and true God.

4. ALLOW IMAGERY FROM SCRIPTURE TO SHOW YOU WHO GOD IS.

We usually tend to seek out biblical texts that correspond to our distortions of God and concentrate on them. But we may have a great deal of difficulty taking in the vast, rich, diverse texts that speak of God's love, grace and compassion.

I have found it helpful to spend focused time with biblical images of God and to write my personal thoughts and feelings in response. Biblically balanced images of God that provide a clear contrast to the previously held distressing images can be especially meaningful to you.

Read the following verses and let them help you to reconstruct the distorted images of God. I would even recommend that you memorise these scriptures, embedding them into your psyche.

> "For you are a people holy to the Lord your God. The Lord your God has chosen you out of all the peoples on the face of the earth to be His people, His treasured possession. The Lord did not set His affection on you and choose you because you were more numerous than other peoples, for you were the fewest of all peoples. But it was because the

Lord loved you and kept the oath He swore to your forefathers that He brought you out with a mighty hand and redeemed you from the land of slavery, from the power of Pharaoh king of Egypt. Know therefore that the Lord your God is God; He is the faithful God, keeping His covenant of love to a thousand generations of those who love Him and keep His commands" (Deuteronomy 7:6-9).

"But you are a chosen people, a royal priesthood, a holy nation, a people belonging to God, that you may declare the praises of Him who called you out of darkness into his wonderful light" (1 Peter 2:9).

"The Lord your God is with you, He is mighty to save. He will take great delight in you, He will quiet you with His love, He will rejoice over you with singing" (Zephaniah 3:17).

"You who bring good news to Zion, go up on a high mountain. You who bring good news to Jerusalem, lift up your voice with a shout, lift it up, do not be afraid; say to the towns of Judah, 'Here is your God!' See, the Sovereign Lord comes with power, and He rules with a mighty arm. See, His reward is with Him, and His recompense accompanies Him. He tends His flock like a shepherd: He gathers the lambs in His arms and carries them close to His heart He gently leads those that have young" (Isaiah 40:9-11).

"Can a mother forget the baby at her breast and have no compassion on the child she has borne? Though she may forget, I will not forget you!" (Isaiah 49:15).

"He came to that which was His own, but His own did not receive Him. Yet to all who received Him, to those who believed in His name, He gave the right to become children of God" (John 1:11-12).

This may have been a painful chapter for you. The distorted images of God may have come up, and you may have realised, perhaps for the first time, that these distorted images were created because of your family or friends who betrayed you, or perhaps the church that let you down.

Perhaps you now breathe a sigh of relief, but on the other hand this may have led to a new resentment toward others. Let me suggest to you as your own pastor, nobody intentionally led you astray, but rather, they allowed their convictions to dominate your thinking. Being angry with them will only result in a spirit of bitterness.

Let me suggest another, alternative way to react in this situation: *Celebrate the new image of God that you have now come to understand from the Scriptures.* However, be warned that, as time goes on, the older images will try to creep back into your mind. This means that you need to celebrate the new understanding of God on a regular basis.

Talk about your new understanding of God. Tell others what you have discovered. Be an agent of healing, presenting what you have found—a Bible-based, true and powerful image of God—to others.

Chapter Eleven

A New Identity in Christ

I DEEPLY APPRECIATE THAT you have tagged along with me up to this point in our journey toward healing. At this stage, I want you to prayerfully read and embrace the concepts that I will be sharing with you. I urge you to pause and ask the Holy Spirit to lead you to understand all the concepts that are highlighted in this chapter, so that it will not be mere cognitive information, but a reality that you will embrace and celebrate on a daily basis.

This chapter is written so that you will,

- **Believe** in your new identity.
- **Celebrate** your new identity.
- **Exercise the authority** that is vested in you.
- **Serve the people** that God has entrusted to you.

A. BELIEVE IN YOUR NEW IDENTITY.

We often speak of our "personal identity" as what makes us the person we are. Your identity, in this sense, consists roughly of what makes you unique as an individual and different from others. Or it is the way you see or define yourself or the network of values and convictions that structure your life.

Based on what we have discussed in preceding chapters, it is possible that you have allowed your identity to be developed based on circumstances in which you were placed, what people said about you or how you were treated in the past. We need to deal with this for total healing and freedom. In this chapter, I want to work with you in reconstructing your true identity in Christ Jesus.

Know your true identity in Christ Jesus, so that you can replace the old, warped identity.

> "Therefore, if anyone is in Christ, he is a new creation; old things have passed away; behold, all things have become new. Now all things are of God, who has reconciled us to Himself through Jesus Christ, and has given us the ministry of reconciliation, that is, that God was in Christ reconciling the world to Himself, not imputing their trespasses to them, and has committed to us the word of reconciliation" (2 Corinthians 5:17-19, NKJV).

- Therefore, if anyone is in Christ, *he is a new creation*
- *Old things have passed away*
- Behold, *all things have become new.*

Let's take a closer look at this passage. The key idea in this paragraph is reconciliation. Because of his rebellion, man was the enemy of God and out of fellowship with Him. Through the work of the cross, Jesus Christ has brought man and God together again, and God has turned His face in love toward the lost world.

The basic meaning of the word reconcile is "to change thoroughly." It refers to a changed relationship between God and the lost world. God does not have to be reconciled to man because that was accomplished by Christ on the cross. It is sinful man who must be reconciled to God. "Religion" is man's feeble effort to be reconciled to God—efforts that are bound to fail. The only person who reconciles us to God is Jesus Christ, and the place where He reconciled us is His cross.

Another key idea in this passage is "imputation" (in the King James Version). This is a word borrowed from banking and simply means "to put to one's account". When you deposit money in the bank, the computer (or the clerk) puts that amount to your account or to your credit. When Jesus died on the cross, all of our sins were imputed to Him—put into His account. He was treated by God as though He had actually committed all those sins.

The result? All of those sins have been paid for, and God no longer holds them against us, because we have trusted Christ as our Saviour. But even more startling is this truth: God has put to our account the very righteousness of Christ! "For He hath made Him [Christ) to be sin for us, who knew no sin; that we might be made the righteousness of God in Him" (2 Corinthians 5:21). However, this does not mean that the consequences of a rebellious life will immediately change. We need to work at change.

Ravi joined the army as a teenager in the 1950s. His journey to alcoholism began with a "social" drink with friends, but he soon became an extreme alcoholic, violent and abusive. When he returned home in the evening, his wife and children would escape to the nearby jungles and spend the night sleeping out, or until he fell into a drunken stupor and it was safe for them to return home.

A series of events led to his conversion, and he reconciled with God and thereafter, with his family. With reconciliation, he experienced a new status with God—he became a child of God. He was forgiven and sanctified. But the consequence of his excessive drinking over a long period of time continues its toll on his physical body. This is inevitable. In fact, as I write this chapter, he is experiencing the full effects of his alcoholic past. But this physical disadvantage does not negate his new identity in Christ.

Here's a passage of Scripture that I would like to share with you to celebrate your new identity in Christ.

> "As for you, you were dead in your transgressions and sins, in which you used to live when you followed the ways of this world and of the ruler of the kingdom of the air, the spirit who is now at work in those who are disobedient. All of us also lived among them at one time, gratifying the cravings of our flesh and following its desires and thoughts. Like the rest, we were by nature deserving of wrath. But because of His great love for us, God, who is rich in mercy, made us alive with Christ even when we were dead in transgressions—it is by grace you have been saved. And God raised us up with Christ and seated us with Him in the heavenly realms in Christ Jesus" (Ephesians 2:1-6).

Please also read these verses of Scripture and meditate on them.

- Psalm 139:14
- Ephesians 1:1
- Matthew 5:13-14
- Romans 8:1-2
- Philippians 3:20
- Romans 8:31-34
- Ephesians 2:6
- Romans 8:35-39
- 2 Corinthians 1:21-22
- John 15:16

B. CELEBRATE YOUR NEW IDENTITY.

Since we're reconciled to God, we must celebrate our new identity. All of the circumstances that surrounded you in your past may have left you with many negative images of yourself, of others and even of those in authority.

We can allow these to dominate us, take away our joy and alienate ourselves from people. This would be a sad outcome. But I propose at this stage that we adopt a strategy of replacing all negative images with positive ones based on what God says about us. This is possible when we believe His word, meditate on it and live according to it.

In Ephesians 4:1-3, God says, "Live worthy of the calling." You are now a son or daughter of God. Living worthy of this calling does not permit you to dwell any further on the past identity you may have established about yourself. You are now a child of God. Practice being a child of God, rather than allowing the negative images to control you.

This may sound ridiculous at this stage, but it is good for you to inform yourself every morning, "I am a child of God." And whenever negative images or circumstances cause you to belittle yourself, learn to remind yourself that you're a child of God. As you continue to practice this concept, soon you will constantly live in the understanding that you are a child of God.

When we celebrate an important occasion, we treat it as special, invite our friends to share the joy with us and take time to celebrate together. You are now a child of God, and I urge you take time to celebrate this wonderful fact on a daily basis. To me, this is one of the most important realities of my walk with God.

Living in a broken world, and among broken people, the pressures and the disappointments of life are severe. In the midst of these disappointments, there is only one unchanging reality: God and my relationship with God. Focusing on my new identity gives me sanity to continue with a sense of renewed hope for the future.

A child of God lacks nothing. This does not mean you will be flooded with the luxuries of the world, but whatever God has called you to do, He will ensure you have all you need to fulfil that calling.

Stop comparing yourself with others. Stop competing with others. In the family of God there are many children, and each of the children has been entrusted with a unique call. Your value is not based on what you do, but rather on the fact that God called you. Say goodbye to a performance-based mindset. Relax and know that you are a child of God.

C. EXERCISE THE AUTHORITY THAT IS VESTED IN YOU.

> "When you were dead in your sins and in the uncircumcision of your flesh, God made you alive with Christ. He forgave us all our sins, having canceled the charge of our legal indebtedness, which stood against us and condemned us; He has taken it away, nailing it to the cross. And having disarmed the powers and authorities, He made a public spectacle of them, triumphing over them by the cross" (Colossians 2:13-15).

In verse 13, Paul identifies our former position as being "dead in your sins and in the uncircumcision of your flesh," and in 13b, he states, "He forgave us all our sins."

This is an interesting passage of Scripture, and Paul is using a practice within the legal system of his time to highlight our new position in Christ. In ancient Rome, when someone was found guilty of a crime and was sentenced to prison, the court clerk would write out the charges against him. He would then nail the charges on the door of the cell holding the prisoner. When the prisoner had completed his sentence, the court clerk would come and tear down the charge sheet and release the prisoner.

That is why, in verse 14 Paul says, "Having canceled the charge of our legal indebtedness, which stood against us and condemned us." Our collective sins were the charges that were nailed to the cross, and which Jesus paid in full, thereby releasing us from the sentence of death.

Praise God, we are forgiven! Nothing of my past is held against me. It could be the darkest sin a human being could imagine. It could be all of the distorted sexual practices you indulged in, or all of the hatred and jealousies that you allowed to control your life and behaviour. Or it may be all of the wicked scheming you did, because of your hurt, to get even with others. All of it is now over. Do not dwell anymore in the past.

Be aware that Satan will constantly bring back old memories, haunt you with your past and accuse you of your sins. He will torment you with the question, "How could God have forgiven you of all you have done?"

Rejoice and read with me:

> "And having disarmed the powers and authorities, He made a public spectacle of them, triumphing over them by the cross" (Colossians 2:15).

Paul is again using his cultural context to explain a theological concept. During Paul's time, the Roman emperors would send their armies to conquer smaller nations. When the war was over, the defeated king would be brought to Rome where he would be marched in shackles in front of Caesar, while the jeering crowd would humiliate and insult him. And as they approached Caesar, he would determine their fate and punishment.

On the cross of Calvary the powers of darkness were defeated, humiliated and exposed. They are no longer in authority but are subject to the authority of God and to the saints of God. You are chosen, you are cleansed and you have power and authority over the demonic realm.

You may have listened to the powers of darkness and its suggestions in the past and believed Satan's lies, but today he is a defeated foe. Would you now believe what God says about you, or would you rather succumb to the lies that Satan has been telling you all these years?

Satan will come to you over and over, sometimes as an angel of light, to deceive you. This is what happened in the Garden of Eden. He deceived Eve to believe a lie. Satan has no real authority, because you are a child of God, but he will cleverly employ deception to bring you down. He will do all that is within his power to deceive you again, because a false understanding of yourself will undermine your call and the authority that God has vested in you.

Based on these theological truths, there is no reason for you to ever imagine that you cannot overcome your past. The evil one and your past will tell you it is not possible. But this is only a subjective feeling, not an objective reality. The truth is that God has delivered you from the powers of darkness and given you authority. How about using it for a change?

D. SERVE THE PEOPLE THAT GOD HAS ENTRUSTED TO YOU.

God did not save you only so that you can go to heaven. But rather, He has commissioned you to be a blessing to your fellow human beings. You are called to be salt and the light. You are called to be an ambassador of the gospel of Jesus Christ. You are called to love your neighbour as yourself. Some of your neighbours are people who are hurting very deeply. Perhaps their stories are even worse than your own. God is looking to you to make a difference in their lives.

God never determined a strategy to help people from heaven. He came to this world and became man so that He could feel like a man, identify with humanity and serve a person like you who has now experienced the joy of forgiveness. Another believer who had experienced the love of God made you his priority, and that is the reason you have now experienced the love of God.

Now, God has ordained you to be the bearer of good news to your community. You have gone through pain, so now you can understand the pain of others. And you are best equipped to help them overcome this pain.

Jeremy was born with a twisted leg, which resulted in his left leg being shorter than his right. He walked with a limp, and as he grew up and started going to school, he would always be the quiet boy who sat on the sidelines watching others play. One day his father saw an advertisement in the newspaper for a litter of golden Labradors and thought that perhaps caring for a puppy would be something his son would enjoy. Jeremy was thrilled at the idea and accompanied his dad that afternoon to the address given in the advertisement.

There were six beautiful pups that came tumbling out of the small kennel as soon as it was opened, eagerly rushing about and playing with each other. Jeremy's father and the dog owner started discussing the merits of each pup, but Jeremy was still peering inside the kennel. "C'mon Jeremy, its time to pick your pup," said his father. "There's still one more, look, inside the kennel," said Jeremy, pointing. "Oh that one's got a bad leg—there's always one bad one in a litter. You won't want him," said the owner. But Jeremy continued to stand there, and finally the owner opened the door wider and the small pup, slightly limping, came out the kennel slowly and cautiously.

For several more minutes the adults discussed the puppies, and finally, it was time for Jeremy to choose. Very quietly he said, "I choose him," and pointed to the lame puppy. "Oh son, you don't want that puppy. He's no good. C'mon look at these others," said the owner. But Jeremy was resolute. As Jeremy's father paid the money, the dog breeder again asked Jeremy, "Son, why would you want this puppy?" Jeremy slowly raised his trouser to show his bad leg and said, "I'm lame too. The puppy is perfect for me."

Only someone who has gone through hurts and emotional pain can truly understand and empathise with another hurting person. Stop making excuses and reach out to another hurting person today!

Chapter 12

Decision Time!

YOU HAVE TAKEN TIME to read this book, and perhaps your emotions are now quite mixed up as you come to its end.

For some of you, the pain of the past may have surfaced and is tormenting you again. For others, it may be a relief that you finally understand why you think and act differently with those around you. Some of you may have experienced a freedom and breaking of the shackles and might even be looking to the future with great anticipation.

But let me caution all of you, no matter what emotion you are experiencing at the moment. You are well informed of your problem. You have grappled with me, seeking a solution. The decision for total healing is now in your hands. You have a choice to make: find permanent healing, or wrap yourself in self-pity and defeatism again.

HEALING IS A MATTER OF YOUR WILL

I have taught this material and counselled many. I have had the joy of seeing some be totally healed and restored to God and the community. But I have also found some who never experience victory. The difference is that one group was committed to seeing victory, and they made a decision to achieve it.

For the other group, their hurt became an integral part of their own identity. Their problem was their crutch, and they depended on it so much for attention, that they could not let go. They would rather continue in the pain than lose that identity.

There is a believer in our church in whom I have invested myself for over 25 years. She continues to live in utter defeat, bitterness and anger. She was a young child when her parents divorced. Both are deceased now. The mother was an extremely bitter person. Of course, she may have had reasons for her bitterness, but she never dealt with the issues. Because of the separation, the children experienced extreme poverty. It was my privilege to step in and help the family, together with other colleagues. We saw her through school, and she was able to finish her education and marry a Christian worker.

But like her mother, she never gave up her anger and bitterness. She left a trail of hurting people and unresolved issues but tried to worship and serve God fervently. Since I was involved with the family, I confronted her on many occasions, challenging and sometimes pleading with her to let go of her past and all its bitterness and embrace her new identity in Christ. She had a choice to make, but she opted for the choice of not dealing with her bitterness and anger. It finally caught up with her—she continues to believe in God, but is certainly a poor ambassador of the gospel of Jesus Christ.

I have also witnessed others who refused to let go of their pain and accept this new reality of forgiveness and healing. In a shame-based culture, letting go of the painful past would be seen as equal to giving up their right to getting "their pound of flesh." Or it could be seen as a defeat in one's quest for justice.

Even at this point, let me tell you: let go and embrace your new identity.

Over the years, I have seen many like the woman above, and it becomes obvious to me that they have made a choice to live defeated lives. I sometimes wonder if they are using their past as a crutch, a crutch without which they cannot live in the present, defining their identify and perhaps providing a sense of security by living in the known rather than venturing out in faith, to break free.

A story is told of an African man who was known throughout the continent as being wise and always being right. A young boy thought he would, for once, prove that this man could not give the right answer. The boy caught a butterfly in his hand and went up to the wise man and asked him, "Is the butterfly dead or alive?" The wise man looked deeply into the boys face and replied, "If I say the butterfly in your hand is alive, you will crush it to death. And if I say it is dead, you will set it free. All I will say is that life or death, it is in your hands. It is your choice." What wise words these were, and they are words that I too will say to you: life or death, it is in your hands. It is your choice.

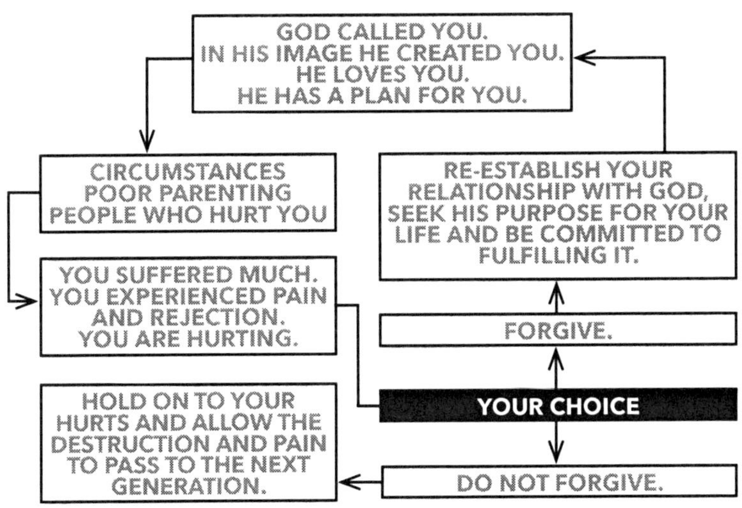

I hope your choice is to seek freedom, victory and a productive future of serving God and countless millions that are hurting very deeply.

CPSIA information can be obtained at www.ICGtesting.com
Printed in the USA
LVOW12s0335090914

403016LV00003B/3/P

Dennis Laney

Leica®

LENS PRACTICE

CHOOSING AND USING LEICA LENSES

First Edition 1985

Second Edition 1993

Hove Books
34 Church Road, Hove
East Sussex BN3 2GJ

British Library Cataloguing-in-Publication Data

A catalogue record for this book is available from the British Library

ISBN 1-897802-01-3

Design and typesetting: *Facing Pages, Brighton*

Printed in England by *FotoDirect Ltd, Brighton.*

Distribution in U.S.A.

The Saunders Group

21 Jet View Drive

Rochester, N.Y. 14624-4996

Fax: (716)328-5078

Distribution in Canada

Amplis Foto Inc.

22 Telson Road

Markham, Ontario L3R 1ES

Fax: (416)477-2502

Contents

Acknowledgements

The Author and Publisher would like to thank Leica Camera GmbH for their kind co-operation during the preparation of this book. We also wish to thank the Company for permission to use their Registered Trademarks; these are:-

ABSORBAN®	LEICA®
LEICAFLEX®	SUMMILUX®
ELMAR®	TELYT®
ELMARIT®	SUPER-ANGULON®
HEKTOR®	PA-CURTAGON®
NOCTILUX®	REPROVIT®
SUMMICRON®	VISOFLEX®

The following photographers have provided pictures to illustrate the applications of LEICA lenses:- Julius Behnke, Rudolf Seck and John Robert Young. All pictures not otherwise credited are by courtesy of Leica Camera GmbH.

Cover Pictures

Front cover: The 180mm, f/3.4 Apo-Telyt-R gives its peak performance in the distant focusing range, but even near its closest focusing distance edge sharpness is outstanding.
Dennis Laney

Back cover: 50mm, f/1.4 Summilux-M

Preface

Many changes have taken place since the first edition of this book in 1985. Leica cameras and lenses are now made by a new company, Leica Camera Group, in a new factory at Solms, five miles from their old home at Wetzlar. The company is independent of Leitz, but the traditions of quality, and many of the personnel remain the same.

The Leica M6 continues virtually unchanged as the ideal compact camera for photo-journalists and all amateurs who aspire to their style of photography. Its range of lenses remains the same too, from 21mm to 135mm, with some redesigned and a superb 35mm, f/1.4 with aspherical surfaces offered in addition. The R-cameras have gone through several model changes, leading to higher specifications, and now comprise three models. The Leica R7 is the top electronic model, with the Leica RE offering a simpler specification. Meanwhile the Leica R6-2 is a purely mechanical model but still with TTL metering, in the mode of the M6, for those photographers who prefer never to have to rely on batteries. Many R-lenses have been redesigned and some very interesting new ones added to the list.

Autofocus may rule now in the amateur world, and appeals to many professionals, but Leica continues to serve the needs of those photographers who want total control over their cameras and the benefits of superb Leica optics.

Dennis Laney

Brighton, July, 1993

For a photojournalist on an assignment where there must be the least possible disturbance, where it is essential to be silent and inconspicuous, the Leica M-camera is the ideal instrument. John Robert Young used the 21mm lens for most of his shots for this project on modern monastic life.

1. The Leica Philosophy of Lens Design

This chapter explains why we, who use Leica lenses and believe they are so special, are not deluding ourselves. Sound optical principles back our judgement. Readers may prefer to skip this chapter at first and go straight on to the practical information in Chapter 2 and the rest of the book. Come back to it later at leisure.

Leica lenses have always had a high reputation for their image quality, but many people are puzzled as to why their performance in comparative lens tests, as reported in photo and consumer magazines, is never outstanding. They have always been up with the very best, but never seemed to outperform them in the tests in a way to justify their reputation for sheer image quality among professional and discerning amateur photographers.

If those responsible for lens design at Leica are asked why Leica lenses never seem to stand out in conventional magazine tests, the reply will be "How often do you want to photograph patterns of black and white lines?". Subjects we photograph are very rarely black and white, or indeed in a single plane. They will be in all shades of grey, they will be in colour, they will be in all manner of solid shapes, they may be distant, misty, dimly lit, backlit, have high degrees of contrast or very little. A good *photographic* lens must project not only the detail onto the film, but also the factors which convey the tone and mood of the subject as faithfully as possible. The ultimate criterion for judging a photographic lens must be the quality and faithfulness of the photographic image, and that is the criterion they set out to meet at Leica.

The Leica objective is to provide a well balanced selection of superb objectives that will match the capabilities of the two camera systems, and will meet the needs of the majority of professional and serious amateur photographers. The general principles underlying Leica lens design may be summarized as follows:-

* Image quality comes first. Weight and size come next in importance, but not at the expense of image quality.

* Maximum aperture is always a proper working aperture. It is *never* just a status aperture that gives a degraded image unless stopped down.

* Lenses are corrected to give their best performance when focused at infinity, unless they have been specifically designed for close-up work.

* Very high speed lenses are designed to yield their peak performance at, or close to, maximum aperture. They are intended for use in poor lighting conditions. Slower lenses are better where critical definition is important at small apertures or in close-ups.
* All lenses have a consistent and neutral colour rendition. There is no such thing as a "warm" or "cold" Leica lens. This means that in colour slides the same colour will be consistent, with the same film, whatever lens is used.
* Above all: lenses are designed for total overall photographic performance, not to do well in one particular test or another.

Aspects of Lens Design

Two things happen to a ray of light when it passes through a glass surface in its passage through a lens. One is that it is bent through an angle. The degree of bending depends on the angle of incidence of the light ray at the surface, and on what is known as the "refractive index" of the particular glass. The higher the refractive index, the greater the degree of bending. It is the bending of light rays in this manner which allows a lens to focus an image. Modern lenses, particularly very fast ones and those of extreme focal length, require glasses of very high refractive index.

Light is also dispersed when it passes through a glass surface. This means that light of different wavelengths (light of different colours) is bent to different degrees. The consequence of dispersion in a lens is that light of different colours will be brought to focus at different points: in a simple single-element lens this will show as colour fringing round the image. Clearly, if a camera lens were to bring different colours in an object to focus at different points the result would be a fuzzy negative or transparency. This is why the lens designer is always searching for glasses of higher refractive index, but with the lowest possible dispersion.

Thirty-five years ago Leitz set up their own glass research and glass-making facilities to find such glasses. High refractive index usually means high dispersion too, so the task was not easy. Furthermore, many of the most promising compositions do not have satisfactory physical properties. They may result in glasses which are too soft, for example. Others may fail to form glasses of sufficient transparency. Nevertheless, Leitz had a number of notable successes and new Leitz glasses have been incorporated in Leica lenses since the early 1950's. Sometimes new glasses have led to improvements in existing lenses, but they have also enabled outstanding new lenses to be produced which would have been impossible to compute without them. Examples of the latter are the very wide aperture, very long focus and "apo" designs.

Advances in lens design, helped by new glasses, are demonstrated by these two versions of the 28mm, f/2.8 ELMARIT-M. The 1993 version on the left is more compact and has a better performance than its predecessor on the right. An interesting feature of the new design is the slightly concave front surface.

Benefits brought by the new glasses are numerous. Designs have been simplified by a reduction in the number of elements, with the benefit of reduced weight and reduced number of surfaces, and hence reduced danger of internal reflections.

Aspherical surfaces, which are difficult and expensive to make, have generally been avoided. Calcium fluoride and other crystalline salts, employed in long telephoto lenses by some lens manufacturers to overcome chromatic aberrations, are avoided together with their concomitant disadvantages of thermal instability and softness. In lens types which require elements of very short focal length, it used to mean sharply curved surfaces, which either made them very thick and heavy or they had narrow rims, leading to less precision in mounting and less secure fixing. Steeply curved surfaces are also often accompanied by high tolerance sensitivity; in other words, very small errors produce a disproportionately deleterious effect on performance. Highly refractive glass avoids all these disadvantages by enabling short focal length elements to have much more shallow curvature.

In the old days the lens designer had to carry out multitudinous calculations using logarithm tables to trace the path of a ray of light through a lens. The angle of refraction had to be calculated for each surface for rays passing through the centre and the periphery of the lens. Ingenious formulae were developed to reduce the number of calculations, but the process was still very time-consuming and tedious. Lens design was a matter of trial and error, based very much on experience and hunch. The early lenses designed for the Leica by Max Berek came about in this way. Leitz were one of the first optical companies to apply computers to the problem of lens design, at about the same time as the glass research laboratory was set up.

These days a lens design is developed entirely on the computer and a prototype will not be built until the design has been optimized first on paper. The twin assets of the Leica company which give it its unique strength in photographic lenses are its knowledge of glass and its computer programmes. These programmes now enable the designer to explore many more variables than was ever possible before. A lot of the trial and error is now carried out on computers in a fraction of the time, enabling the designer to spend more of his time in exploring new concepts and principles. He can go on to forecast the side effects, such as the likely degree of vignetting in different points in the lens at different apertures.

Another fruitful aspect of earlier Leitz research was the development of "ABSORBAN" cement for the cemented elements in a lens. ABSORBAN also has the property of absorbing ultra-violet light, thus making a u.v. filter unnecessary, except at extreme altitudes or to protect the front surfaces of a lens. In can also be used for correcting the colour rendering of a lens, although this is more usually done nowadays through the medium of the anti-reflection coating.

The mechanical components of Leica lenses are as vital to high image quality as the optics. All mechanical linkages with the camera body, such as the rangefinder/viewfinder frame-selection cams in M-lenses and the automatic diaphragm and meter couplings in R-lenses, are kept safely inside the lens barrel. They do not protrude to be vulnerable to damage. Focusing mounts on the modern lenses have parallel operation, that is, the lens head does not rotate during focusing, but simply moves in and out. This means that lens attachments such as polarizing filters remain correctly aligned during focusing. The exceptions are two of the zoom lenses.

Lens diaphragms run on anti-friction-coated ball bearings. The automatic diaphragms fitted to R-lenses operate in a different way to that of most other makes. The more usual manner of operation is for the mechanism to hold the iris fully open until the shutter release is pressed. A device in the camera body then stops it down to the selected aperture. Leica R-lenses operate on the opposite principle which results in a shorter delay between pressing the shutter release and the opening of the shutter. The iris is spring-loaded so that it closes to the selected aperture when a locking device is tripped on pressing the shutter release. After the exposure the mechanism in the camera body returns the iris to the full aperture position and holds it there until the next operation of the shutter release, or the depth-of-field lever. The maximum time for the diaphragm to close from maximum to minimum aperture is 38 milliseconds. The iris blades in Leica R-lenses have an extra long travel from maximum to minimum aperture compared with other SLR lenses with automatic diaphragms. This helps to reduce further the risk of extra exposure due to blade bounce.

Apochromatic lenses

The term "*a*chromat" as applied to a lens has been familiar since the beginning of photography. The image formed by a simple lens with white light will have colour fringes due to the dispersion of the light by the lens. In the eighteenth century John Dolland and others had found that by combining two lenses, one made from crown glass and the other from flint glass, this could be corrected for the portion of the spectrum to which the eye was most sensitive, yellow and green. Daguerre had been able to specify an achromat for his first camera in 1839. Practically all photographic lenses are now achromats, although the precise colours for which they are corrected has been varied to match the changing colour sensitivity of black-and-white films. This still leaves a secondary spectrum, which becomes more serious as focal length increases. *Apo*chromatic lenses are corrected for three colours, and although they have been known for some time they have only been introduced into general photography in recent years.

The term "apochromat" was originally defined in connection with telescopes and microscopes. Both of these are instruments with narrow angles of view, and hence relatively small image fields. The classical definition of "apochromatic" requires that a lens, to be described as such, must be fully corrected for all three primary colours for longitudinal and spherical chromatic aberrations: but these aberrations only occur with subjects which are on the optical axis, ie., in the centre of the image field. Some lens manufacturers do not even adopt this limited definition when ascribing the term "apo" to their lenses.

In a photographic lens we are equally concerned with subjects which are at a distance from the optical axis; in other words, which are over the whole image field. In these circumstances no fewer than five other possible forms of chromatic aberration become significant as we move towards the edges of the picture. A lens which conforms only to the limited classical definition of apochromatic correction may not then be free of all colour errors, and these can be particularly serious in long-focus lenses.

Leica apply more rigid standards and a lens to which they attach the description "Apo" will meet the following criteria:-

An extender is an invaluable addition to any outfit to increase the focal length of lenses of 50mm or more focal length, and of maximum aperture f/2 or smaller. The quality of LEICA extenders may be judged by comparing these two pictures. The one on the left was taken with the 280mm, f/2.8 APO-TELYT-R, stopped down to f/4, and the one on the right with the same lens set to the same aperture

but with the 2x EXTENDER-R added, giving an effective aperture of f/8 at 560mm. Enlargement is 16x. These half-tones cannot do justice to the really crisp images of the original prints because the screen pattern obscures the sharpness and contrast of the horizontal and vertical lines of the roof tiles.. *Rudolf Seck*

* It will exhibit almost perfect monochromatic correction as far as is physically and technically possible (this means it will be free of distortion, astigmatism. etc.).
* It will meet the classic definition of apochromatic.
* The colour fringes in the whole image field, not only round the optical axis, will be attenuated to such a level that the lens will satisfy the most exacting requirements in practice.

To the layman all this adds up to an extremely crisp image with very high contrast. It must be remembered though that such a stringent specification can only apply when the lens is used for applications for which it was designed. This generally means when it is focused at infinity, or at least in the longer focusing range.

Extenders

Tele-converters, or extenders, have been known for a long time but were notorious for poor image quality. New highly refractive glasses enabled Leica to design extenders which would have a performance compatible with Leica lenses, and their first one appeared in 1980. The scope for ultimate correction of optical systems with negative focal lengths, as with an extender, is very limited. The slight negative field curvature cannot be corrected. In a normal telephoto lens in which the negative component at the rear is, in effect, playing the part of an extender, the residual aberrations in the rear component are compensated for by aberrations of an opposite nature which the designer deliberately leaves in the front component of the lens. With a separate extender this cannot be done and the picture quality given by a lens-plus-extender will be adversely affected to a greater or lesser extent. Leica have reduced these adverse effects to a minimum by carefully matching the extender to the degree of correction of the lenses for which it is suitable. This is why each extender is only recommended for certain lenses.

Sharpness and lens aberrations

The ordinary professional or amateur photographer does not need a detailed knowledge of the many aberrations that affect the performance of a photographic lens in order to take good pictures. What does matter is the collective effect of the aberrations on image formation. They may manifest themselves as distortion, colour cast, or lack of sharpness. Distortion is most easily recognized in pictures of rectangular objects when lines which should be straight are curved. Distortion is virtually absent from even modestly priced modern lenses of normal focal length; but it can be present in ultra-wide-angle and zoom lenses,

The LEICA M6 with its silent shutter and a 50mm, f/1.4 SUMMILUX-M unobtrusively secured this picture in Chartres cathedral. The bright candles, even at the edges of the frame, betray no coma or flare, faults which are often present in fast lenses.
John Robert Young

A 35mm, f/1.4 SUMMILUX-M is one of the most useful lenses to have on the camera if you carry no others and dont't know what to expect. On a visit to the Leitz works in Wetzlar, it captured this shot of small scale production of one of Leitz' special optical glasses. *Dennis Laney*

One of the greatest joys of the R-system is the ease with which close-ups can be taken, especially with the macro lenses. You can switch instantly from landscape or general photography to a close-up of something that catches your eye. No other accessory equipment is needed, and if the light is reasonable the camera can be hand-held. Focus approximately for the framing required and then sway your body gently to and fro. When the subject jumps into sharp focus, press the release. Above: 100mm, f/2.8 Apo-Macro-Elmarit-R; below: 60mm, f/2.8 Macro-Elmarit-R. *Dennis Laney*

and is a feature of fisheye lenses. Colour changes brought about by a lens may be more subtle, but they can be measured by relatively simple standard instruments. Lack of sharpness is a lot more difficult to define. The eye can recognize it in an unsatisfactory image, and can detect the differences in images produced by different lenses. However, what the eye actually sees when we describe an image as being unsharp has been a matter of controversy for years.

It is very important for the lens designer to be able to identify and measure those characteristics of a photographic image by which the eye judges its quality. He knows all about coma and astigmatism and chromatic aberration, and so on, and if they could all be removed he would be a long way down the road to producing the perfect lens. But reality is not like that; lens design is a matter of balancing compromises; the removal of one form of aberration is likely to aggravate another. The skill of the lens designer lies in his ability to create a lens which will give as near perfect an image as possible, within its anticipated range of applications. Thus, a very fast wide-angle lens will have been designed for available-light photography, probably in confined spaces, or for candid portraits, or theatre pictures, or photo-journalism, but it should not be expected also to give first class results in close-up work or copying. In order to begin to understand what "quality" in a photographic image means in physical terms, the designer must know what this lack of sharpness is that the eye can discern; how does it manifest itself? How can he detect it and measure it with physical instruments so that he will know what he must aim for? How can he compare one lens with another in quantitative rather than in qualitative terms?

The importance of contrast has always been emphasized by Leica and they have always given it a higher priority than resolution, provided the result was a better lens photographically. Astigmatism and curvature of field can both lead to lower resolution in terms of lines per millimetre. Some lens manufacturers endeavour to keep these to a minimum, but this can often only be done at the expense of contrast. Lens-testing charts are two-dimensional objects and the lenses from makers who adopt this policy will perform well in the conventional resolution tests. Leica, on the other hand, if they have to find a compromise, will choose the solution that gives the best *photographic* results with three-dimensional objects, even if that means sacrificing some flatness of field to achieve maximum contrast.

Resolution is usually quoted in terms of Modulation Transfer Function, or MTF. An image produced by the lens under test of a very narrow bright line against a dark background is scanned electronically and the MTF obtained by a mathematical process known as Fourier transform. The results are presented as a set of curves showing the contrast and resolution at various apertures and at the centre and the edges, or at any other part of the image. MTF curves are very difficult for the layman to interpret.

Other aberrations of a lens, which cannot be expressed by MTF, are indicated by Phase Transfer Function (PTF). Interpretation of PTF is even more difficult for the layman. MTF and PTF together give what is known as the Optical Transfer Function (OTF). It is generally agreed that OTF correctly describes the image-forming properties of a given lens, but up to now no one has been able to develop a method of interpretation which is agreed by all experts world-wide. OTF is a complex function, in the mathematical sense, and although it may be understood mathematically as describing what is happening to light rays passing through a lens, it is very difficult, if not impossible, to visualize what it means in terms of the photographic image. Therefore, in routine testing, and certainly in lens tests published in magazines, the PTF is ignored and only MTF is considered. This means that in most published lens reports certain potentially serious defects are simply treated as if they did not exist. One of these is coma, which can be a serious defect in wide-aperture lenses. If coma is present in a lens the effect is best seen when point sources of light occur near the edges of the picture in night shots – the very circumstances in which wide-aperture lenses are often used. The points of light will be spread out in a tangential direction relative to the centre of the image, forming the characteristic "flying bird" shape. The effect of coma gets progressively worse towards

Coma is a common aberration in wide-aperture lenses, but it is not revealed by MTF measurements and therefore is totally ignored in lens reports which rely on MTF alone. Both the above pictures, which are from the top left quarters of the original negatives, were taken with f/1.4 lenses stopped down to f/2. The lens on the left suffers from severe coma. The effect is most marked in the string of lights on the top left and in the lights strung along the windows of the Sparkasse shop. Although coma is most the edges. This spreading of point sources means, of course, that all points in the image, whether bright ones or not, are similarly spread and the sharpness of the image is greatly reduced as a consequence.

Lens tests for ultimate image quality

Leica take the view regarding photographic and consumer magazine lens reports that, under the special conditions chosen by the magazine, one lens may be shown to be better than another but it will not necessarily be better under all circumstances. What really matters is the total *photographic* performance of the lens. The standard lens tests, MTF and so on, are very important for them and they employ them all the time, but they do not tell the whole story about a photographic lens. It is true enough that resolution is important and contrast is very important. If you take pictures of the same scene, on the same film, and at the same time with two different lenses, one corrected for maximum resolution and the other corrected for maximum contrast, then the more unfavourable the lighting conditions are, the more detail you will be able to pick out in the photo taken with the high-contrast lens than in the photo taken with the high-resolution lens. But these measurements alone do not provide an objective, physical method for measuring the sharpness of the best lenses and distinguishing them from lenses which give just as good, or even better, results in conventional tests, but which yield inferior images. Leitz, in the days before Leica was set up as a separate company, set out to find a method for measuring the image-

apparent in images of point light sources, it affects all the image points which are also spread in a similar way and reduces the sharpness and contrast of the whole image. Compare the images of the television antennae and the railings of the balcony on the top floor of the Sparkasse building in the picture on the left with that on the right, where coma is virtually absent. The right-hand picture was taken with the prototype of the 35mm, f/1.4 SUMMILUX ASPHERICAL.

forming properties of a lens that could be directly related to the photographic image.

They started from the proposition that photographic subjects are likely to be landscapes, people, animals, buildings, technical objects, and so on. Except in special applications such as copying, all the subjects we record in the outside world are three-dimensional. The images of such subjects will be complex; they will consist of innumerable areas of different densities and different colours, with a jumble of boundaries between them. The density differences at some of the boundaries will be very small. The boundaries themselves may be straight or curved, ragged or smooth, and will generally lie in all directions throughout the image. What governs our perception of the degree of sharpness in the image will be the acuity of the transition from one side of a boundary to the other. If the transition is less acute than in the original subject, the boundary will appear less sharp. In optics the term "edge" is used for such boundaries.

For simplicity, consider a transparency of a tree with the sky as a background. Then consider the image on that transparency of an individual leaf on the outside of the tree, so that it is seen against the sky. Assume that the leaf was sharply focused in the camera. The leaf will appear dark in comparison with the bright sky. The outline of the leaf will be the boundary between the dark leaf and the light sky and so it will be an "edge" in the image on the transparency. The light from the sky, as focused by the camera lens on the film, will have had a higher intensity, or brightness, than the light from the leaf. If the lens had been a perfect photographic objective the two bundles of light rays, those from the leaf near its edge and those from the sky close to the leaf, would have been sharply separated. If one then drew a graph of the light intensity falling on the film at this point of the image, across the boundary between the leaf and the sky, it would be in the shape of a step, as in Fig. 1.

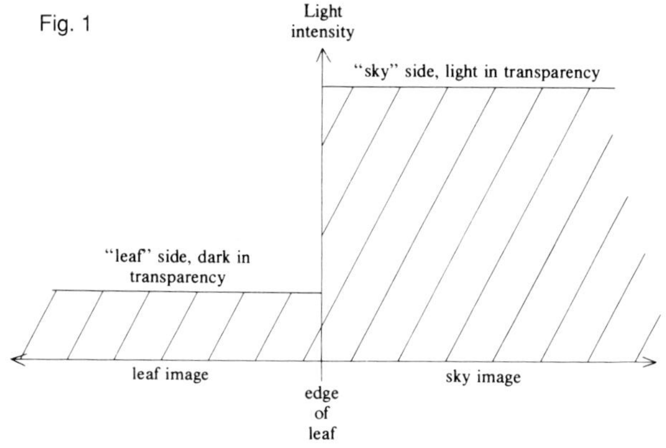

If the lens is not ideal and spreads the light rays a little so that some of the higher intensity ones fall on the "leaf" side and some of the lower intensity ones fall on the "sky" side, then the edge will be blurred; it will no longer be sharp, but spread out a little on either side. A graph of the light energy falling across the edge would take on an "S" shape, as in Fig. 2.

Fig. 2

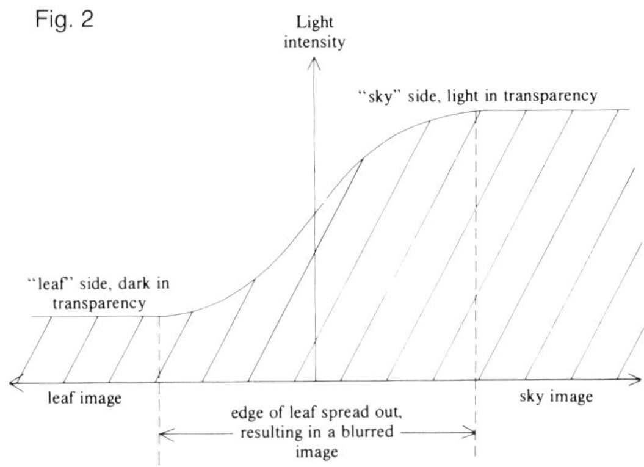

Leitz found that the edge image gives a more critical evaluation of lens aberrations than the line image which is used in MTF measurements. Furthermore, the shape of the curve gives a visual indication of both edge sharpness and contrast. If the curve is as in Fig. 2, then both sharpness and contrast would be low. If, on the other hand, the middle portion of the curve is steep but the "tails" spread a long way either side of the edge, as in Fig. 3, indicating that light is spilling over for some distance on the wrong side of the boundary, then the edge image will appear sharp but the contrast will be low. Whereas if the tails are very short, as in Fig. 4, then the edge image will appear sharp and the contrast will be high, indicating a very good lens. No lens will ever give the ideal step-shaped curve because of diffraction and because of the compromises that have to be made in lens design, but the nearer the step-shape is approached the better is the lens. These curves are called the "Edge Spread Function".

Fig. 3

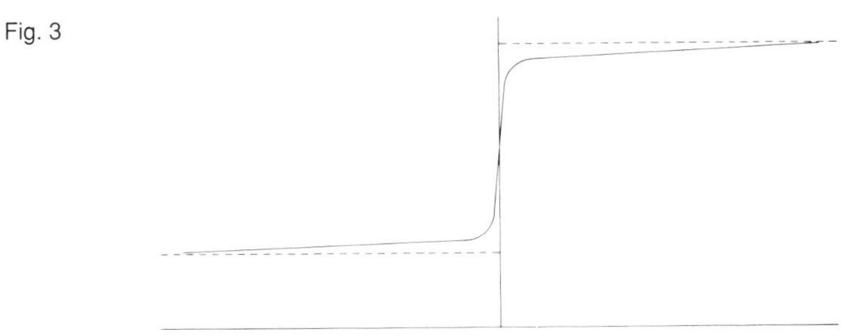

Fig. 4

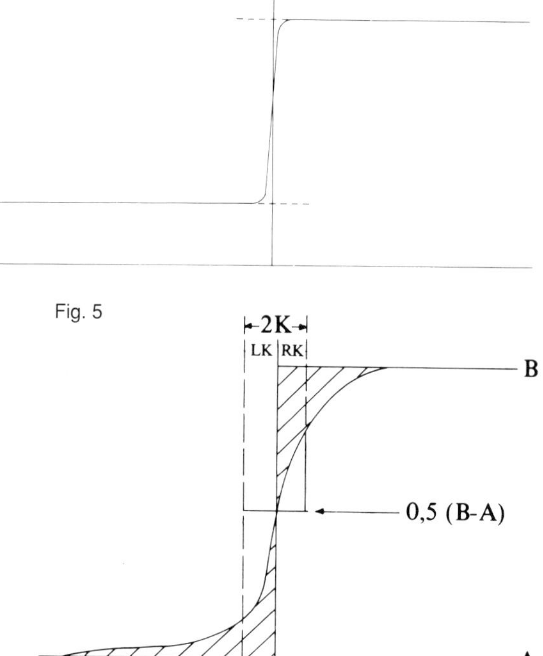

Fig. 5

The areas under the curve indicated by the shaded portions in Fig.5 at A and B represent the degree of spreading on each side of the edge. Leitz showed that the width of a rectangle of equal area to the area under the curve, drawn from the 50% point, can be taken as a convenient and representative measure and they called this the "Edge Spread Width", represented by the symbol "K", from the German *Kante* meaning "edge". K is therefore a measure of lack of image quality. A value for K may be found for each side of the edge, left and right; "LK" and "RK". If LK and RK are unequal, the difference between them represents the degree of asymmetry in the lens. Asymmetry may be due to coma, for example, inherent in the design, or it may be caused by centring errors during assembly. A value for the overall Edge Spread Width of a lens is given by:

$$\frac{LK + RK}{2}$$

K gives a greater weighting to contrast defects than to edge sharpness defects. A second quality criterion has therefore been added which indicates sharpness only, but it is derived from the same set of measurements. The curve between the points 25% and 75% up the step has been found from experience to be relatively straight (Fig. 6) so the horizontal distance between the curve and the vertical axis at the 25% point can be taken as the "Left Edge Sharpness", or LKS, and that at the 75%

Fig. 6

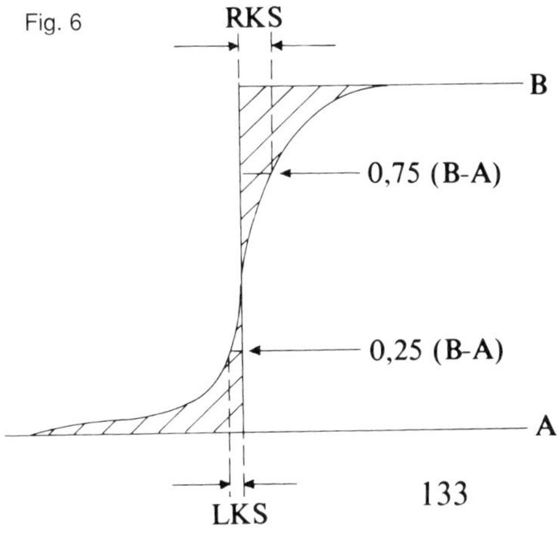

point as the "Right Edge Sharpness", or RKS. The overall Edge Sharpness, KS, is then given by:

$$\frac{LKS + RKS}{2}$$

If we restrict our measurements at a particular point in the image to radially and tangentially oriented edges only (see Fig. 7) we will obtain four values for Edge Spread Width and four values for Edge Sharpness – two of each for each edge. These will be LK and RK for each of the radial and tangential edges, and LKS and RKS for the same two edges.

A radial edge is any edge which lies on a radius of the image circle, and a tangential edge is one which is perpendicular (at right angles) to a radius.

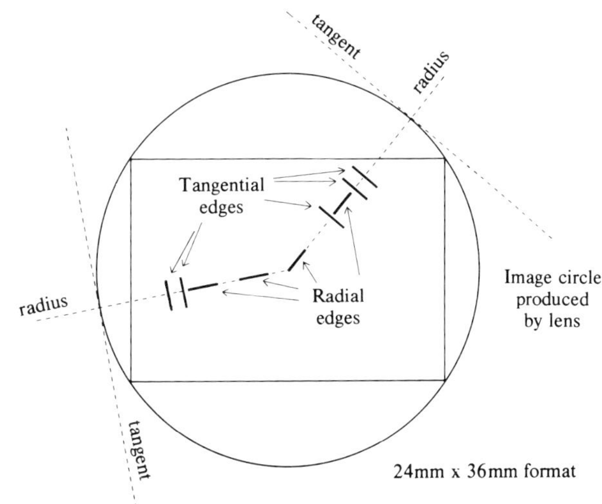

Fig. 7. Illustration of radial and tangential edges in an image.

The image of a radial edge will be degraded by lens aberrations which produce their effect in a tangential direction, and that of a tangential edge by lens aberrations operating in the radial direction. Coma, as an example, is radial, and affects tangential edges. In reality, edges in a photographic image will be randomly oriented in all directions: those not precisely oriented either radially or tangentially will be affected by both sorts of aberrations.

Even by restricting our measurements, taken at a single point, to radial and tangential edges only, the mass of numbers obtained would be difficult to assimilate, but they can be represented graphically in quite a striking manner. Two axes are drawn, the horizontal one representing the radial direction at the point in the image where measurements are taken, and the vertical one representing the tangential direction at the same point. The four values for each edge are plotted on the appropriate axis, ie; those for the tangential edge on the horizontal axis because a tangential edge is spread in a radial direction, and those for the radial edge on the vertical axis because the radial edge is spread in a tangential direction. A suitable scale might be 1 mm to represent 1

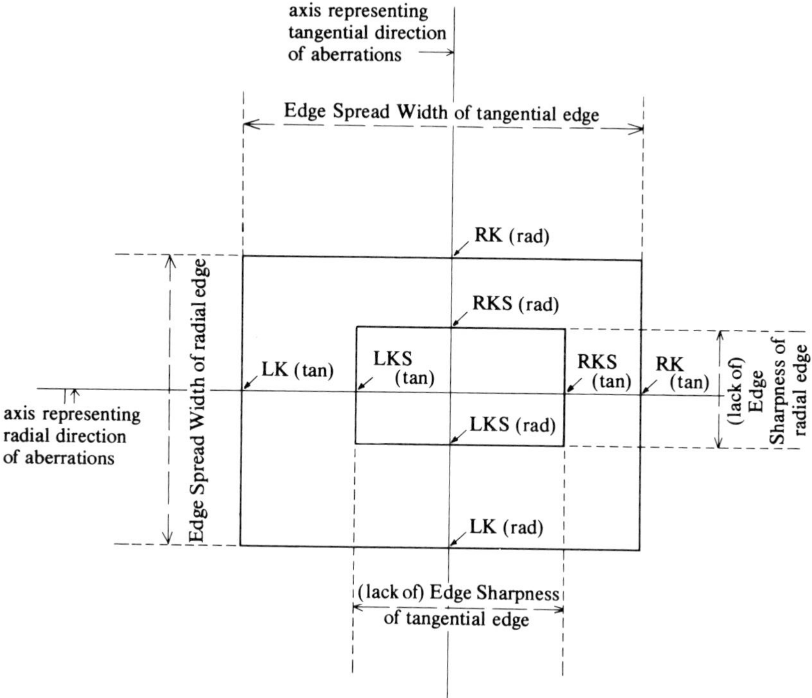

Fig. 8. The Leica computer-generated box diagrams, as described in the text, graphically illustrate the lack of sharpness (inner rectangle), lack of contrast (outer rectangle) and any asymmetry at one point in in an image as measured in a radial and a tangential direction. Such diagrams afford a visual analogue of the overall effect at that point of all the aberrations present in a lens.

micron. Perpendiculars are then drawn from these points extending on both sides of the axes. Two rectangles are obtained, as in Fig. 8.

The size and form of these rectangles, the differences in their size and proportions, and their asymmetry relative to the axes and relative to each other, show very clearly, at a glance, the image-forming characteristics of the lens at that particular point. The outer rectangle is a visual analogue of the lack of contrast and the inner rectangle is a visual analogue of the lack of sharpness. Such a diagram represents the total effect at that point of all the aberrations in the lens which lead to lack of sharpness and contrast. From the photographer's point of view this is what matters. He is not normally interested in how each of the individual aberrations in his lens manifests itself, but in the overall influence of all the aberrations on the quality of his photographs.

Sixty years ago the 50mm SUMMAR was introduced as the first f/2 lens for the Leica. It was not so sharp as the old 50mm, f/3.5 ELMAR, but over twice as fast. Its softness at full aperture was an acceptable price to pay for the increased speed. Fig. 9 shows the SUMMAR compared with a

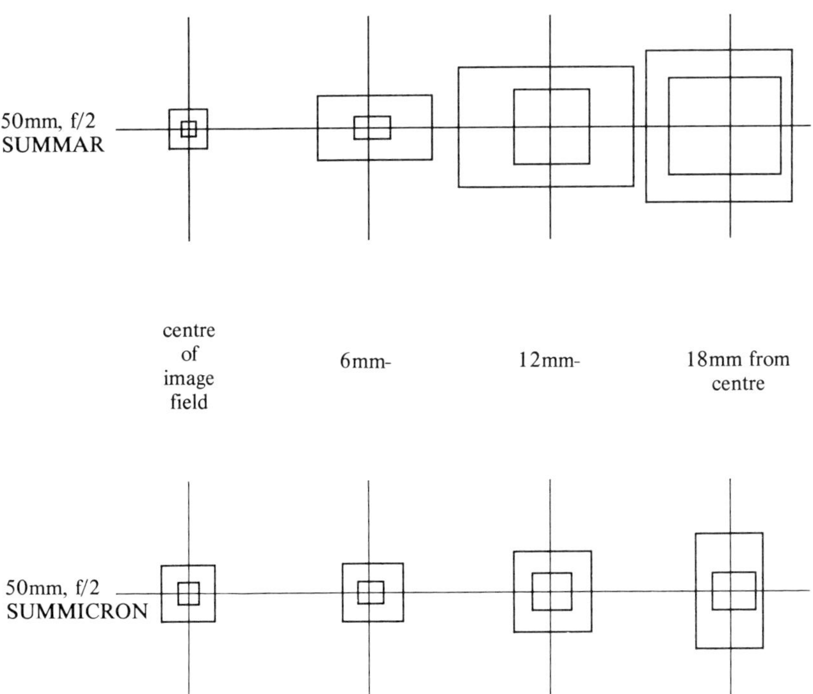

Fig. 9. Comparison of 50mm, f/2 SUMMAR and SUMMICRON-M lenses at full aperture. The inner rectangles represent the blurring of an edge leading to lack of sharpness, and the outer rectangles represent spilling of light beyond the edge, which shows as lack of contrast. The performance of the SUMMICRON is extremely good and uniform for a lens of its angle of view and speed. Scale: 1mm = 2 microns

modern 50mm, f/2 SUMMICRON-R, both at full aperture. The left-hand box diagram for each lens refers to the centre of the image field, in other words on the lens axis. The three box diagrams to the right refer respectively to points 6mm, 12mm, and 18mm, from the image centre. The scale of the original computer diagrams has been reduced to half for these illustrations, so 1mm on the printed page represents 2 microns (1 micron = 1/1000mm).

Compared with the SUMMAR, the SUMMICRON gives much better sharpness in the field away from the lens axis. Its contrast is also much higher than that of the SUMMAR and the performance of the lens is much more uniform over the entire image field. When these lenses are stopped down the sharpness and contrast of the SUMMICRON improve uniformly over the whole image field, whereas the performance of the SUMMAR improves radically in the centre of the field, but to a much lesser extent in the outer regions of the image.

Both these lenses have a wide acceptance angle (45°) and are fast (f/2). When the acceptance angle is reduced by increasing the focal length, and the maximum aperture is also smaller, it is possible to design a lens with a better performance than is attainable with a 50mm, f/2. The current 90mm, f/2.8 ELMARIT-R is an outstanding example (Fig 10). Not only are sharpness and contrast extremely good at full aperture, but they are uniform over the whole image field. Stopping down improves it further.

Macro lenses are normally corrected to give their best performance in the close-up range. One normally needs to stop them down for optimum sharpness at infinity. The 100mm, f/4 MACRO ELMAR-R was originally designed to be used with focusing bellows on LEICA reflex cameras and has been around for about twenty-five years. Because of its good performance at infinity it was later made available in a normal focusing mount as well. More recently LEICA introduced a new 100mm, f/2.8 APO-MACRO-ELMARIT-R, twice as fast as the 100mm MACRO-ELMAR-R. This lens at its full aperture of f/2.8 has outstanding performance at infinity, as well

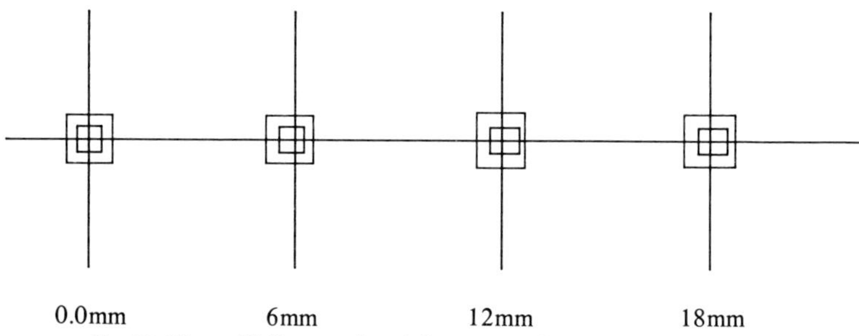

Fig.10. 90mm, f/2 ELMARIT-R at full aperture. Scale: 1mm = 2 microns.

as at its closest focusing distance where the reproduction ratio is 1:2; It can thus be used as a normal medium long focus lens.

In Fig. 11 the upper diagram shows its performance when focused at infinity and the lower diagram at a reproduction ratio of 1:2.

When the focal length is increased further, chromatic aberration becomes a problem in telephoto lenses. However this has been virtually eliminated in the 280mm, f/2.8 APO-TELYT-R which has an incredible performance for such a fast lens of this focal length, as is demonstrated in Fig. 12.

This lens is already giving close to its best performance at full aperture. Stopping down produces only a marginal improvement.

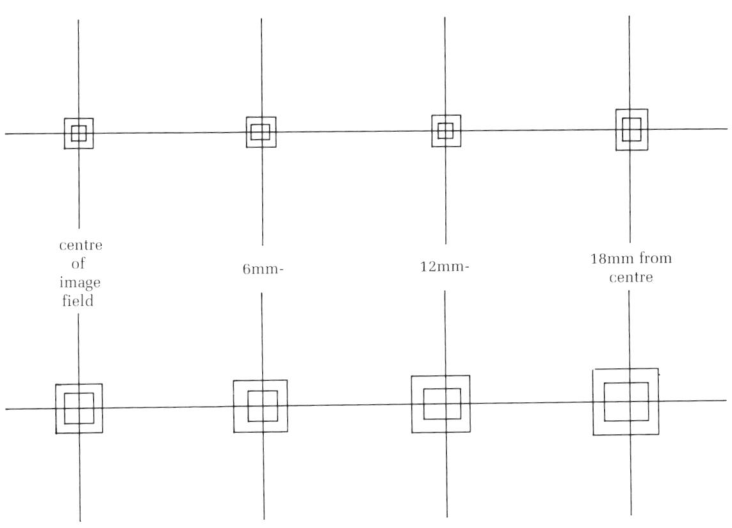

Fig. 11. 100mm, f/2.8 APO-MACRO-ELMARIT-R. In the upper diagram it is focused at infinity and in the lower one at 45cm to give a reproduction ratio of 1:2, in both cases at full aperture. Scale: 1mm = 2 microns.

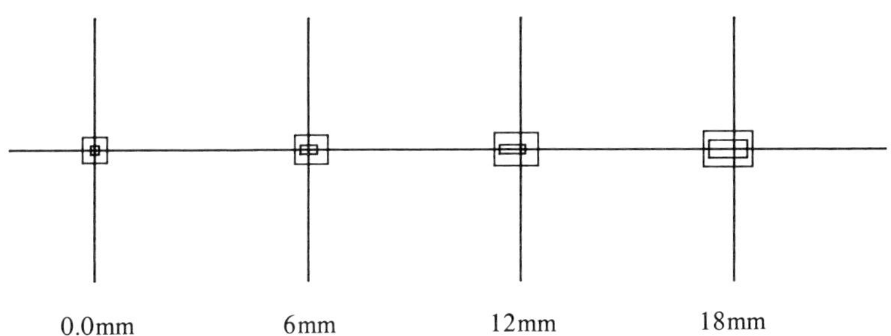

Fig. 12. 280mm, f/2.8 APO-TELYT-R at full aperture. Scale: 1mm = 2 microns.

Quality control

All these features which give Leica lenses their unique optical qualities would be of little practical value if quality was not strictly controlled during the manufacturing process and the finished lens carefully tested to make sure it met its specification. The finer the lens is optically, the more care is needed in its manufacture and assembly.

There are eight distinct stages in the production of a Leica lens. These are:-

1.Manufacture or purchase of the various types of glass.

2.Formation of the glass discs with parallel faces for making into the individual lens elements.

3.Grinding and polishing of the discs to form the spherical or aspherical surfaces, convex or concave.

4.Centring of the elements, which means grinding the edges so that they are parallel to the optical axes.

3.Ultrasonic cleaning and surface coating of the elements.

6.Fixing together of any cemented groups.

7.Manufacture of all the mechanical components and the making of sub-assemblies, such as the iris diaphragm.

8.Assembly of the optical elements into the focusing mount, together with the iris diaphragm, linkages, cams, etc.

Lack of precision in any of these processes will degrade the performance of the lens: the better and finer the design of the lens, the greater will be the deleterious effect. The best evidence of the standards reached by Leica lens specifications is the fact that in many respects they meet military requirements without modification. Examples are in their requirements for reduction in internal reflections, climatic endurance, and resistance to fungoid growth. Leica specifications also demand that a lens must be able to withstand temperature shock by cooling from +20°C to -20°C and warming back again to +20°C. The completed lens is checked on no fewer than 75 points, optically and mechanically. Thus a Leica lens is a superb optical instrument and one which will continue to perform to the same standards under the most adverse conditions.

Quality control begins as soon as the prototype design of a new lens is turned into a production product. The specification for every optical and mechanical component is laid down to very narrow tolerances. Mechanical components are tested by the normal methods common in high precision engineering, but Leica, and Leitz before them, have often had to develop methods themselves for testing optical components. Despite the use of modern, computer-controlled machinery wherever possible, the production of a lens to Leica standards requires individual craftsmanship of the highest order. Small-batch production methods have to be used because of the relatively small numbers made of any one type, and also because of the continuous inspection of every component at every stage of manufacture.

Several types of glass are necessary in any one lens. A glass may be supplied by one of a few optical-glass manufacturers in the world, or it may be a special Leica glass developed and made in their own glass laboratory. Bought-in glass will be accompanied by a certificate that it meets specification; a batch of Leica's own glass will be analysed for chemical purity and tested for correct optical properties. These days the majority of glass for camera lenses is supplied as moulded blank discs, already to size.

When the blank discs have been ground to form their two optical surfaces, and have been checked for precise curvature, they are polished with progressively finer abrasives until the surfaces are perfect. They are then placed in an instrument, invented formerly by Leitz, which finds the exact optical centre of a lens element and grinds the rim until it is parallel with the optical axis. This ensures that the elements will be precisely aligned when they are mounted.

The next stage, after thorough removal of all contaminates in cleaning baths with ultra-sonic vibration, is the application of the anti-reflection coatings. This operation must be very accurately controlled because the thickness of the coating layers is very critical. It is a quarter of the wavelength of the light which is to be affected by the coating.

Elsewhere in the factory the metal parts for the lens mount are being fabricated. Besides the various barrels and rings and helical screws that go to make the body, there are the numerous small parts, such as the diaphragm blades. The helical focusing mounts of Leica lenses have a reputation for being durable and for having a smooth, silky movement. One part of the mount is machined from a special aluminium and the other from brass. The brass accounts for some of the greater weight of Leica's lenses compared with similar lenses from other makers. They are machined to very close tolerances, the focusing mount for an individual lens being formed from two components individually lapped together. In this way only a very thin film of lubricant is required; Leica do not need to pack their lens mounts with grease in order to prevent wobble or play between the two parts of the mount. Special alloys are used for external parts which allow the application of a special electroplated finish which is more wear-resistant than chrome, paint or lacquer, and is also more attractive. The bayonet fittings are made from a brass alloy which is then given three hard metallic coatings for durability. Iris diaphragms are assembled by hand and carefully adjusted for accuracy at all apertures. In the case of R-lenses, they must also be adjusted to eliminate bounce in their automatic stop-down move-

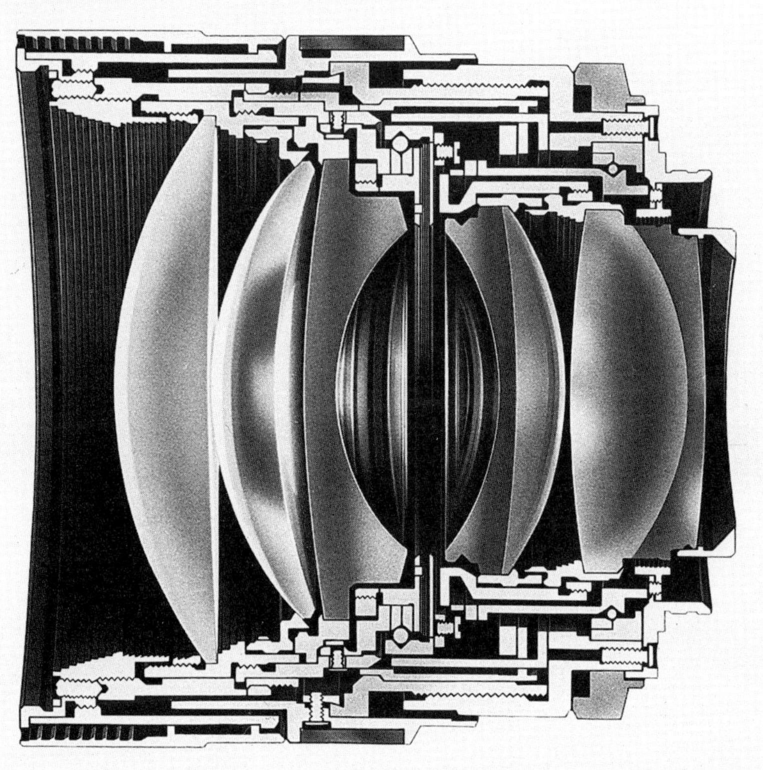

This cross section of the 80mm, f/1.4 SUMMILUX-R demonstrates the complexity of the mechanism of LEICA lens mounts that ensures smooth focusing and accurate, bounce-free diaphragms. One part of the helical focusing mount is machined from a special aluminium and the other from brass. The two parts for each lens are individually lapped together so that only a very thin film of grease is required for a very smooth and durable movement.

ments. Leica have their own patented method for doing this. Bounce of the diaphragm blades after closing would produce exposure error.

Most lenses contain at least one cemented pair. These are assembled after coating. When they are going to form part of a cemented doublet the individual elements do not need to have such close tolerances as they would if they were free-standing, but the cemented combination must come within very tight tolerances. The elements for a cemented group are selected so that the combination will meet closer tolerances than the individual components.

Lens assembly takes place in dust-free rooms under a slight positive air pressure to prevent entry of dust. When the lens is complete the iris diaphragm is finally adjusted to give the correct aperture at every stop engraved on the mount. Checking, testing and adjusting at these final stages take a high proportion of the total manufacturing time and, together with the hand assembly, go a long way to account for the consistency and reliability, and price, of Leica lenses.

The completed lens is taken over by the Quality Assurance Department, which has the responsibility to make sure that it matches specification in every respect, both optically and mechanically. The Quality Assurance Department has its inspectors in the production shops who will have already checked and passed the separate components as they are made, but once the lens is assembled it becomes, as it were, the "property" of Quality Assurance who alone have the authority to release it for sale. The significance of this is that *every individual* LEICA lens is fully tested to make sure it matches specification before it reaches a customer.

In the final Quality Assurance tests a lens must match in performance the Master Lens for its type. This is one of the prototypes which meets in all respects the specification laid down by the designer and yields an image quality commensurate with that for which he was aiming. Once it had been selected, the Master Lens is kept in the Quality Assurance Department as the standard by which all other lenses of its type will be judged.

Samples of completed lenses, and individual components, are taken at intervals for more extensive testing by the Quality Assurance Department and the Lens Testing Laboratory to detect trends towards departure from specification. This is because, although all the lenses in a batch may be within specified tolerances, if the measurements are all tending towards one tolerance extreme, rather than being randomly distributed within the tolerance limits, it could be an indication that all is not well in the manufacturing procedures. It might, for example, be a forewarning of wear in a piece of plant or machinery. If such a trend is identified, an enquiry will be set in train to find out the cause.

Provided it has passed all these tests, the lens is sealed in its polythene bag by the Quality Assurance Department. It will then be passed for sale. No one else will touch it until it reaches its customer.

These same strict quality control standards are applied to those lenses which are made for Leica, to Leica specification, by other manufacturers.

2. The Two LEICA Lens Systems

Leica produce a comprehensive range of lenses, in terms of focal length and maximum aperture, for the R- and M-camera systems. Each range has been carefully chosen to cover all likely fields of photography for which the cameras are suitable.

The LEICA R-system of lenses embraces a very wide range of focal lengths. Compared to the LEICA M-system, it is not constrained by the number of bright-line frames that can be accommodated in the viewfinder, nor by limitations on the accuracy of focusing imposed by the base-length of a rangefinder. The reflex screen is the best method for focusing with long focal lengths, and for viewing with very short focal lengths. It is less suitable for rapid focusing with the mid-range focal lengths, particularly in poor light, the very circumstances in which the M-camera is at its best. On the other hand, the reflex camera does not require cumbersome accessories for close-up work.

Reflex lenses are bulkier than their rangefinder equivalents because a larger diameter bayonet mount was adopted for the first LEICAFLEX. This was in order not to constrain the development of wide-angle and wide-aperture lenses. The lens barrel has to accommodate the automatic diaphragm mechanism as well as the cams for coupling to the exposure meter. However, the larger diameter of the reflex lenses has allowed built-in extensible lens-hoods to be incorporated in the majority of lenses now whenever the configuration of the lens has permitted. This is a very great convenience for the user.

The M-series lenses enjoy a considerable weight advantage over the reflex ones, particularly at the wide angle end. For the longer focal lengths it has been possible to incorporate extensible lens-hoods when the lenses have been redesigned.

To sum up: The LEICA R-system is the universal camera system offering the widest range of applications. The reflex screen eliminates the need for all the ingenious accessories and adapters that used to fill the Leitz catalogues and now delight Leica collectors. Relatively few accessories are needed to extend the scope of a reflex Leica to close-up, technical or scientific work. The Leica M-system on the other hand has returned to the original concept of the Leica as a robust, light-weight and handy tool for quick work with accurate focusing, particularly in poor lighting conditions, for recording what Henri Cartier Bresson called “the decisive moment”. In this respect it is now virtually unique, notwith-

How to exploit an ultra-wide-angle lens to convey the peaceful atmosphere of a scene. In these circumstances many photographers would have chosen a longer focal length to fill the frame with the chateau of Azay le Rideau, Loire valley, France. 21mm, f/2.8 ELMARIT-M. *John Robert Young*

Left and above: A medium long focus lens and a close-up facility is often the best equipment for crowded events. The crowds prevent a close approach with a wide-angle lens and the best alternative is to stand further off and await your opportunity, but it is easy to get in close for the detail shots as at this gathering of historic railway locomotives. 100mm, f/2.8 APO-MACRO-ELMARIT-R. *Dennis Laney*

Above: The grandeur of Victorian engineering in a confined space captured by the 19mm, f/2.8 ELMARIT-R. *Dennis Laney*

standing today's highly sophisticated compact cameras. It offers a choice of very fast lenses in the shorter focal lengths for close-quarter work in available light, including the 50mm, f/1 NOCTILUX-M – the fastest lens in the world for general photography. These lenses, which render flash unnecessary in many situations without resorting to very fast films, together with the virtually silent shutter, enable the reporter armed with a LEICA M-camera to work unobtrusively.

The Leica R Lens System

LEICA R-lenses manufactured between 1976 and 1986 were fitted with three control cams. This meant that, with few exceptions, they were compatible with all LEICA reflex cameras. An exception was the less expensive version of the 50mm, f/2 SUMMICRON-R which had only cam-3 for the LEICA R3 and later models. The lenses made for the original LEICAFLEX, discontinued in 1968, had only a single cam, but with the introduction of the LEICAFLEX SL in 1968, which had its coupling lever in a different position, a second cam became necessary for lenses to be compatible with both models. The LEICAFLEX SL2, discontinued in 1976, also employed this second cam. The advent of the LEICA R3 in 1976 brought the need for a third cam, of stepped shape, because it had a different type of coupling mechanism. In 1986 Leitz announced that they had reviewed their policy and could no longer justify tying up the production capacity needed to make and fit three precision cams to every lens. Since then the following lenses have been fitted only with cam-3 for LEICA R-models: 28mm, f/2.8 ELMARIT-R; 35mm, f/2.8 ELMARIT-R; 50mm, f/2 SUMMICRON-R; 50mm, f/1.4 SUMMILUX-R; 60mm, f/2.8 MACRO-ELMARIT-R; 80mm, f/1.4 SUMMILUX-R; 90mm, f/2.8 ELMARIT-R; 90mm, f/2 SUMMICRON-R. The three extenders – APO-EXTENDER-R 1.4x, APO-EXTENDER-R 2x and EXTENDER-R 2x – as well as the MACRO-ADAPTER-R also now only have cam-3. These lenses have a modified bayonet mount which only LEICA R-cameras accept. See the Lens Directory at the back of the book for the camera compatibility of each lens. Additional cams can be fitted to some lenses by a Leica Service Centre or authorised workshop of a Leica agency, but it is as well to check first before buying.

Certain wide-angle lenses have a rear element which protrudes further into the camera body than is normal with R-lenses. These lenses have a modified bayonet mount so that they cannot be fitted to the LEICAFLEX or LEICAFLEX SL, otherwise they would obstruct the mirror mechanism. On the LEICAFLEX SL2, and all the LEICA R-models, the mirror is positioned further back so that they can accommodate these lenses, and their bayonet mounts have been modified accordingly to accept them.

Lenses unsuitable for the LEICAFLEX and LEICAFLEX SL are the 15mm Super-Elmar-R, 16mm FISHEYE-ELMARIT-R and the 24mm ELMARIT-R. In addition the following lenses are unsuitable for the original Leicaflex: 19mm ELMARIT-R, 21mm SUPER-ANGULON-R, 28mm PC-SUPER-ANGULON-R, 35mm PA-CURTAGON-R, 100mm MACRO-ELMAR-R, 100mm APO-MACRO-ELMARIT-R, 250mm TELYT-R, 280mm, f/2.8 APO-TELYT-R, 350mm TELYT-R, 400mm and 560mm, f/6.8 TELYT-R, 500mm MR-TELYT-R, 800mm TELYT-R, 28-70mm VARIO-ELMAR-R, 35-70mm VARIO-ELMAR-R and 70-210mm VARIO-ELMAR-R.

Original LEICAFLEX lenses with cam-1 only will fit SL, SL2 and all R-cameras, but the diaphragm setting ring will not be coupled with the meter. Two-cam lenses will fit Leica-R cameras, but metering will not be automatic.

As mentioned above, most LEICA R-lenses, except for certain wide-angle ones, have built-in, extensible lens-hoods. Newer R-lenses, and redesigned older ones, carry the M55x0.75 filter thread, when the diameter of the front element allows it. This permits the use of both E55 screw-in and Series 7 filters (the latter requires the [14225] filter adapter). A set of lenses can be chosen with focal lengths ranging from 35mm to 180mm that require only one set of filters and ELPRO close-up attachments.

Lenses in the LEICA R-system embrace focal lengths from 15mm to 800mm, or to 1600mm with a 2x extender. Three zoom lenses allow continuous focal length adjustment from 35mm to 210mm, or 28mm to 210mm, depending which pair are chosen. In addition there are three extenders, or tele-converters; a 2x and 2x and 1.4x apochromatic ones. Among the long focal length lenses there is a choice between fast, apochromatic lenses giving the finest image quality, or light-weight fast-focusing lenses, or conventional telephotos. In the most commonly used focal lengths the photographer must weigh up the factors he considers most important and then choose a lens which best suits his purposes: whether for work in poor light, whether the close focusing range matters, how important are weight, compactness or price. This book is to help in making such choices.

General points concerning the R-system are discussed in this chapter, but details of the characteristics and main fields of application of the individual lenses are given in the Lens Directory at the back of the book.

Mention must be made of a very useful accessory recently introduced by Leica. This is an eyepiece that fits on the bayonet of R-lenses of 50mm focal length or longer to produce a telescope. It is described at the end of the R-lens section in the Lens Directory.

Standard Focal Length: 50-60mm

50mm, f/2 Summicron-R

50mm, f/1.4 Summilux-R

60mm, f/2.8 Macro-Elmarit-R

The 50mm, f/2 Summicron-R fully maintains the reputation set by its M-namesake and in its current version continues to set the standard by which other standard lenses are judged for image quality. A Leica RE, fitted with a 50mm, f/2 Summicron-R, represents the least expensive entry to Leica reflex photography: it is also compact, with the lens-hood built-in. The addition of Elpro screw-in near focusing attachments, which are also compact and light in weight, extend its scope right into the close-up range – to a reproduction ratio of 1:2.6 with Elpro No.2.

The high speed standard lens is the 50mm, f/1.4 Summilux-R. It is an all-purpose lens, twice as fast as the Summicron and comparable to it in performance at similar apertures, but of course it more expensive and heavier. It is not suitable for macro work.

The lens which has become very popular as a standard lens for the general photographer is the 60mm,f/2.8 Macro-Elmarit-R. This is fast enough for most applications and more versatile than the Summicron in that it can be focused down to 27cm (about 10.5in) to give a reproduction ratio of 1:2 without any additional accessories. With the Macro-Adapter-R it can reach a ratio of 1:1. The angle of view is only 6^{0} less than that of a 50mm lens and some think it gives a more pleasing perspective.

Photography with these standard lenses presents no problem to the photographer coming to interchangeable lenses for the first time because the angle of view corresponds approximately to the natural view of our eyes. Handling is simple and requires no special technique. They offer high speeds, are compact, relatively light in weight, and give an excellent optical performance.

Wide-angle R-Lenses

Leica's views on the design of wide-angle lenses have already been mentioned. A comprehensive range of focal lengths is available for the reflex cameras, including one fisheye and two perspective control lenses. It extends from the traditional Leica focal lengths of 35 and 28mm, the normal wide-angles, to the ultra-wide 15mm.

The type of scene for which the standard lens is perfect, with the water taking away the problem of unwanted foreground. 50mm, f/2 Summicron-M.
Rudolf Seck

Moderate wide-angle: 28-35mm

35mm, f/2.8 ELMARIT-R

35mm, f/2 SUMMICRON-R

35mm, f/1.4 SUMMILUX-R

28mm, f/2.8 ELMARIT-R

The SUMMILUX is the fastest LEICA R wide-angle lens and will be the preferred choice as a snapshot lens or for hand-held interior work, but at a penalty of greater weight and cost compared to the other two. The SUMMICRON has all the well known characteristics of its 50mm namesake and likewise offers the best compromise between speed, versatility, weight and price. If speed is not a prime consideration then go for the ELMARIT because it will give a first class performance, will be lighter to carry around, and the cost saving can go towards another lens. Either the SUMMICRON or the ELMARIT partnered with the corresponding 90mm lens, and omitting the standard focal length, makes a high-quality basic outfit that will cover a wide range of photographic applications. These three 35mm lenses are the shortest focal length LEICA R-lenses with built-in extensible lens-hoods.

For photographers who want a somewhat wider angle, and perhaps more contrast with the standard lens, but without going to extreme wide-angles and the greater care they require in use, there is the 28mm, f/2.8 ELMARIT-R. It is much lighter and smaller than any of the extreme wide-angle lenses. Whereas 35mm lenses, like standard lenses, give a view which appears natural as regards scale and perspective, with a 28mm lens the typical wide-angle characteristics are beginning to be apparent.

Perspective-control lenses (shift lenses)

35mm, f/4 PA-CURTAGON-R

28mm, f/2.8 PC-SUPER-ANGULON-R

These lenses are for the specialist, such as the architectural photographer, who wants to avoid converging verticals, or the advertising or display photographer who can create particular perspective effects with them. They are useful too in landscape and townscape photography. These shift lenses are made for Leica, to Leica specification, by Schneider of Kreuznach who specialize in this type of lens. The lenses actually have a greater coverage than is normal for their 35mm or 28mm focal length. The diameter of the image circle of the PA-CURTAGON is 57mm instead of the 43mm which is normal for a 35mm lens. The lens unit itself can be shifted in its special mount by up to 7mm in any direction from its normal position on the optical axis of the camera. The image circle of the PC-SUPER-ANGULON is 62mm and the lens unit can be rotated in its mount and shifted in its dovetail guide by means of a micrometer drive by up to 11mm horizontally and vertically and 9.5mm diagonally. By these means, with either lens, one can select that portion of the bigger image which is desired. Thus when photographing a tall building the lens unit is shifted upwards until the whole of the building is contained within the frame without tilting the camera. Both lenses can be focused as close as 30cm.

Extreme wide-angle: 15-24mm

24mm, f/28 ELMARIT-R

21mm, f/4 SUPER-ANGULON-R

19mm, f/2.8 ELMARIT-R

16mm, f/2.8 FISHEYE-ELMARIT-R

15mm, f/3.5 SUPER-ELMAR-R

Choice here rests solely on what is the most suitable focal length(s) for the purpose in mind. The optical configuration of very short focal length lenses is complex and they must have very large diameter front elements to avoid vignetting as far as possible, which inevitably means bulk and weight. On the other hand they do open up very exciting prospects in photography. Relatively fast, low distortion, extreme wide-angle lenses have been available long enough now for the novelty to have worn off and their value in creative photography to have been thoroughly explored. The images which at one time seemed unreal, now are readily accepted and indeed have influenced some landscape artists.

The 24mm, f/2.8 ELMARIT-R is the easiest to handle pictorially and might be considered an alternative to the 28mm ELMARIT, particularly if one already has a 35mm. It is, however, firmly in the ultra-wide-angle class and will display marked wide-angle perspective effects. Generally speaking, the shorter the focal length of a wide-angle lens, the greater the degree of skill that is needed to use it. Apart from their technical and architectural uses these extreme wide-angle lenses can give dramatic pictorial effects with strong emphasis on the foreground and a rapidly receding, sharply focused background.

Special mention must be made of the redesigned 19mm, f/2.8 ELMARIT-R. The original model was one of the memorable milestones in the progress of LEICA lenses. The image quality of the new version is even more outstanding for its focal length and speed, whilst the lens itself is much more compact and handier than its predecessor.

The extreme wide-angle 15mm, f/3.4 SUPER-ELMAR-R is a high performance, true wide-angle lens, not a fisheye. It gives a normal rectilinear image and has particular applications in technical work, but it can also be a very exciting pictorial lens. It has a protruding front element and a short vestigial lens-hood to protect such a vulnerable feature. The lens-hood has cut-outs for the wider dimension of the picture which means that, with the camera in the horizontal position, the lens is shaded only from above and below and not from the sides. Even that amount of shading is slight, because any bigger hood would obstruct the angle of view, so the camera position must be carefully chosen so that the lens is in the shade. For the same reason it has built-in filters in a turret mount.

Fisheye

In a different class to the others is the 16mm, f/2.8 FISHEYE-ELMARIT-R. Its high speed is remarkable for its focal length and it has a very high degree of correction. Its image fills the entire frame, unlike some fisheye lenses which produce a circular image within the normal rectangular format. However, the image field it does produce is barrel-like in form. Straight lines which cut the optical axis, that is those which pass through the centre of the picture, will be rendered as straight lines; but straight lines which do not pass through the centre will be curved in the image, and the further away they are from the centre the more curved they will be. The FISHEYE-ELMARIT-R can be a very good pictorial lens with a carefully chosen subject, with the fisheye distortion only being apparent on careful inspection of the picture, provided the camera has been held absolutely level. Its angle of view is 180°. The filters are built-in, because a filter mounted on the front would cause vignetting, and it has a vestigial lens-hood, like the 15mm ELMARIT, more to protect the front element than to shade it effectively.

Long Focus R-Lenses

The Leica programme of long focus lenses for the R-system has been well thought out. It offers a wide selection of well-spaced focal lengths that cater for all photographic needs. There are lenses that are very fast for their focal length and lenses that can be hand-held at shutter speeds slower than would normally be thought possible for their focal length. There are lenses that can be focused more rapidly and readily than is normally the case with telephoto lenses so that fast moving subjects may be easily followed. There are apochromatic lenses giving the finest image quality.

The term "telephoto" is often used now to refer to any lens of longer than standard focal length. Leica tend to use this terminology. A true telephoto lens is one whose overall length is shorter than would normally be the case for its focal length. This requires an optical construction which is more complex and heavier, although more compact, than a conventional design. Leica continue the Leitz policy of always selecting the optimum compromise of weight, length and maximum aperture for their long focal length lenses, depending on their primary purpose. Several of their very long lenses are not of telephoto construction.

Moderately long-focus: 80-180mm

80mm, f/1.4 Summilux-R

90mm, f/2.8 Elmarit-R

90mm, f/2 Summicron-R

100mm, f/4 Macro-Elmar-R

100mm, f/2.8 Apo-Macro-Elmarit-R

135mm, f/2.8 Elmarit-R

180mm, f/4 Elmar-R

180mm, f/3.4 Apo-Telyt-R

180mm, f/2.8 Elmarit-R

These are the longest focal lengths for general photography and Leica offer a wide choice. All these lenses can be easily hand-held, provided the shutter speed is fast enough to avoid blurring due to shake. Many photographers use a moderately long focus lens for most of their work because they can achieve tight, frame-filling compositions which are especially important for slides. Many choose two, say a 90mm and

The 100mm, f/2.8 Apo-Macro-Elmarit-R focuses down to give a reproduction ratio of 1:1. The dedicated Elpro 1:2-1:1 attachment extends the close-up range to 1:1 whilst preserving the apochromatic properties of the lens.

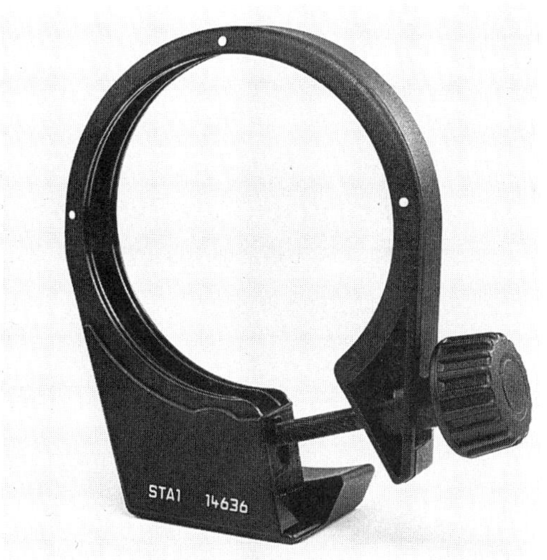

The STA1 Tripod Clamp was designed for the 100mm, f/2.8 Apo-Macro-Elmarit-R but may be used to fit any long focus lens rigidly to a tripod or the Universal Handgrip.

180mm. The choice depends on whether you are more interested in light weight and compactness, or close-ups, or high-speed work in poor light, and at what distances you are likely to be working from the subject. Among the shorter focal lengths the fast lenses are the 80mm, f/1.4 SUMMILUX-R and the 90mm, f/2 SUMMICRON-R (which is very compact for its speed). The smallest and lightest-weight lens in the group is the 90mm, f/2.8 ELMARIT-R, which is a very good companion for the 35mm, f/2.8 ELMARIT R, the pair forming a minimum but versatile outfit.

Photographers keen on close-ups will choose the 100mm, f/2.8 APO-MACRO-ELMARIT-R which besides being a superb medium telephoto lens with apochromatic correction, focuses down to a reproduction ratio of 1:2. With its special attachment, ELPRO 1:2-1:1, the close-up range is extended to life-size at 1:1. The 100mm focal length offers an advantage over the 60mm MACRO-ELMARIT in affording a greater working distance, which can avoid frightening small creatures or trampling plant habitats. The STA 1 TRIPOD CLAMP was designed for this lens.

A cheaper alternative would be the 100mm, f/4 MACRO-ELMAR-R which will focus down to give a reproduction ratio of 1:3, or with the MACRO-ADAPTER-R to 1:1.6. A special version, without a focusing mount, is supplied for the FOCUSING BELLOWS-R and the AUTOMATIC BELLOWS-R, by which it can be focused continuously from infinity down to a reproduction ratio of 1:1.

If a slightly longer focal length is preferred there is the classic Leica length of 135mm offered in the 135mm, f/2.8 ELMARIT-R; but for reflex photography many people now prefer to go to a 180mm because it gives a more useful spacing from a 90mm lens. Leica recognize the importance of this focal length in offering a choice among three. Each has unique characteristics to suit different types of photography.

The 180mm, f/4 ELMAR-R offers light weight and compactness, whilst the 180mm, f/2.8 ELMARIT-R has the highest maximum aperture and its performance surpasses even that of the ELMAR; in fact it is an outstanding lens of exceptional speed for the focal length. The third member of the trio is another one of those Leica milestones in progress which marked significant advances in lens quality. The 180mm, f/3.4 APO-TELYT-R has aprochromatic correction, giving outstanding colour brilliance and crispness of image at full aperture. The colour correction also includes the infra-red region, thus no focusing compensation is necessary with infra-red film.

Very long-focus: 250-800mm

Leica have a most interesting selection of lenses of very long focal length. They are all for clearly defined purposes and it is more convenient to discuss them by type rather than focal length.

LEICA lenses with focal lengths of 250mm and longer do not have a stop at the infinity setting. The focusing ring can be turned beyond the infinity mark. This is to allow easier focusing on objects which are at that particularly critical distance just short of the point where they would have been in focus with the lens set at infinity. The absence of an infinity stop makes it possible to find the point of sharpest focus by focusing to and fro, beyond infinity and back. These long lenses (except the 500mm MR-TELYT) also have a rotating collar with a tripod bush, or a rotating bayonet mount, to enable ready switching between horizontal and vertical formats when mounted on a tripod or shoulder stock.

250mm, f/4 TELYT-R

350mm, f/4.8 TELYT-R

These are conventional telephoto lenses, with relatively large maximum apertures for their focal lengths and type. They enjoy a considerable price advantage over the two apo-lenses described below. In fact you could buy both of them for the price of the 280mm, f/2.8 Apo-Telyt-R and still have some change left! Both lenses have a comparatively short focusing travel for their wide focusing range, making quick focusing easy.

The Universal Handgrip and Shoulder Stock is a very useful and versatile accessory. Developed from the stocks used with the 400mm and 560mm, f/6.8 follow-focus lenses in their sliding focusing mounts, it can be used to advantage with most long focus lenses or with the focusing bellows for hand-held shots. It enables slower shutter speeds to be used than would normally be considered wise with such lenses. Finally, it converts into a sturdy mini tripod.

280mm, f/2.8 APO-TELYT-R

400mm, f/2.8 APO-TELYT-R

Developed with press, sports and wildlife photographers in mind, these lenses are in a class by themselves. They are fast for lenses in this focal length range and at the same time they produce "apo" quality images. When television cameras needed very high levels of lighting, press photographers at sports and other events could get properly exposed colour pictures, with a fast enough shutter speed, with a lens of maximum aperture about f/5.6. Nowadays T.V. cameras can operate at much lower lighting levels and the lighting intensity provided in sports halls and similar places has been correspondingly reduced. Hence the need for a fast long-focus lens. Creative photographers of course find many other uses for these lenses in applications such as fashion photography, taking advantage of the paper-thin depth of field at maximum aperture.

The lenses are supplied in aluminium cases strong enough to stand on and big enough to hold the camera body with motor drive and the two Apo-Extenders. Carrying straps are also provided which fit onto lugs on the lenses and by which the camera/lens combination should be carried. The 280mm APO-TELYT-R is intended to be used on the Shoulder Stock [14239] and is supplied with a detachable palm grip which rests in the left hand at the point of balance in such a way that focusing can be done with the thumb of that hand. The total rotation of the focusing ring needed between infinity and the closest focusing distance of 2.5m is very short. The 400mm APO-TELYT-R may be preset on a shortest focusing distance, such as the nearest goal-mouth, so that it can focus normally over the rest of the field but be switched instantly to the preset distance. These lenses have internal focusing, which means that the overall length of the lens remains constant and thereby the point of balance is also stable. They are provided with a filter slide for Series 5.5 filters. The NDx1 filter provided must be in place if no other filter is to be employed because it is part of the optical system. A special circular polarizing filter is available which may be fitted in place of the filter slide and be rotated from the outside. With the Apo-Extenders very long and fast lenses are created:

400mm, f/6.8 ("Follow Focus") TELYT-R

560mm, f/6.8 ("Follow Focus") TELYT-R

400mm, f/6.8 TELYT-R in NOVOFLEX mount

560mm, f/6.8 TELYT-R in NOVOFLEX mount

Each of these lenses consists simply of two elements, cemented together, forming an achromat and having only two air-to-glass surfaces. Achromats have a slight curvature of field at full aperture which causes the plane of sharp focus at the margins of the picture to be shifted slightly nearer the camera. The effect is reduced somewhat on stopping down. This field curvature is sometimes regarded as an advantage because the gain in sharpness in the foreground gives a more satisfying picture.

Not being of telephoto construction, the length of lens and camera combined is roughly equivalent to the focal length. On the other hand they are very light, and they have a type of focusing mount which can be hand-held and which is very quick in action, so that fast-moving distant subjects can be followed easily and kept in focus. The lenses should be mounted on the Universal Handgrip and Shoulder Stock [14239] and handled like a rifle. The left hand supports the lens barrel and at the same time focuses it by sliding the lens tube back and forth. In this way focusing is quick and it is easy to keep a subject in focus

The Novoflex rapid focusing mount is an alternative to the Leica sliding mount for the 400mm and 560mm, f/6.8 follow-focus lenses. Focusing is by trigger action.

even when it is moving rapidly towards or away from the camera. The lens barrels are too long for an automatic diaphragm to be practicable. However, such long focus lenses hand-held are likely to be used at maximum aperture in order to allow the fastest possible shutter speed. If they are being used on a tripod, for instance in architectural work, then there is going to be plenty of time to set the aperture manually. Both lenses dismantle into two parts, a tube about six inches (15cm) long and common to both which carries the shoulder stock fitting, and the respective lens unit with its focusing mechanism.

An alternative version of these lens heads is used with a NOVOFLEX focusing unit. This has a rear handgrip with a spring-loaded trigger. Normally the spring keeps the lens focused at its nearest distance, but squeezing the trigger focuses the lens by drawing the front section back into the rear tube. Focus can be locked by turning the wheel above the rear tube: this can be done by brushing it with the ball of the thumb. The front grip has a button to trigger the camera via a cable release. The camera can be rotated for vertical shots and the stock serves as a chest or shoulder support. A filter slot accepts special Novoflex or Helioplan filters

500mm, f/8 MR-TELYT-R

Another way to overcome the problems of chromatic aberration in very long-focus lenses is to use a mirror construction in which curved mirrors rather than lenses are used to bring light rays to a focus, as in the Newtonian type of astronomical telescope. Because the light rays are not passing through glass they are not refracted, and so light of different wavelengths is not separated. The mirror surfaces also have the effect of folding the light rays so that a very short and compact lens can be designed. The weight will also be much less than that of a conventional lens of equivalent focal length and aperture. This sounds like a photographer's dream, a very compact and light-weight very long focus lens. Mirror lenses have disadvantages however, and the shrewd photographer will weigh these against the benefits in relation to his type of photography. One disadvantage is a comparatively small maximum aperture, in this case f/8. They cannot be fitted with an iris diaphragm, so there is no means of stopping them down. The only way that exposure can be controlled, other than by shutter speed, is by the use of neutral-density filters. Even 1/1000th second may be too long at f/8 in bright conditions, and so a filter to reduce the light transmission to 25% is normally provided with the lens and this is the case with the MR-TELYT-R. The other potential shortcoming of mirror lenses, although creative photographers will take advantage of it, is that out-of-focus point light sources in the picture will appear as rings instead of blurred discs.

This lens is for people for whom minimum weight and compactness are the most important considerations, such as travellers and mountaineers.

800mm, f/6.3 Telyt-S

Occupying the extreme end of the Leica R-range, this lens was another of those Leitz milestones in lens development. Its image quality approaches apochromatic quality. It gives an outstanding performance in long-distance photography – at an outstanding price. It is available to special order only, and the price is determined not only by the very large optics, but also by the complexity of the mount. Such a large lens must be very rigidly supported and accurately mounted, but its mount dismantles into five parts for transport in the fitted metal case which is included in the price. The lens was the first of the long Leitz achromats, although in this case, with three elements cemented into a single component, and the remarks about achromats in the paragraphs above on the 400mm and 560mm Telyt-R lenses apply to this 800mm Telyt-S.

Extenders

Apo-Extender-R 1.4x

Apo-Extender-R 2x

Extender-R 2x

An extender has the effect of multiplying the focal length of a lens by its stated factor when it is placed between that lens and the camera. In effect it converts a lens into a telephoto lens by acting as the negative rear component in a telephoto configuration. No Leica extender is optically compatible with lenses of focal length less than 50mm or faster than f/2. The Apo-Extender-R 1.4x was designed specifically for the 280mm and 400mm Apo-Telyt-R lenses, but it can also be combined with the 100mm, f/4 Macro-Elmar-R, the 180mm, f/2.8 Elmarit-R and the 800mm, f/6.3 Telyt-S. Trying to combine it with any other lens could result in damage because of the protruding front element. The two 2x extenders are compatible with a wider range of lenses of 50mm and above. The Apo-Extender-R 2x should be employed with apo-lenses in order to preserve their apochromatic characteristics, although the Extender-R 2x will yield perfectly acceptable results with apo-lenses if the utmost reproduction quality is not demanded. Lens compatibility of the three extenders is summarized in the Table 1.

The price one pays for the convenience of an extender is that the effective aperture of the master lens is reduced by one stop with the 1.4x extender and by two stops in the case of the 2x extenders. This is because the area of the opening in its iris diaphragm remains the same and is

Compatible LEICA R-Lenses	With APO-EXTENDER-R 2x	With EXTENDER-R 2x	With APO-EXTENDER-R 1.4x
f/2/50 mm	f/4/100 mm	f/4/100 mm	-
f/2.8 /60 mm	f/5.6/120 mm	f/5.6/120 mm	-
f/2/90 mm	f/4/180 mm	f/4/180 mm	-
f/2.8/90 mm	f/5.6/180 mm	f/5.6/180 mm	-
f/4/100 mm	f/8/200 mm	f/8/200 mm	f/5.6/140 mm
f/2.8/100 mm APO	f/5.6/200 mm APO	f/5.6/200 mm	-
f/2.8/135 mm	f/5.6/270 mm	f/5.6/270 mm	-
f/2.8/180 mm	f/5.6/360 mm	f/5.6/360 mm	f/4/250 mm
f/3.4/180 mm APO	f/6.8/360 mm APO	f/6.8/360 mm	-
f/4/180 mm	f/8/360 mm	f/8/360 mm	-
f/4/250 mm	f/8/500 mm	f/8/500 mm	-
f/2.8/280 mm APO	f/5.6/560 mm APO	f/4/400 mm	f/4/400 mm APO
f/4.8/350 mm	f/9.6/700 mm	f/9.6/700 mm	-
f/2.8/400 mm APO	f/5.6/800 mm APO	f/5.6/800 mm	f/4/560 mm APO
f/8/500 mm	f/16/1000 mm	f/16/1000 mm	-
f/6.3/800 mm	f/12.6/1600 mm	f/12.6/1600 mm	f/8.8/1120 mm
f/3.5/35-70 mm	f/7/70-140 mm	f/7/70-140 mm	-

Table 1. Compatibility of Leica R-lenses with Leica extenders, with resulting focal lengths and maximum apertures.

therefore reduced in relation to the focal length with an extender attached. The lens aperture is governed by the area of the opening in the iris, which is proportional to the square of its diameter, and so the effective aperture is reduced to one-half when the focal length is multiplied by 1.4 (approx √2), or to one-quarter when the focal length is doubled.

The big benefits offered by extenders are their convenience and the extra pictorial opportunities. At a cost of an additional modest lens, say the 135mm, f/2.8 ELMARIT-R, an extender can double the number of focal lengths above 50mm available in your outfit. They are very convenient for the traveller because they are so small and light. An extender is also the best solution if you have only occasional need for a very long focus lens. For instance, if the longest lens you possess is a 180mm, f/2.8 Elmarit-R, the EXTENDER-R 2x will convert it into a 360mm, f/5.6.

Zoom Lenses

28-70mm, f/3.5-4.5 VARIO-ELMAR-R

35-70mm, f/3.5 VARIO-ELMAR-R

70-210mm, f/4 VARIO-ELMAR-R

An alternative choice to the prime lenses described above are Leica's zoom lenses. They offer focal lengths from the wide-angle to the near long-focus with only two lenses. They give the photographer the ability to frame pictures precisely within these limits, but with a penalty in

With the 70-210mm, f/4 VARIO-ELMAR-R, frame-filling portraits can be taken from a discreet distance, as with this fisherman at Peter's Port, in the Western Isles of Scotland. *John Robert Young*

The 28-70mm, f3.5-4.5 VARIO-ELMAR-R is one of the most versatile, general purpose lenses in the R-system; very handy if you only want to take one lens on holiday and leave the camera bag behind. It is good for landscape, here at the 70mm setting (at 28mm with a clear blue sky it does exhibit a little vignetting), and at the wide-angle end for interesting shots in towns. It also has a useful close-up facility, focusing down to 50mm. *Dennis Laney*

weight, bulk and comparatively slow speed. The 28-70mm, f/3.5-4.5 VARIO-ELMAR-R costs little more than half as much as the 35-70mm,f/3.5 VARIO-ELMAR-R and is a versatile alternative to the 50mm SUMMICRON to partner with a LEICA RE to form a budget outfit for an outlay of an extra 15% or so. On the other hand the non-rotating focusing mount of the 35-70mm lens (making the use of polarizing and graduated filters much more practicable), the constant aperture throughout the focal length range, and the superior optical performance in more critical situations, mean it will be the choice of professional and more ambitious photographers, despite its more limited focal length range.

Either of these lenses, together with the 70-210mm zoom, will cover all the most commonly used focal lengths. Some people, on the other hand, prefer prime lenses for their photography in the standard and wide-angle areas, but partner them with the 70-210 because of its ability to be able to frame subjects precisely when they are further away and it is more difficult to move the camera position.

Telescope eyepiece

To add to the general usefulness of Leica-R lenses, Leica offer a fully corrected telescope ocular which attaches to the bayonet mount of Leica-R lenses. The lens must have a focal length of 50mm or more.

A most useful accessory is the telescope eyepiece that can be fitted to the bayonet mount of any R-lens of 50mm or more focal length.

The Leica M-Lens System

The LEICA M-system covers focal lengths from 21mm to 135mm. These limits are unlikely to be exceeded because 135mm is about the longest focal length which can be focused accurately with a rangefinder with a base length of that of the M6, whilst 21mm is the shortest practicable focal length for a rangefinder camera, although there was once a 15mm, f/8 available for a short time. M-lenses from 21mm to 135mm automatically couple to the rangefinder when they are locked home in the bayonet mount of the camera. At the same time the appropriate bright-line frame appears in the viewfinder, except for the 21mm lens for which a separate bright-line finder is available to fit into the accessory shoe. The bright-line frames appear in pairs in the LEICA M6 viewfinder (see Fig. 13). Earlier M-series LEICA cameras, except the M4-P, were less comprehensive in their provision for different focal lengths in their viewfinders, but M2, M4 and M4-2 cameras may be found with 28mm and 75mm frames added as a factory conversion. The whole story of Leica M viewfinders is summarized in Table 2.

Leica provide two separate accessory bright-line finders. The 21mm already mentioned, showing the subject field at 0.3x magnification, and a 28mm finder for earlier M models showing the subject field at 0.5x magnification. Both have an additional line marking for parallax compensation at distances below about 2m (6.5ft).

The Leica M-system offers maximum speed or minimum volume and weight, although no M-lens is very bulky. It reflects the purposes for which the rangefinder camera is at its best: quick focusing, often at close quarters, in poor light, with moving subjects. The choice of focal length is much more limited than with the R-system and is confined to those focal lengths for which the rangefinder system is superior to any focusing screen for focusing accuracy.

The basic choice facing the photographer from 35mm to 135mm is whether he needs high-speed lenses that will be used mainly at maximum aperture; or whether lighter and less expensive lenses would suit better. At the wide-angle end there is no choice, it is simply a question of which focal length best suits the intended purpose, bearing in mind that a separate viewfinder is required for 21mm.

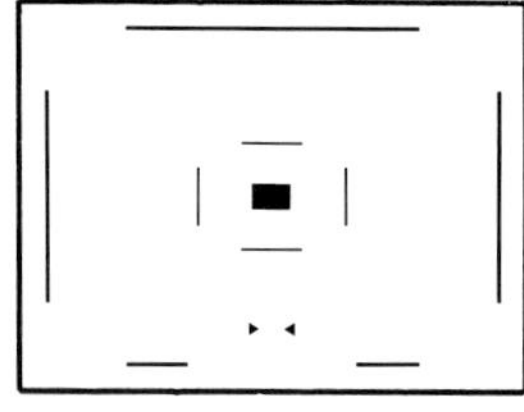

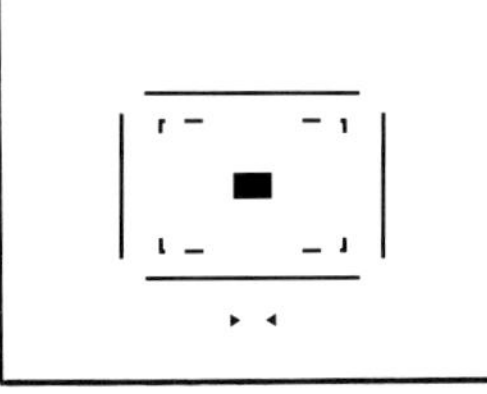

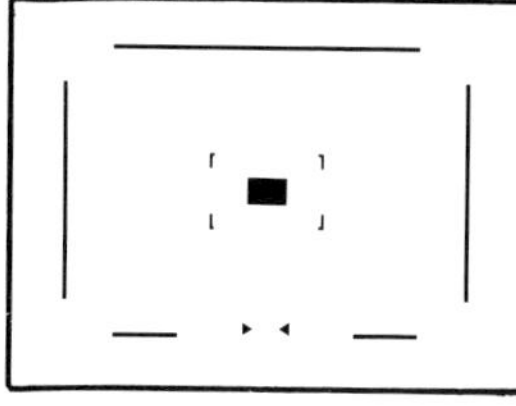

21mm & 90mm 50mm & 75mm 35mm & 135mm

Bright-line viewfinder frames in the Leica M6 and M4-P viewfinders. The two small triangles in the lower portion represent the two LED's of the M6 TTL metering system.

Table 2. LEICA-M Viewfinders

LEICA M-camera	*Viewfinder Frames provided*						
	21	28	35	50	75	90	135
M6	(a)	28	35	50	75	90	135
M4-P	(a)	28	35	50	75	90	135
M4-2	(a)	(a, e)	35	50	(f)	90	135
M4	(a)	(a, e)	35	50	(f)	90	135
M5	(a)(b)	(a, b, e)	35	50	(f)	90	135
M3	(a)	(a, e)	(c)	50	(f)	90	135
M2	(a)	(a, e)	35	50	(f)	90	(d)
MP	(a)	(a, e)	(c)	50	(f)	90	135
MP(SP)	(a)	(a, e)	35	50	(f)	90	(d)
M1	(a)	(a)	35	50	–	(a)	–
MD MDa MD-2	No viewfinder, intended for use with VISOFLEX						

Table 2. Viewfinder frames in Leica M-cameras

Notes to Table 2:

(a) Separate viewfinder available to fit into accessory shoe.
(b) Early 21mm and 28mm lenses had protruding rear element which could damage the metering arm in the camera body.
(c) Special 35mm lenses were produced for this model. They had a "spectacle" attachment with two oculars. One of these was centred over the rangefinder window and the other over the viewfinder window where it had the effect of converting the 50mm frame to indicate the 35mm format. (These special M3 lenses can also be used on M2, M4, M4-2, M4-P, M5 and M6 models; the correct frame is selected but the view is minified, having the effect that the 35mm frame on these cameras is easier to see for spectacle wearers.)
(d) The 135mm,f/2.8 Elmarit-M is fitted with oculars similar to those described in note (c) above. These have the effect of magnifying the viewfinder and rangefinder images to the same size as if a 90mm lens were in use. In fact the 90mm frame comes into view when the lens is attached. The results are an image which is easier to see and greater accuracy in focusing.
(e) If a 28mm lens is fitted, the 90mm frame will show in the viewfinder.
(f) If a 75mm lens is fitted, the 50mm frame only will show in the viewfinder.

All lenses of focal length 75mm or longer have built-in extensible lens hoods. There is less standardisation with filter sizes among the M-lenses than in the R-series, but it is possible to select four with focal lengths from 35mm to 135mm which will only require one set of E39 filters.

Owners of chrome M-cameras will be pleased to know that Leica are re-introducing the satin-chrome finish for some M-lenses. At the time of writing the 35mm, 50mm and 90mm f/2 SUMMICRON-M lenses are available in satin-chrome.

Owners of LEICA M-cameras with a silver-chrome finish will be glad to know that Leica have reintroduced silver-chrome as an alternative finish on some M-lenses. So far the 35mm, 50mm and 90mm, f/2 SUMMICRON-M's are available in silver-chrome.

Standard Focal Length: 50mm

50mm. f/2 SUMMICRON-M

50mm, f/1.4 SUMMILUX-M

50mm, f/1 NOCTILUX-M

A focal length of 50mm was chosen by Oskar Barnack as being ideal for the 35mm format and it became the standard focal length for the LEICA and most other 35mm cameras. There are three 50mm M-lenses, differing in maximum aperture.

The first 50mm, f/2 SUMMICRON appeared in 1953, when it created a sensation and helped to establish the reputation of the LEICA M3 in the same way that the 50mm, f/3.5 ELMAR did for the original LEICA nearly thirty years earlier. The SUMMICRON revolutionized our ideas of what could be expected of the image quality from a fast lens (f/2 was regarded as fast in those days). It was one of the first fruits of Leitz post-war glass research, and further glass developments have enabled it to be improved several times since. It is the perfect general-purpose lens for the M-camera, fast enough for most purposes, and performing extremely well at infinity or close to, at full aperture or stopped down.

For those who require a faster lens there is the 50mm, f/1.4 SUMMILUX, twice as fast and more expensive than the SUMMICRON, but indispensable for available-light work. It is designed to be used at, or near maximum aperture, although it can be stopped down for general use

The 50mm, f/1 NOCTILUX-M is the supreme lens for low light situations and the M-camera rangefinder enables it to be focused accurately in the dimmest of light. At f/1, as here, the depth of field is very shallow so that tjhe subject is sharply isolated from its background.
Rudolf Seck

when no difference will be noticed, compared with the SUMMICRON, for most subjects. The fastest lens of all produced by Leica, or any other manufacturer for general photography, is the 50mm, f/1 NOCTILUX. It is for the photographer who needs to work, probably unobtrusively, using only available light in the dimmest of conditions. It is four-times as fast as the SUMMICRON. The NOCTILUX will reveal more details in photographs taken in poor light than could have been distinguished with the naked eye. It is solely a poor light lens and should be seen as complementary to, rather than as an alternative to a SUMMICRON.

Wide-angle: 21-35mm

35mm, f/2 SUMMICRON-M

35mm, f/1.4 SUMMILUX-M ASPHERICAL

35mm, f/1.4 SUMMILUX-M

28mm, f/2.8 ELMARIT-M

21mm, f/2.8 ELMARIT-M

It is convenient to consider all the wide-angle M-lenses together, rather than separate the sole extreme wide-angle example. Some people prefer a 35mm as their standard lens because its wider angle of view compared with the 50mm can cope with a greater variety of circumstances. It can also suit the snapshot, candid photographer better because the greater depth of field allows more latitude in focusing. As to the choice between the 35mm, f/2 SUMMICRON or the 35mm, f/1.4 SUMMILUX, the same remarks apply as to the 50mm lenses above. The 35mm SUMMILUX ASPHERICAL will give a superior performance compared with the plain SUMMILUX, but then it costs twice as much.

As with the R-system, a compact and versatile outfit would comprise a 35mm and a 90mm lens, leaving out a standard lens. If high speed was the requirement, then one of the two 35mm SUMMILUX lenses together with the 75mm SUMMILUX-M would be an ideal combination.

For a wider angle and a bigger contrast from a 50mm lens, the 28mm, f/2.8 ELMARIT-M would serve many people better. It is the shortest focal length provided for in the Leica M6 and M4-P viewfinders. This lens, together with the extreme wide-angle 21mm, f/2.8 ELMARIT-M, is popular for reportage or candid photography at very close quarters because general background noise will mask the very soft action of the LEICA M shutter. With such short focal lengths, zone focusing (setting the focal scale at the average distance) will be sufficiently accurate, and with some practice viewfinding can be dispensed with so that the camera can be used without raising it to the eye. The 21mm lens will reproduce the characteristic extreme wide-angle perspective effects which are often used by photo-journalists to give emphasis in close-up portraits.

Long-Focus: 75-135mm

75mm, f/1.4 SUMMILUX-M

90mm, f/2.8 ELMARIT-M

90mm, f/2 SUMMICRON-M

135mm, f/4 TELE-ELMAR-M

135mm, f/2.8 ELMARIT-M

The 75mm,f/1.4 SUMMILUX-M is ideal for reportage and all those situations where more reach is needed in poor light, such as places or occasions when the LEICA M is the only camera allowed, on account of its quiet shutter, and flash is forbidden, such as in certain theatres and American courtrooms. As a companion to a 35mm, f/1.4 SUMMILUX, it provides a compact and versatile high speed outfit. The focal length was chosen to be 75mm because a longer one with an even bigger front element would obscure part of the viewfinder's field of view. The LEICA M6 and M4-P are provided with a 75mm frame, but with other M models the 90mm frame can be used to frame the subject really tightly (the 90mm frame will have to be kept in position by a finger of the left hand on the field-selector lever).

At the two longer focal lengths the 90mm, f/2.8 ELMARIT-M and the 135mm, f/4 TELE-ELMAR-M offer minimum weight and bulk. Photographers needing faster lenses in these focal lengths can select the 90mm, f/2 SUMMICRON-M, which has all the well-known SUMMICRON qualities, as well as the 135mm, f/2.8 ELMARIT-M. This latter lens is unique among current lenses in having a pair of oculars attached, which fit one in front of the viewfinder and one in front of the rangefinder windows. The oculars have the effect of magnifying the normal viewfinder image by 1.5 times and increasing thereby the accuracy of focusing and the speed of operation. The lens is rather heavy and the oculars make it awkward to stow, but for the photographer who needs this focal length in poor light it is the ideal lens.

3. Applications of Leica Lenses

Modern creative photographers, particularly photo-journalists, advertising and fashion photographers, television and film cameramen, have had a tremendous impact on our ideas of the photographic image. All the previous rules about what lens should be used for what subject have been thrown out of the window. They have explored the limits of extreme focal lengths, both long and short, and extreme aperture, and used them to convey mood, atmosphere, drama, or just emphasis. These adventures are also open to the amateur. One of the joys of photography is finding out what can be achieved with one's existing equipment and exploring the possibilities of a new lens.

The professional photographer will know exactly what he wants to do and will carefully select his set of lenses accordingly. Every lens has to earn its keep. The amateur has, in many ways, a more difficult problem of choice. Other factors come in, such as pride of ownership, and the urge to collect. If there is a clear subject interest, the choice is easier; if his interest is in the practice of photography and the subjects are general, then the choice is more difficult.

A modest selection of three or four moderate focal lengths will see the average amateur through all his photographic needs. If he is a specialist, then he will choose specialized lenses for his purpose. If he is a creative adventurer, then any lens will be pushed to its limits to see what can be achieved with it, and the more extreme the lens the greater will be its challenge.

Throughout the book we consider Leica lenses in broad categories according to focal length. There is nothing fixed or conventional about these groupings, they have simply been chosen because it simplifies matters when discussing applications. Standard focal length lenses form one natural grouping; they have an angle of view near to that of human vision, they are the easiest lenses to master, and most people start their photography with some sort of camera fitted with a standard lens. Wide-angle lenses, of focal length between 28mm and 35mm, form another category because the so-called wide-angle perspective is not too apparent and they are fairly easy to handle; also their application is fairly general. Furthermore, 35mm or 40mm is now common for lenses on compact cameras, so people graduating from a compact to an S.L.R. or Leica M will be more accustomed their angle of view. These, together with one or two lenses from the moderate-long-focus group, up to 180mm, will fill most people's requirements, especially if a

2x EXTENDER-R is available for occasional use when something longer is needed. A well-balanced outfit might consist of one wide-angle, one standard, and one or possibly two lenses from the moderate-long-focus group.

Lenses with focal lengths outside these limits in the extreme-wide-angle and extreme-long-focus groups have a much more limited application for the general photographer, and require considerably more skill in use. They are lenses more for the specialist, either amateur or professional, for whom such lenses are essential to pursue particular interests. For instance, the wildlife photographer must be able to bridge long distances; the architectural photographer has to work in confined spaces. The general amateur photographer will usually find his interests developing towards particular subjects and that is the time to invest in the more esoteric lenses. The creative pictorial photographer will choose such lenses for different reasons; they offer the greatest scope to experiment with perspective.

Similar considerations should govern the choice of maximum aperture. The extreme large-aperture lenses will not be so versatile in general photography as the more modest ones, although they do give tight control over depth of field. They will generally not be so good for close-up photography, they cannot be used with an extender, and their weight and bulk will probably mean they will be left at home more. But if your interests develop into available-light work, when they will be used frequently at maximum aperture, then they are marvellous tools and will become constant companions.

Applications of Standard Focal Lengths: 50-60mm

Because standard focal length lenses have an angle of view which corresponds approximately to that of our own eyes, one obtains the most natural looking effects and perspectives with them. Many critics regard this as boring, but some of the greatest photographers of the twentieth century have done all their work with a standard lens. The ready availability at moderate prices of a wide range of different focal lengths for the 35mm SLR camera may have given rise to the view that the possibilities of the standard lens were exhausted, and that only wide-angles or telephotos could be seriously considered nowadays for really creative work. This is not true. However, with a standard lens the photographer does need to vary the camera position more. By exploring the possibilities of different viewpoints and perspectives one discovers that the standard lens offers plenty of opportunity for achieving striking pictorial effects.

8x Enlargement

The 60mm, f/2.8 MACRO-ELMARIT-R, as well as being a superb lens for close-ups, is also an excellent general purpose lens that can replace the normal 50mm standard lens in an outfit. As demonstrated here, stopped down to f/5.6, its performance at infinity is faultless. Film: Kodak Technical Pan.

Rudolf Seck

16x Enlargement

32x Enlargement

The "natural" angle of view makes the standard lens the easiest focal length for the beginner to master. Its universality means that if one were taking a single lens on an expedition and it had to cover all eventualities, then the standard lens would be the choice. It is very suitable for landscapes and townscapes. It is not very suitable for head-and-shoulder portraits because one has to get too close in order to fill the frame, with the result that facial features nearer to the camera, such as the nose or an ear, are over-emphasised. However, for full or half-length portraits and groups they are perfectly satisfactory. It can also be used for snapshots and candid portraits because the depth of field allows them to be pre-focused so that the moment is not lost during the time required for careful focusing. They cannot be used so easily as a 35mm or 28mm lens for the unobtrusive snapshot without more practice than is needed with the shorter lenses.

The high-speed lenses of standard focal length (f/1.4 or f/1) extend the scope to poor lighting conditions and for work with available light. Unless such lenses are to be used frequently at maximum aperture they are an expensive luxury, but they do open up greater possibilities for photographic adventure. With a NOCTILUX and high-speed film, colours and detail will be revealed of a very dimly-lit scene that were not apparent at the time. But don't regard them only as poor-light lenses. In ordinary lighting they allow higher shutter speeds and hand-held exposures when one would otherwise have to resort to a tripod. The shallow depth of field at maximum aperture also has creative possibilities by isolating a subject from its background. This is particularly marked with the NOCTILUX, only available for the Leica-M with its long-base rangefinder which is perfect for quick, accurate focusing in poor light. These very fast lenses will never quite match a SUMMICRON for sheer definition, however much they are stopped down, nor are they suitable for close-up work, but they are unbeatable for their intended role.

Many people these days with a LEICA reflex camera choose the 60mm, f/2.8 MACRO-ELMARIT-R as their standard lens. If it is expected that a stop faster than f/2.8 will only be used rarely, then the macro-lens offers more scope. You can always use a faster film on occasions when more speed is required. The 60mm, f/2.8 MACRO-ELMARIT-R can focus down to give a reproduction ratio of 1:2. Although it has been computed to give its best performance in the near focusing range, it is perfectly satisfactory for subjects at infinity. Some people also prefer its slightly narrower angle of view, 6° less than that of a 50mm lens, making it a little more satisfactory for portraits. It is an excellent lens for exploring and learning about the world around us. On a walk in the country you can take the normal subjects and then examine them in close-up without having to change lenses or carry special attachments. Having the close-up facility available at all times like this encourages you to be more adventurous and the rewards can be very satisfying. You can examine the structure of things in a way that you might not if extra attachments were involved. With the macro-lens you can take the whole, such as a rose bush or a house, then pick out interesting features such as an individual flower or a doorway, and then go right in to reveal the detailed structure of the petals or the texture of the brickwork. Hand-held close-ups are the forte of this lens: it sits firmly in the palm of the hand and quite slow shutter speeds are possible. With the MACRO-ADAPTER-R the reproduction ratio is extended to 1:1.

Applications of Moderate Wide-angle Lenses: 28-35mm

No LEICA photographer should be without a "35" or a "28". The greater depth of field allows focusing to be less critical than with a 50mm. If the focus is pre-set to an average distance at which action might be anticipated, say 2 to 3m (6 to 10ft), on a walk round a town, then a picture can often be snatched which would have been lost if time were taken to focus. All the above are good snapshot lenses. The faster ones obviously offer more scope for grabbing a picture in poorer light.

The view of these moderately wide-angle lenses are regarded by many people as normal these days, as much as 50mm used to be. We are more attuned now to the wide-angle shot which we see every day on television, in magazines and in advertising. Exploration of the dramatic perspective effects of wide-angle lenses can begin with the "28's" and, because the exaggeration will not be too great, the beginner in this aspect of photography is not likely to become frustrated.

The 35mm lenses have an angle of view which is not much wider than our own, which is roughly that of a 45mm lens, so the standard 50mm lens "sees" a slightly narrower angle of view. If you go out with no specific photographic plans in mind, with only the one lens on the camera, then a "35" could be the most useful. It will cope with landscapes, it is particularly good about town, it has the snapshot ability we talked about above, and it is more likely to be of use in interiors. But with a 35mm as the sole lens one must get in close if the pictures are to be more than general views. Alternatively it can be partnered with a suitable 90mm lens to give a versatile two-lens combination, which is very convenient for the traveller.

Before we leave the subject of snapshots with these moderately wide-angle lenses, there is a technique for the unobtrusive candid snapshot which is made possible by the depth of field and the consequent focusing latitude. If the LEICA is slung on its strap round the neck in the horizontal position in the usual way, so that it is at waist level, then

35mm, f/2.8 ELMARIT-R

The two extremes of the wide-angle range. The 35mm lens is used by many people as their standard lens. Its perspective looks natural, although with somewhat more emphasis on the foreground than with a 50mm lens, and its angle of view is still fairly close to that of our eyes.

15mm, f/3.5 SUPER-ELMAR-R

The 15mm shot, on the other hand, taken from the same spot. has all the emphasis on the foreground and the background has become merely incidental. However, everything is in focus, and if the picture is held as close to the eye as possible for it still to be focused sharply, one gets the impression of actually standing in the picture and the perspective then looks normal.

a 35mm lens focused at 3m, or 10ft, will take in a scene 3m wide. In other words, the width of the scene covered is the same as the distance from it. the height will be 2m, or 6½ft, that is somewhat more than the height of a standing figure. With a little practice at keeping the camera level you can wander about with the thumb on the shutter release and take fascinating character studies without the subject being aware that you are taking photographs. After a little experience you can move in closer, estimating the subject area for the new distance and raising the camera on its strap so that it rests higher on the body, for head-and-shoulder portraits.

The same thing can be done with even wider-angle lenses, but you then need to get very much closer in. The LEICA M, with its near silent shutter, is ideal for this, but in a place where there is some noise, such as a market, the soft *clunk* of the Leica R mirror will not be heard either.

With all the excitement about snapshots and candid pictures we must not forget the traditional role of wide-angle lenses: that is to cover more of a subject than is possible with a 50mm lens. This usually means buildings, interiors, landscapes and portrait groups. The effects of tilting the camera become more prominent the shorter the focal length, so great care must be taken to keep the camera level if verticals, such as with a building, form an important part of the composition. If converging verticals cannot be avoided then it is better to make it obvious that the effect was intended. Keeping the camera level is more difficult the wider the angle of view of the lens, and the small spirit level (or case level) which can be bought for mounting in the accessory shoe is a very useful aid. The old Leitz "DOOLU" is ideal, if a collector can be persuaded to part with one!

If you want a moderately wide-angle lens which gives a substantially different field of view from your standard lens, then a 28mm would be the focal length of choice. It would open up more opportunities for extending the range of pictures you can secure in landscapes, townscapes, interiors, etc., while at the same time it can be an excellent snapshot lens. It will also give a somewhat more marked wide-angle perspective than a 35mm. Choice is easy because there is only one lens of this focal length in each of the R- and M-systems.

Choice among 35mm lenses is much wider and depends on maximum aperture. Both the 35mm SUMMICRON-R and -M lenses have a performance equivalent in all respects to their 50mm counterparts. They would be the lens of choice for general photography and technical work, whilst allowing fast shutter speeds for snapshots, candid pictures, etc. When the main application is going to be available-light work in poor lighting conditions, then a 35mm, f/1.4 SUMMILUX must be the preferred lens, but a SUMMILUX has no advantage if it is not to be used at an aperture wider than f/2. For critical photography with M-cameras, when a

This picture by John Robert Young from a helicopter about to land on H.M.S. *Ark Royal* demonstrates how to use a fisheye, the only practical lens in the very cramped circumstances. Everything is in focus from a few inches to the far horizon. The horizon being curved hardly matters, in fact it suggests the curvature of the earth. The ship, on the other hand, shows no distortion because its axis passes through the centre of the image. It is in the nature of fisheye lenses that straight lines passing through the lens axis remain straight, but curvature of straight lines gets progressively greater the further from the lens axis they are. 16mm, f/2.8 FISHEYE-ELMARIT-R.

A shift lens is essential for architectural photography, not only for preventing leaning verticals, but also for "looking round corners" on cramped sites. A high wall is only a few feet away from the south side of this church at Alciston, Sussex, and the ground falls away steeply on the other side of the wall, preventing photography of this side of the church from further away. Furthermore, the gardener's shed inside the wall, opposite the memorial tablet, restricts any approach along that side. The 28mm, f/2.8 PC-Super-Angulon-R, shifted to its maximum upwards and to the left, permitted this picture to be taken showing the memorial tablet in its unusual position on the outside of the south wall of the chancel, where because of its location few visitors would see it.

The 35mm, f/4 PA-CURTAGON-R as a snapshot lens – more convenient in this role than the 28mm PC-SUPER-ANGULON. With the lens shifted downwards the camera could be kept horizontal and the picture appears to have been taken from closer to sea level than was actually the case.
Dennis Laney

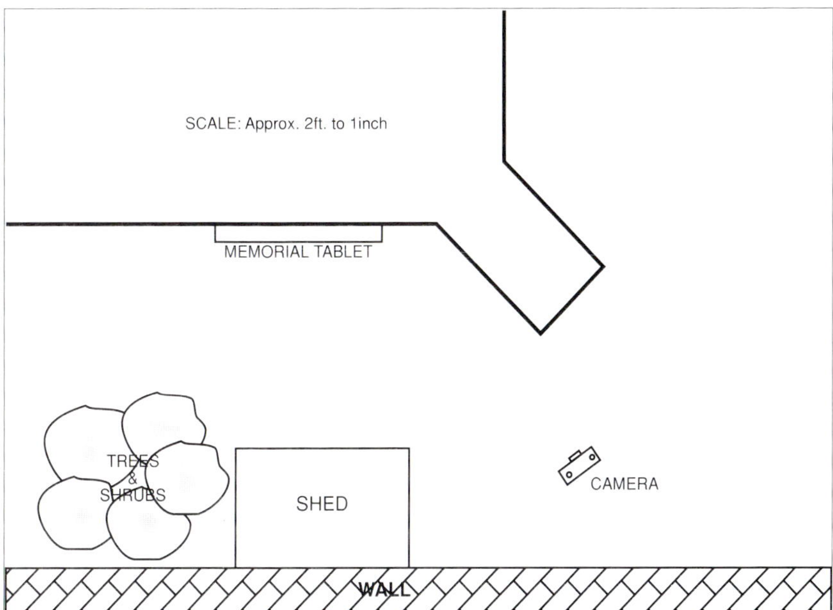

For the picture above of a night landing by a Sea Harrier on *Ark Royal*, John Robert-Young used the 280mm, f/2.8 APO-TELYT which has ensured reproduction of the finest detail in the very poor light.

fast lens is needed, particularly when definition and lack of coma at the edges of the picture are important, then the 35mm, f/1.4 SUMMILUX-M ASPHERICAL is the lens of choice.

For Leica-R cameras the 35mm, f/2.8 ELMARIT-R is another option. It has similar applications to the SUMMICRON and will perform as well in technical work, but it has only half the maximum speed; however, it is light, compact, and relatively inexpensive, and is an ideal lens for travel.

Focusing wide-angle lenses on the LEICA reflex cameras is best done with the split-image rangefinder in the centre of the field. Focusing on the ground glass can be very difficult because details are rendered so much smaller than with longer lenses. Always check that the focus is right by a glance at the focusing scale. At medium apertures focusing errors are unlikely to affect the result because of the depth of field.

Applications of Shift Lenses

Shift lenses, otherwise known as perspective-control lenses, are a specialised form of wide-angle. Their operation has been explained in Chapter 2. The problem with photographing tall buildings from ground level, if the camera is not to be tilted, is that the lower half of the picture, usually uninteresting foreground such as a bare roadway, will be unwanted. This is simply because the camera at eye level is at the base of the building. The answer to this problem for the architectural photographer is a shift lens. To photograph a tall building set the camera on a tripod and then operate the shift upwards until the desired composition is on the focusing screen. But these lenses have many other uses whenever the desired centre point of the subject cannot be aligned on the optical axis of the lens. For example, you can take a street scene from an upper window instead of street level to avoid the heads of crowds or parked cars, or use it to "look round the corner" when it is physically impossible to move sideways to get the desired view, such as on a river bank. Advertising photographers also find shift lenses useful for photographing products with interesting perspectives. Pictures of antiques or objets d'art, for example, can look better when taken from slightly above and a shift lens enables the sides to remain parallel instead of receding as they would with a normal lens.

Applications of Extreme Wide-angle Lenses: 15-24mm

First-rate photographers have extended the scope of pictorial photography with their achievements using extreme wide-angle lenses. Unfortunately, others with less skill and experience have worked the theme to death, but in the hands of a master the extreme wide-angle lens can produce pictures with tremendous impact, or drama, or convey the atmosphere of a place or event in a way that cannot be done any other way photographically.

They take in a wider and wider angle of view as you move down the list. These lenses are intended for getting in all of the subject when space is confined, such as with architecture and interiors. The very wide ones also have special technical uses: recording aircraft instrument panels, for example. The problem of unwanted foreground applies with greater force the wider the angle of view. Similarly, even the slightest camera tilt becomes greatly exaggerated the wider the angle of view. Hence these lenses require much more careful handling than the more moderate wide-angles.

These very short focal length lenses can be used for candid portraits at very close range. For instance, a 21mm or 19mm will give full length pictures of fellow passengers in a lift (elevator). Unless conditions are fairly noisy, the LEICA M is really essential for this type of candid shot. They are much used by photo-journalists for work both in tight spaces and for really close portraits for the emphasis they give to facial features. The most benign politician can be made to look evil when taken from very close up.

The really exciting property of ultra-wide-angle lenses is the pictorial scope they offer by allowing the photographer to move in close and obtain a totally different perspective. A wide-angle lens tends to place emphasis on the foreground and cause the background to recede by being diminished in size. At the same time the great depth of focus allows both foreground and background to be equally sharp. This is the opposite situation with very long-focus lenses which are also used to suppress the background, but by throwing it out of focus. With a long-focus lens one knows the background is there, large and looming behind the blur, whereas with an extreme wide-angle lens the background is sharp and exposed for all to see how small and insignificant is has become.

Because the foreground is so dominant in ultra-wide-angle pictures its composition needs to be very carefully arranged. The slightest camera tilt will ruin the picture with converging verticals or sloping horizon. Therefore, for architectural views, or any other subject in which vertical and horizontal lines are dominant, the camera must be very carefully set up on a tripod. A photographic spirit level mounted in the accessory shoe is very useful, but should not be relied upon without checking in the viewfinder for parallelism with the sides or bottom frames of the screen. For the LEICA reflex cameras with interchangeable screens, the screen with grid divisions [14306] is ideal, but the ground glass is not very suitable for focusing such short focus lenses, and focus and depth of field should be checked by reference to the focusing scale.

In this wide-angle view of the interior of Wetzlar cathedral, taken with a 21mm, f/2.8 Elmarit-M, the lines of the columns and floor tiles remain perfectly straight right to the boundaries of the image field. Any pin-cushion distortion introduced by the lens would be immediately apparent - a good test of a wide-angle lens. The camera was tilted upwards to take in the height and the resulting converging verticals were corrected during enlargement by tilting the enlarging frame
Rudolf Seck

For the average LEICA photographer venturing into the extreme wide-angle field the choice is likely to be between the 24mm, 21mm or 19mm lenses for a LEICA reflex camera. The 24mm ELMARIT takes in a width of the scene which is 2.2x that of a 50mm lens. The 21mm SUPER-ANGULON is the lightest of the three but has only half the speed; it covers 2.5x the width of a 50mm lens. The 19mm ELMARIT has a superb optical performance for its focal length and speed; it takes in 2.7x the width of view of a 50mm lens.

For the LEICA M there is no problem of choice because only the 21mm ELMARIT is available. It is fast for its focal length and is ideal for snapshots, reportage, etc. at close quarters. Alignment is more difficult without a focusing screen so it is less convenient than a similar focal length mounted on a Leica R for architecture or interiors. The accessory viewfinder [12012] is necessary.

A specialised application for lenses in this range is for the photography of architectural models of townscapes or individual buildings. They give a perspective on models that is similar to that presented by the full size buildings viewed from street level. The amateur can make use of the same effect to experiment with table-top photography.

The 15mm, f/3.5 SUPER-ELMAR-R has two distinct roles. It is a specialist's lens for recording instrument panels, or mechanisms, or other technical subjects in very confined spaces. The fact that it is a very high quality, normal wide-angle lens (not a fisheye) makes it ideal for this purpose. It is also used for room interiors when it greatly enhances their apparent size. In its other role it has great appeal for photographers exploring the extreme wide-angle area who are discovering fascinating new creative possibilities.

Applications of the Fisheye Lens

The angle of view of the 16mm, f/2.8 FISHEYE-ELMARIT-R is 180°: you can take a view and include your own feet! Fisheye lenses have been a popular novelty at the cheaper end of the SLR market, often in the form of so-called fisheye attachments. Of course, novelties wear off and as a result fisheyes have tended to be denigrated. This is a pity because in skilled hands they can yield most interesting and aesthetically pleasing pictures that are unobtainable in any other way.

The fisheye lens was first developed for meteorological use in photographing cloud cover. The curvilinear distortion which is characteristic of fisheye lenses was unavoidable in a lens intended to cover the entire sky. The important point to remember about a fisheye is that straight lines which pass through the centre of the image field are reproduced straight. The further they are from the centre of the image field the more curved they will be. The horizon, for instance, if carefully centred in the focusing screen, and with the camera absolutely level, will be perfectly straight and horizontal. Thus by very careful choice of subject and positioning of the camera, pictures can be obtained which will be revealed to have been taken with a fisheye only on close examination. Familiar landscapes can be presented in an unusual, indeed eerie, way. Cloudscapes against a blue sky can be particularly effective. Circular subjects, centred on the centre point of the image are reproduced circular just as they appear to the eye, but the 180° angle of view means that the subject, which might be a flower, can be taken from very close up and the background rendered into insignificance, not only by its small size but also by the curvature.

Very effective fisheye pictures, and pictures with other extreme wide-angle lenses, can be made from close to the ground. For this the right-angle viewfinder is a very useful accessory. Different models are required for the various LEICA reflex cameras, so a LEICA dealer should be consulted about the appropriate one.

Applications of Moderate Long-Focus Lenses: 75-180mm

Long focus lenses have the ability to bridge distance. In doing so they can appear to foreshorten perspective. They are used to tighten the framing of a picture, concentrating on the essentials. They are also used to get closer to the subject, whether the subject itself is far away or close-to. The choice of lenses for the LEICA R- and M-systems looks bewildering, but as with the standard lenses it is quickly narrowed down when you consider the purpose for which you want a long-focus lens.

The traditional longer focal lengths for the LEICA are 90mm and 135mm and the long-time LEICA user tends to think of these two first, but one of the others might well suit better. The reflex camera comes into its own with longer focal lengths when the ground glass screen is ideal for focusing, whereas 135mm is really the limit for accurate focusing with the rangefinder of the LEICA M. A popular focal length now is 180mm, exemplified by the fact that Leica offer a choice of three lenses of this length.

The next most versatile lens after a standard is probably a 90mm. (Although most of the following remarks apply also the 75mm SUMMILUX-M and 80mm SUMMILUX-R lenses, their very wide maximum apertures do limit them for some applications such as close-ups). Many photographers say that the best way to improve your photography is to confine yourself to a 90mm for every picture. In this way you really learn how to pick out the essentials in a subject and you will produce pictures with much greater impact and interest. Another great merit of the 90mm lens is that you can take the same subject as with a standard lens, but with a marked change in perspective, by moving the camera position back to somewhat less than twice the distance from the subject. The scope for moving back is often limited if you want to avoid cropping at the same time.

The 90mm is particularly good for head-and-shoulders portraits. The camera can be sufficiently far away so that features nearer to it, such as the nose, are not emphasised. At the same time the photographer does not become too remote from his sitter and lose the intimacy essential for a good portrait.

Well stopped down, a 90mm lens still gives a good depth of field so that you can obtain sharp reproduction of all details in the picture from foreground to background, which is impossible when the focal length becomes much longer. On the other hand, particularly with the big aperture lenses, the reduced depth of field at full aperture can be used to place emphasis on a subject or a detail.

The 90mm, with its nearby relatives, is excellent for landscapes when the narrower angle of view allows a scene to be captured that cannot be approached close enough with a 50mm, but without the compression effect that can give a false impression with a longer lens. It can also be used to exclude ugly features, such as buildings or poles. In architectural photography a 90mm lens can be used for larger details, such as doorways.

There is a 90mm, f/2 SUMMICRON and a 90mm, f/2.8 ELMARIT in both the R- and the M-systems. The ELMARIT's are light in weight and handy and ideal as travelling lenses, but have only half the maximum speed of the SUMMICRON's. The SUMMICRON's have all the qualities of their 50mm counterparts and are good for reportage. They are ideal snapshot lenses when pictures are to be taken discretely from a distance. Of course, at f/2 the depth of field is shallow and they can be used to pick out the essentials in a scene by throwing the background out of focus. They are also excellent for technical and close-up work, with appropriate attachments, when a longer working distance between camera and subject is necessary. The 90mm ELMARIT-R is also particularly good in this role.

The remarks about 90mm lenses apply also to those with focal lengths up to 15mm either side. The two high-speed lenses, the 80mm, f/1.4 SUMMILUX-R and the 75mm, f/1.4 SUMMILUX-M, have slightly shorter focal lengths to keep the weight and bulk within reasonable limits. They are intended to be used principally at maximum aperture, either for available-light work, particularly in poor lighting, at night or indoors, for stage work, for portraits by available light, and for even greater concentration on details by restricted depth of field.

Armed with a LEICA M6, with its near-silent shutter, fitted with a 75mm SUMMILUX-M the reporter is perfectly equipped to wander unobtrusively and record the variety of life about him, day or night. Even bright light sources within the picture area will not cause flare, nor will they show distortion.

Owners of earlier LEICA M models, without the 75mm frame, can either use one of the old 73mm accessory finders (see *Leica Collector's Guide* for details) or use the middle finger of the left hand on the field selector lever to keep the 90mm frame in view and use it to frame the picture very tightly.

The reflex may not be quite so fast or quiet in operation, but the 80mm, f/1.4 SUMMILUX-R provides twice as much light on the focusing screen as the 90mm, f/2 SUMMICRON-R and makes focusing possible under more adverse conditions.

The 100mm, f/2.8 APO-MACRO-ELMARIT-R and the 100mm, f/4 MACRO-ELMAR-R have been computed to give their peak performance in the near focusing range. They are eminently suitable as well for general photography and with the added benefit of the macro-facility the remarks on applications of the 60mm MACRO-ELMARIT apply. The 100mm APO-MACRO-ELMARIT-R can be focused down to give a reproduction ratio of 1:2, or to 1:1 with the special ELPRO 1:2-1:1 and is clearly the more versatile lens. The 100mm MACRO-ELMAR-R in its focusing mount goes down to 1:3, or with the MACRO-ADAPTER-R to 1:1.6 (there is a version of this lens without focusing mount for use with the bellows). For the naturalist, interested in flowers, small wildlife, etc., who needs to work at a greater distance than is possible with the 60mm MACRO-ELMARIT-R, one of these 100mm lenses is the perfect lens.

The upper limit for rangefinder focusing with the LEICA-M is 135mm and consequently it is an important focal length in the M-system, whereas in the R-system it has been overshadowed by the 180mm family, which offers twice the reach of the 90mm lenses. You might have both a 90mm and a 180mm in an outfit, but if only one lens is to be purchased in this group the 135mm would probably be the better choice. It can be used in much the same way as a 90mm for landscape, architecture, people and animal portraits, etc., but with a greater degree of cropping if the same camera position is used, or a different perspective if the camera is moved back. At the same time its narrower angle of view makes it a useful focal length for bridging greater distances; for example, animals in a zoo, or smaller details in buildings. The f/4 TELE-ELMAR-M in the M-system is light and handy, whereas the f/2.8 ELMARIT-M with its ocular attachment offers more accurate focusing, higher speed and a magnified viewfinder image, but at the expense of weight and less convenience in stowage. The 135mm, f/2.8 ELMARIT-R is identical optically to the M-version.

Using a LEICA R fitted with one of the 180mm lenses is a real adventure. All sorts of fascinating details in familiar subjects are revealed. The advantage of a 180mm lens is that it can still be part of a general photographic kit, whereas the opportunities for using lenses of longer focal length than 180mm are considerably less, unless you specialize in sport or wildlife, for example. Longer lenses need more skill in handling, camera shake is a particular problem, but 180mm is relatively easy to master and with care you can get away with a shutter speed in hand-held shots as slow as 1/125th second if absolute sharpness is less vital than securing the shot. This is why the focal length has become so popular. It is versatile, interesting to use, relatively handy, and doesn't require special techniques.

The 90mm lens is suitable for formal portraits, when the sitter is co-operating with the photographer. The 180mm lens on the other hand is excellent for the informal portrait or character study, when the subject is either unaware of the camera, or sufficiently far away to forget its presence. With the camera held for the horizontal format one can take a head and shoulders from 20ft (6m), but the longer perspective does flatten the features compared to a 90mm lens. Seeing the image filling the focusing screen for the first time you feel that you are intruding and that the subject must be aware, but by watching the subject's eyes you can tell if the camera has been noticed and innocently turn the camera away. A 180mm is a perfect lens for taking camera-shy children, or small animals.

It can really isolate a subject from its background when used at full aperture by throwing background detail completely out of focus so that it becomes an abstract pattern. In this way a distracting background can be removed, but the blurred, mottled effect can be used to advantage to "paint in" a background. For example, a background of trees can be rendered as a pleasing patchwork of greens and browns. In addition the long "reach" of a 180mm makes it ideal for the reporter, journalist, wildlife and sports photographer. It can also pick out inaccessible details in a variety of subjects, such as sculpture on the facade of a building, or the interesting details often missed because they are above eye level. A 180mm lens, in conjunction with the selective metering of the LEICA R-camera is the right lens for the high stained glass windows inside a church.

Of the three 180's in the LEICA catalogue, the 180mm, f/4 ELMAR-R is the lightest in weight and smallest in size of the three, and is fast enough for most outdoor applications. It is therefore the one for the traveller. The 180mm, f/2.8 ELMARIT-R enables you to exploit more fully the advantages of a 180mm lens, hand-held shots in poorer light are possible (it is a favourite of stage photographers) and the greater maximum aperture can be used to restrict the depth of field and put all the emphasis on the subject. The viewfinder image is also brighter, but there is a penalty in slightly greater weight. The 180mm, f/3.4 APO-TELYT-R is in a class by itself. It has a very high contrast, not normally associated with long-focus lenses. When the best possible colour rendering and maximum sharpness and resolution at large apertures, limited only by the film used, are essential, then the APO-TELYT has no rival. It is inherent in the design that it performs best at infinity and is less suitable for close-ups. When stopped down to medium apertures its performance is matched by the other two 180's at the same apertures. The 180mm, f/2.8 ELMARIT-R remains the most versatile 180mm lens, but once you have tried an Apo and seen the results you will not want to part with it.

Applications of Zoom Lenses

The range of the zoom lenses 35-70mm, f/3.5 VARIO-ELMAR-R and 28-70mm, f/3.5-4.5 VARIO-ELMAR-R extends from the wide-angle to the lower limit of the long-focus group, which makes them very versatile and useful universal lenses for the reflex cameras. They are slower than the standard lenses, but if lens speed does not matter and you are interested primarily in people, landscapes or travel, then the variable focal length is an immense asset. Many people are prejudiced against zoom lenses because of their reputation for distortion and their complexity of construction, which can lead to low contrast and faulty alignment; but these disadvantages have been largely overcome in the VARIO-ELMAR lenses. Do not expect them to match a SUMMICRON in exacting technical or reprographic work, but, if the variable focal length would suit your type of photography, try to borrow one to check its performance for yourself on the type of subjects you normally take. The traveller will find the 28-70mm Vario-Elmar-R the most versatile single lens of all, capable of coping with most of his needs whilst taking up minimum space and saving considerable weight and cost compared with two or three prime lenses. It also has a useful close-up extension down to a reproduction ratio of 1:6. Its disadvantage is the variable maximum aperture and rotating mount which makes use of polarizing filters difficult. The 35-70mm VARIO-ELMAR-R is for more critical photography and more convenient for use with polarizing and graduated filters.

The 70-210mm,f/4 VARIO-ELMAR-R can fill the role of two or three longer focal length lenses. In partnership with the 28-70mm or the 35-70mm it will cover all the focal lengths likely to be needed by the average LEICA photographer, and the pair will form a light-weight travel combination. So if high speed is not important and a variety of focal lengths is needed in this range, but multiple lenses would be inconvenient, then the 70-210mm VARIO-ELMAR-R might be the best buy. Zoom lenses also lend themselves to special effects by zooming during a long exposure.

Applications of Extreme Long-Focus Lenses: 250-800mm

Very long focal length lenses such as these are going to be used primarily for bridging distances and will be bought to satisfy special interests. These might be reportage, photo-journalism, sport, wildlife in its natural habitat, detail in architecture, or to photograph buildings from a distance to avoid foreground problems. They enable us to photograph scenes, objects, events, people, animals, that would normally be impossible because we cannot get close enough.

These lenses are very individualistic and serve quite different purposes. Briefly, the 250mm and 350mm TELYT-R lenses are general purpose lenses, the Apo's are for when maximum lens speed and image quality are essential, the 400mm and 560mm, f/6.8 follow-focus lenses, whether in sliding or Novoflex mounts, are light-weight and for keeping fast-moving subjects in focus, the 500mm mirror lens offers extreme light weight – the mountaineer's lens, and the 800mm is for specialist professional use.

There are problems in using very long-focus lenses that must be understood, and the skills practised, before results are obtained comparable to those that would be expected from shorter focal lengths. The longer the focal length the less the opportunity you have to alter the composition and perspective, or the angle, by moving the camera position. The distances you would have to move in order to have an appreciable effect would be too great. For the same reason the subject cannot be made to fill the frame simply by moving closer or further away. For example, with a 560mm lens you may have to walk 100 yards or so to do this. This is why such long lenses must be carefully chosen for the intended purpose. Buying one in the hope that it will serve as a universal lens will result in disappointment. Another factor is that the longer the focal length the more difficult it is to hold the camera steady. The long lens not only exercises a leverage on the arms, which increases any unsteadiness in the hold, but it also magnifies movement of the image caused by camera shake. Hence with very long-focus lenses the highest possible shutter speeds are essential, otherwise they must be mounted on a very stable tripod. This means they will be used mainly at maximum aperture, which is what the longest LEICA lenses are designed for.

Depth of field is very limited with very long-focus lenses, but it is better to avoid stopping down and the risk of camera shake from too long an exposure time. In any case, one of the great assets of long lenses is the way the subject is picked out sharply by selective focusing, which overcomes the inability to be able to move the camera position for a frame-filling shot.

The 800mm, f/6.3 Telyt-S is often used for shots of distant wildlife, but it must be mounted on a very solid tripod, preferably also with a monopod front support.
Julius Behnke

The 250mm, f/4 TELYT-R and the 350mm, f/4.8 TELYT-R are relatively short and handy for their focal lengths and also reasonably fast. Both lenses can be handled in the same way as lenses in the moderate long-focus group, making due allowance for the longer focal length in selecting shutter speed. The focusing travel is short, allowing faster operation. These two lenses are likely to find application in wildlife and sports photography, photojournalism, particularly when bulk has to be kept to a minimum, and for picking out detail in landscape and architectural photography. If the 280mm or 400mm Apo-Telyt-R is not available, then one of these two lenses is the next choice for use in poor lighting conditions.

The 280mm and 400mm APO-TELYT-R lenses are intended for photographers who have to secure the best possible images under adverse conditions. An example would be sports photographers working in indoor arenas or outside in poor weather in winter. Often at big events photographers do not get a place allocated near the action and they have to produce pictures enlarged from a portion of the negative. In these circumstances the apo-quality, high contrast image is invaluable. But their use is not confined to sport. They open up opportunities in any situation where a very fast telephoto lens giving a superb image and colour fidelity can be used, such as wildlife, theatre, ballet, etc. Professional advertising and fashion photographers have also discovered the creative possibilities of these lenses, in the sharp delineation of the subject plane for instance. The 1.4x and 2x APO-EXTENDERS add greatly to their versatility without affecting the image quality. They are inevitably heavy and expensive, but one can be the best companion an action photographer could have to see him through an assignment when he knows he will have little or no control over his camera position or the lighting.

The 400mm, f/6.8 TELYT-R and 560mm, f/6.8 TELYT-R ("follow-focus") lenses are an individualistic pair, unique to Leica, for a different type of action photography. They find their obvious application in sport, reportage, and wildlife, although the latter can include quite small creatures when the special extension tube, common to both lenses, is fitted. They are intended for use mounted on the Universal Handgrip and Shoulder Stock so that the camera and lens combination can be very easily handled like a rifle, and slower shutter speeds are possible than would normally be the case for the focal length concerned. They are also now available with a Novoflex mount which has handgrips and a shoulder stock but is focused by pressing a trigger rather than by sliding the lens sleeve on the traditional Leica mount. Potential buyers should try out both mounts before purchase because it is very much a matter of personal choice which is the easier to use. If a shoulder stock is not available, then a monopod or bean-bag can be used to take the weight of the lens but still allow quick movement, as when following wildlife. It is also possible to obtain perfectly satisfactory results in the absence of any support by sitting on the ground with the left elbow resting on the knee and the lens supported in the left hand. The lenses can of course be mounted on a tripod for more staid and deliberate photography, such as the recording of architectural detail or the taking of distant views, but beware of the curved field if flat surfaces, such as walls, are an essential part of the composition. On the other hand, the simple achromat construction, with only two elements, yields an almost apochromatic quality image in terms of sharpness and contrast. They are not poor-light lenses, but they are light in weight, a delight to use and very fast in action. Their appearance when fitted on the shoulder stock could cause alarm among bystanders at public events and may attract unwelcome attention from the authorities!

The 500mm, f/8 MR-TELYT-R is essentially a lens for people who need a very long lens but for whom compactness and light weight are of overriding importance, such as mountaineers, explorers, back-packers, walkers. It can be used for all the long-distance subjects discussed, but within its limitations of slow speed and fixed aperture. Thus it is an outdoor lens for good lighting conditions. If the light is too bright, as in a snow field, then the 4x neutral-density filter can be put in place to help control the exposure. This will give the lens an effective aperture as far as exposure is concerned of f/16, but of course it will have no effect on the depth of field. The phenomenon by which highlights in out-of-focus portions of the picture have double contours, whereby spots of light for instance appear as rings, has been used by some photographers to creative effect. However, to the average LEICA photographer the advice must be that, unless small size and minimum weight are very important to you, you would have a more versatile outfit by adding a 2x Extender-R to a 180mm or 250mm lens.

The 800mm, f/6.3 TELYT-S really is a specialist's lens. Its price puts it out of reach of all but the most wealthy amateur enthusiast. It must be used with one, or preferably two tripods or other support. It finds its main applications in long distance sports coverage, study of wildlife, and in monitoring and surveillance – for example, inspecting inaccessible parts of engineering structures such as bridges.

The achromat is the ideal form for such long focal lengths, which is why the lens is used for technical applications, but would be useless without the superb quality of design and engineering of the mount. It is clearly not a lens that can be swung into action quickly, but one that needs to be set up in advance. For subjects such as water sports where the distance is inevitably great, or for more inaccessible wildlife, the angle of action is going to be correspondingly smaller and it can be readily followed with this lens, on its tripod, with the aid of the open peep-sight built into the carrying handle. Its optical quality and contrast will yield superior pictures to those of rival photographers using telephotos. In all long-distance photography haze in the atmosphere can seriously reduce the contrast in the image, so a lens that contributes no loss of contrast itself is a great asset. This property of the lens gives it another valuable use in long-distance architectural photography. It is often difficult to photograph a tall building from close-to, because surrounding buildings make it impossible to get the camera far enough back, even with a shift lens. The solution can be to photograph the building from a long distance from which it can be seen rising above its surroundings. A different perspective is also obtained in this way which gives a different quality to the picture. Finally, the 800mm,f/6.3 Telyt-S will produce a good sized image of the moon. Dramatic pictures can also be taken of the sun's disc at sunset – but never photograph the sun at any other time without special protection because the eye can be damaged permanently by looking at the sun through the viewfinder.

Applications of Extenders

Extenders give the opportunity to lift a 135mm or 180mm lens into the extreme long-focus group, to multiply the focal length of a lens in that group, or to give a very useful extension to a lens in the 50mm to 100mm group. Extenders are perfect for photographers who only have occasional need for long focal lengths, or who want to try their hands at some of the extreme long-focus applications. With an extender attached to a familiar lens it is necessary to remember to allow a sufficiently fast shutter speed for the increased focal length to avoid camera shake affecting the image. The automatic diaphragm operation of the prime lens is retained with an extender, so the metering system will compensate for the reduced aperture.

Extenders can be very useful in the nearer focusing ranges. For instance, an extender may bring a flower or an insect within reach when added to a 50mm or 90mm lens, or make a useful adjunct to the 60mm Macro-Elmarit-R or one of the 100mm macro lenses (but remember that the Apo-Extender-R 1.4x cannot be used with the 100mm, f/2.8 Apo-Macro-Elmarit-R). Or they can be used to create space for the arrangement of lights or flash.

Finally, the obvious value of extenders is to lighten the load when travelling.

4. Subjects

Particular types of subject put special demands, or constraints, on the photographer and affect the choice of lens. This choice might be governed by considerations of perspective, or space, or restriction of movement, or low light, or size of the subject or any of a host of other factors.

No one these days attempts to lay down rules for pictorial composition in photography. A book like this can only give guidance. The best photographers have been self-taught and every photographer should experiment continuously. No lens is totally unsuitable for any subject if it is the only one available. However, there are a few general principles that can be teased out from a century-and-a-half of photography and applied to the 35mm format. Rather than list a catalogue of subjects I have taken a few broad categories of subject, each of which makes special demands, and concentrated on them. They are landscape, people, buildings, animals, sport, nature, and low-light situations. Most subjects, leaving aside the professional world of press, fashion or advertising photography, fall into one or a combination of these categories. Thus, for example, when putting together an outfit for travel photography one will need to provide for tackling landscapes, people and possibly buildings or animals, but weight will probably be the overriding consideration.

Landscapes

Landscapes in one form or another are probably one of the most popular subjects for the amateur photographer. Many people start their photographic hobby by taking landscapes, and then other interests often derive from their experience with landscape. Landscapes are also one of the most difficult areas of photography in which to achieve pictures with an interest and impact beyond mere demonstration of technical competence.

Almost any lens can be used for landscape. In fact there is no lens in either system which is unsuitable, but different lenses will produce quite different types of landscape pictures. When faced with a scene which we see as a potential "landscape" picture we tend to look into the middle and distant ground and overlook the foreground, at least until we have learned from experience not to disregard it. The camera sees the scene differently. With a standard lens it puts the emphasis more on the foreground and registers as less significant those more distant features which attracted us to take the picture. When we see

Landscapes with a 50mm lens can be made much more interesting by a careful choice of viewpoint and placement o the horizon. In this example a low viewpoint directs one's interest to the snow-covered rocks in the foreground and gives them even greater emphasis than would normally be the case with a 50mm lens. 50mm, f/2 SUMMICRON-M
Julius Behnke

It may seem unnecessary to use such a superb lens as the 100mm, f/2.8 APO-MACRO-ELMARIT-R on misty scenes like these, but the high-contrast performance of the lens and absence of flare ensures that every detail, from the grasses on the opposite bank to Arundel Castle in the distance, is recorded on the film, despite the sun appearing in the frame. *Dennis Laney*

Above: If the face is in profile, the effects of very long focus lens in flattening facial features are minimised and it is possible to obtain relaxed portraits with the background, in this case foliage, totally out of focus. 400mm, f/6.8 TELYT-R. *Dennis Laney*

Below: The lighting of familiar landscape changes constantly, and choice of lens, wide-angle, standard or long focus, will further influence the mood of the photograph. 180mm, f/3.4 APO-TELYT-R. *Dennis Laney*

landscapes in this way, with the interest on the middle distance and beyond, we would be better off with a longer focus lens, a 90mm or even a 135mm. Some of the most satisfying landscape pictures are indeed produced with these lenses. The only way to treat distant hills or mountains if we want them to be as impressive in the photograph as they are in reality is to use longer focal lengths to bring them forward. The standard lens will diminish them and the results will always be disappointing. So if we are confined to a standard lens we must always have regard to the immediate foreground and incorporate it in a meaningful way into the picture. In recent years many photographers have explored the opposite view and put all the emphasis in their landscapes on the foreground by adopting wide-angle lenses and/or low camera angles.

We have a choice of three different angles of perspective in a landscape, which gives even more variety in the ways we can use our different lenses for interesting and creative effects. The central perspective is the most commonly used. It is the view we take when we stand up with the camera level at the eye. But if we get right down and take a "worm's eye view" we obtain a totally different impression of the scene. Similarly, if we are able to get a higher viewpoint, perhaps by climbing a hill, we can take a "bird's eye view" and obtain yet a third different impression of the scene.

A further choice we have is where to place the horizon. In reasonably flat country, with the camera level, the horizon will cross the middle of the picture, dividing it neatly into two equal halves, one land and the other sky. Generally the effect is most uninteresting and it would be difficult to find a masterpiece with such proportions by one of the great painters. If the camera is tilted back slightly, the horizon will be shifted to near the base of the image and the sky above will acquire enormous volume and become the dominant feature. The picture will convey an atmosphere of a land under wide open skies; it will transmit any feeling of loneliness, of timelessness, that was experienced by the photographer. On the other hand, if the camera is tilted slightly downwards the horizon will be near the top of the picture and the landscape will have great depth. The eye will travel on a tour of exploration from the foreground, through the intervening landscape to the distant horizon. Wide-angle lenses can be particularly effective here because they allow everything to be in focus from the immediate vicinity of the observer to the far distance. Do though make sure that the horizon is parallel with the top of the frame.

With all this choice of camera position the standard lens comes back into its own for landscapes. It can offer just as much in the way of creative opportunities as the longer or shorter focal lengths when used in this way.

One of the macro lenses is particularly good to have available when seeking, or just hoping to find good landscape subjects. Besides landscape views it can also secure close-ups of detail, such as flowers or leaves, texture patterns of rocks, mosses, etc., which add so much interest to a slide show because they give the viewer the experience of actually being there and feeling he could reach out and touch them.

Not only close-up detail, but distant detail as well adds interest to a slide show. Often the terrain makes it impossible to approach such detail closely enough, particularly in hilly or mountainous country, or country criss-crossed by dykes. Such detail might be a clump of trees, or a curve in a river, or a mountain peak. Perhaps such features are already part of the composition in one of our views, but it would be nice to be able to zoom in and take a closer look. We will wish we had a really long lens with us but wanted to avoid weight. This is where an extender really pays for itself; they are so small, light and pocketable there is no excuse for leaving it at home. Alternatively, a long and a short zoom enable a landscape to be thoroughly explored and the best views selected, but at the cost of greater weight.

Almost any lens can be used for landscape. If they are available, experiment with them. See how the fisheye can change the mood of familiar country – a hint of menace in that peaceful valley. Change the scale with extreme wide-angles; push the background right back and increase the feeling of space; make that tuft of grass the most important object in the scene. Bring those mountains, those trees, right up close with an extreme long focus lens; let us see their stature and grandeur. Remember, however, that the foreground can rarely be sharp in landscape photography with very long-focus lenses.

A polarizing filter is very useful when using colour film on days when the sky is so pale that it destroys the colour balance of the picture. Denser transparencies with more saturated colours will be obtained by slightly underexposing colour transparency film. For black-and-white landscape work a LEICA yellow-green filter is indispensable. It increases the contrast between clouds and blue sky and also lightens greens when trees or grass dominate the composition.

More than in any other type of photography, landscapes involve walking or climbing so weight of the equipment is an important factor. If it is too heavy we will simply find reasons to leave it at home. Two lenses, or at the most three, plus an extender, will generally be adequate. Fast lenses will not be needed. The actual choice of focal lengths to take on a landscape expedition will depend on the type of country. In mountainous areas we may find our subjects are either a long way off, so an investment in a 500mm MR-TELYT-R may be worth while, or close-to because it is impossible to step back, in which case a wide-angle is necessary. In flat open country, such as the polder lands in Holland,

East Anglia in England, or the Great Plains in the U.S.A. and Canada, we will probably want to bring out the sense of space so that short focal lengths will be the first choice. In rolling country with scattered settlements, woods and other features, all on a modest scale, the mid-range focal lengths, from moderate wide-angle to moderate long focus, will cope with most of our needs. Depending on the type of country, either a short or the long zoom would keep weight and bulk to a minimum, and the relative slowness of these lenses would be unimportant.

People

The biggest single benefit to photography deriving from the invention of the LEICA was to liberate it from the formal, posed and stiff portrait. As a result our descendants a hundred years hence will know exactly what sort of people we were. They will know what we looked like as we went about our daily business, how we dressed, how we played, how we worked, how we brought up our children. They will also have a very good idea of our emotions and our reactions to events as they happened. Just as the invention of photography itself has allowed us to know far more about the appearance of our Victorian ancestors than we know about any previous people, so the LEICA, by leading the way to 35mm photography with its fast action and wide aperture lenses, has opened the window so much wider on our own generation. If we study nineteenth century portrait photographs closely we can gain some insights into the sort of people the sitters were, and particularly how they saw themselves. In our own time, from the early thirties, photography has laid us bare. The LEICA pioneers, Wolff, Kertesz, Cartier-Bresson, Rothstein, Eisenstaedt, and many others showed the way. Now it is open to everyone.

Many people now find that on their holidays abroad they get the greatest pleasure not from photographing the scenery, but from recording the local life, the characters, the trades and crafts, the little daily dramas, happenings and tableaux that are the fascination of a visit to another country. On returning home they find they are much more aware of life in their daily surroundings and they develop new photographic interests on their own doorsteps.

Even with a LEICA the formal portrait still has a place. By "formal" I mean a portrait taken with the full co-operation of the sitter, but not the stiff studio portrait of the past. In such portraits the sitter wants to be seen as he or she thinks they are, although the best portrait photographers are able to reveal the personality of their subjects. By contrast, candid pictures, taken with the subjects unaware, show people as they really are. The standard lens is all right for a three-quarter length posed portrait taken from about six feet (two metres) away, but if the camera is moved nearer to the sitter for a head-and-shoulders, or even closer for the head alone, the resulting perspective will be unsatisfactory because facial features nearer to the camera, usually the nose, appear disproportionately large. The ideal focal length for portraits with a 35mm camera is 90mm. It is perfect for a head-and-shoulders taken from about six feet, although 80mm or 100mm will do as well. Fast lenses used at full aperture, and precisely focused on the eyes, can give pleasing results with good modelling to the face; the shallow depth of field makes even the ears slightly blurred, thus giving a good sense of depth. A soft-focus attachment on the front of the lens will give a softer, more flattering portrait, particularly of women. But don't, please, smear the front element of your LEICA lens with grease as is sometimes recommended in magazines! A 135mm lens will cover the head alone from six feet. If the camera is moved further away to get in the shoulders as well, then the new perspective has the effect of flattening prominent facial features nearer to the camera: a tip for producing a more flattering portrait of someone with a large nose.

Longer focal lengths, such as 180mm, will also give perfectly satisfactory portraits with slightly flatter rendering of features. But as the distance becomes greater the photographer can lose touch with the sitter. Successful portrait photography depends on a rapport being established between the photographer and the sitter, which is not easy from twelve feet or more away. This is why the 90mm lens is fortuitously ideal in another way. The distance from which it compels you to operate is near enough to encourage this rapport, but not so close as to be intrusive. Out of doors, the longer focal lengths, 135mm or 180mm, can be advantageous when the background is confused, as with foliage, and it can be thrown out of focus with the longer lens. Alternatively, very wide apertures can be used for the same purpose.

For the semi-formal portrait when the subject, although aware of the presence of the camera, is going about his normal business, the standard focal length lens is often the most suitable. It may be a craftsman in his workshop, or a musician practising, or your grandmother knitting; in all these cases the activities of the hands are as important as the face and a lens of about 50mm is just right. When the subject has relaxed and resumed his or her task we can get on with the photography.

Despite all that has been stated above, and written in other books, about the golden rules of focal length in portrait photography, very effective portraits can be seen in exhibitions and magazines taken with wide-angle lenses. These are not candid snapshots, but pictures taken with the full co-operation of the subject. Sometimes the perspective with the wide-angle can tell us more about a person than a more conventional shot. Good photographers know when to break the rules.

To return to the true LEICA "people pictures" that we started to discuss. For these one is concerned with catching the moment; capturing that fleeting instant on film that will tell a whole story. The right lens now is the one that enables you to do it. Wide-angle lenses let you be right in with the action, no bother with focusing, just pre-set the focus at a suitable distance and let the depth of field take care of the movement. With practice a wide-angle lens can even be used without raising the camera to the eye. Pictures can be taken close to people without their knowing the camera is being used at all, especially if it is a LEICA M. The faster the lens, the greater the opportunity for extending picture hunting to indoor or night-time locations, but beware of the reduced depth of field when the lens is wide open.

With a wide-angle lens the photographer is part of the group. He is part of the picture in the sense that his presence must influence the behaviour of his subjects. On the other hand when the photographer only wants to observe he must work from a distance and the moderately long focus lenses will take over. The 75mm, f/1.4 SUMMILUX-M or the 80mm, f/1.4 SUMMILUX-R are perfect because they extend the scope to the maximum degree in all lighting conditions.

The secret of success in this type of candid/reportage/travel photography is to be generous with film. The opportunity only occurs once and it will be pure luck if a single shot produces the picture you wanted. People's expressions are continually changing, they make innumerable small movements, particularly of the eyes and mouth. It is much better to get in as many shots as you can because then at least one is likely to yield the picture that records the moment you remember. A motor-winder is invaluable for this. You can hold the camera steadily to the eye, concentrate entirely on the subject, and either fire off half-a-dozen shots on automatic, or operate the release manually, knowing that you can push the release as fast or as slowly as you like and the camera is always ready. This technique works well too with children, but it is very important to remember that the camera must be down at their level if they are not to appear dwarfed.

We generally know what the attitudes of people in our own country will be when we attempt to photograph them. In foreign countries, especially those where cultural differences are much greater, there is a need to be much more circumspect when setting about photographing the population rather than the tourist sights. Reactions may be friendly, co-operative – too much so sometimes – hostile, or shy. Longer focal lengths, particularly the 180's, will then be more practicable. The 70-210mm zoom is very useful because it enables you to operate initially from a distance and then to move in closer once your presence has been accepted. With the motor-winder in place, observe the intended subject at one side of the viewfinder and release the shutter, then swing the camera to bring the subject into the centre of the viewfinder and let the winder do the rest. People feel uneasy if they may be the subject of a photograph, but will relax when they hear the shutter.

Success in this type of photography depends on the photographer having sympathy with his subjects, and respect for them. The camera poses a threat, particularly with a long lens. Although the whole nature of the game is to be able to grab the opportunities for pictures when they present themselves, it is also very important to know when *not* to take a picture.

Unobtrusive, full-frame, natural portraits can be obtained by using very long lenses, 250mm or longer, or by using an extender on a 135mm Or 180mm. However, the longer the lens the less mobile the camera can be, but such lenses enable it to be operated from a fixed position whilst interesting faces can be picked out without the subjects being aware of the camera at all.

Architecture, Buildings, Townscapes

In photographing buildings we are concerned with straight lines and right-angles, instead of curves and irregular shapes as with landscapes and people. The angles from which curved or irregularly shaped objects are photographed do not matter much, provided the result is a pleasing

If it is necessary to tilt the camera for an architectural subject, then tilt it boldly, even going in much closer to emphasize the tilt.

picture. When rectangular objects are photographed, however, the angle from which they are taken is of prime importance and affects the choice of lenses.

A rectangular object, such as the facade of a building, will only be recorded as a rectangle on film if it is absolutely parallel with the film plane. If it is not parallel its image will be trapezoid shaped. If we take a photograph looking along a street with a rectangular building facade along one side, its image will be in the form of a trapezium. It will not worry us because it will look natural and tells us that the part of the building at the narrow end of the trapezium is further away, in fact the phenomenon gives the picture its three dimensional depth.

If we then, instead of looking along the building, look up at it and take a photograph in the direction of our gaze, again it will come out as a trapezium, but this time with its narrow side at the top. This will give the impression that the building is leaning backwards. These different impressions are all in the brain and nothing to do with the lenses. We must be acutely aware in architectural photography of the effects of photographing buildings from an angle; sometimes it looks right and sometimes it looks wrong. Sometimes by tilting the camera up at a building a very effective picture results, sometimes it just looks like carelessness. Most of the problems in architectural photography arise when it would definitely be wrong to tilt the camera.

In architectural photography, whether inside or outside, we are generally forced to use wide-angle lenses. The more cramped the space in which we have to work in relation to the size of the building, the shorter the focal length lens we need. But the shorter the focal length the more exaggerated is the effect of any tilt. A tripod and spirit level are essential for keeping the camera absolutely level. If you have an R-camera with interchangeable screens, then fit the screen with grid lines [14306] which will make the job much easier. The wide-angle lens will produce images which give a sense of spaciousness that may not correspond with reality, and again the effect is greater the shorter the focal length. This is particularly noticeable in interiors. Everyone will have experienced the disappointment on walking into a small room which looked so spacious in the hotel brochure.

In a wide-angle shot of a building taken from the ground with the camera level the lower half of the picture will consist of unwanted foreground. With negative film the unwanted portion can be lost during enlargement, but with slides we have to try to arrange some interest in the foreground to complement the main subject. Unfortunately the wider the angle of the lens the more the foreground objects will dominate and reduce the building to a mere background. A higher viewpoint, as from an upper window in a nearby building, is rarely available and the only real solution is to use a shift lens, either the 35mm,

A shift lens is indispensible to the architectural photographer, or to the tourist with an interest in buildings. The verticals stay vertical and unwanted foreground, usually bare road, is removed. 35mm, f/4 PA-CURTAGON-R. *Rudolf Seck*

f/4 PA-CURTAGON-R or the 28mm, f/2.8 PC-SUPER-ANGULON-R. They offer lens movements similar to those found on a technical or view camera. With these lenses you set up the camera absolutely level on the tripod, and then raise the lens in its mount until the desired proportion of subject and foreground is on the focusing screen.

Their use is not confined to the prevention of converging verticals when photographing buildings from the ground. Sometimes the view from street level may be obstructed by parked cars or passers-by. A shift lens can then be used from a higher level, such as a roof or upper window of a building opposite. In this case the lens is shifted downwards to remove the excessive area of sky and get in the extreme lower levels of the building. Similarly the sideways movements of the lens enable one to "look round corners" and take pictures from one side if it is physically impossible to operate from a central position.

After all that has been said about avoiding camera tilt, there are situations where deliberate tilting is very effective. It can give drama to a building, especially a tall one. The intention to tilt must be obvious, and usually the more tilt the better.

Another way to avoid converging verticals is to take the picture with a long focus lens from further away, provided you can back off far enough and there is no haze. It helps if there is a slight rise in the ground so that the lens axis can be near the centre of the building. The perspective will be different to that achieved with a wide-angle lens.

If atmospheric conditions are right and there is no haze or shimmer, then a completely different approach to architectural photography is to employ a very long focus lens from a long way off. The ideal would be the 800mm Telyt-S, or one of the 280mm or 400mm Apo-Telyt-R lenses or 400mm or 560mm follow-focus lenses with an extender. High maximum aperture does not matter in architectural photography because the camera will be firmly supported on a rigid tripod. Such long-distance shots reveal buildings in a quite different manner from pictures taken from near by. Sometimes it is the only way to appreciate a tall building in its setting.

The other role for long focus lenses is to record details, windows, doorways, statues, cornices, etc., outside as well as inside. Tilt cannot be avoided, and indeed is likely to be very effective because we generally have to look up at such items and they have been designed to be seen from below. Hand-holding may be more convenient and a fast lens is then invaluable, provided there is sufficient depth of field.

Filters are useful in architectural photography. With black-and-white film a yellow or orange filter will make a white building stand out more against a blue sky, although the effect has been overdone in the past in extolling the virtues of concrete. A green filter will lighten foliage which might otherwise be too dark and take attention off the building, for instance if there is a tree in front of it. A polarizing filter will be useful with black-and-white or colour film to control reflections from windows or other bright surfaces (but not metal), and bring out the texture.

Finally, a specialized area of architectural work is the photography of models to give clients and others an idea of what a building will look like from street level. The extreme wide-angle lenses, from 21mm to 15mm, when used to photograph a model, will give the same sort of perspective to the model as the full-sized building when viewed from street level.

Animals

The same general principles regarding perspective when photographing people also apply to animals. Animals are essentially horizontal creatures, as opposed to vertical man, so they suffer even more from distortion caused by the injudicious choice of too short a focal length. Apart

The "follow-focus" lenses are ideal for wildlife, whether in a Leica sliding mount or a Novoflex mount. They are light in weight, allow rapid, accurate focusing and enable the photographer to follow fast moving subjects, even when they are going towards or away from the camera. In these circumstances they are best used on the shoulder stock. 560mm, f/6.8 Telyt-R. *Julius Behnke*

from that, animals, like children, make the most interesting and natural pictures when they are left to their own devices and are unaware of the camera. Longer focal lengths are therefore called for; for domestic pets such as dogs and cats this means 90mm or 135mm. Small animals are best photographed from their own level, so an adequate distance is needed in order not to attract their curiosity when you get down on the floor: the longer lens provides it. A 180mm is needed for studies of heads of dogs and cats and similarly sized creatures. Perhaps the best lens for animals which are playful and moving about is the 70-210mm VARIO-ELMAR-R. It can be kept focused on the highlights of the eyes and then zoomed to fill the frame with either a close-up of the head or of the whole animal. The slow speed does not matter because a large depth of field is needed and medium apertures will be used.

For animals in captivity in zoos or safari parks, bigger distances have to be bridged and a focal length of at least 135mm is needed for the larger animals. Something even longer, or an extender, is necessary for the smaller ones. If bars or mesh cannot be avoided in the foreground, they must be put right out of focus by using the widest possible aperture.

Capturing animals or birds in the wild on film is a most thrilling experience. They are normally shy, they might be dangerous. In any case very long focal lengths are necessary and in the LEICA R-system there are two perfect ones. Despite their length, the 400mm and 560mm, f/6.8 "follow-focus" TELYT-R lenses are light in weight and very handy. They have been designed to be hand held, with the aid of a shoulder stock, and fast moving subjects can be kept in focus whichever style of focusing mount is employed – the Novoflex mount or the LEICA sliding mount. The image of an animal on a slide should occupy at least a third of the format if it is to be other than a "Landscape with Animal". A useful tip is that a 35mm slide mount held at arm's length will approximately frame the field of view of a 560mm lens.

These two lenses will focus down to cover quite small object fields, enabling small creatures such as birds, squirrels, etc., to be photographed from 20ft (7m) or so. With the 60mm extension tube one can approach even smaller subjects. Small animals and reptiles will flee when they detect rapid movement, but they can often be approached really closely if one moves very slowly and evenly. One of the 100mm macro-lenses may then be used for revealing close-ups.

There is no doubt that the 400mm and 560mm "follow-focus" lenses are by far the best for following fast moving animals, particularly if they are going towards or away from the camera. The 280mm and 400mm APO-TELYT-R lenses can also be focused rapidly by their short-travel focusing rings, but they are too heavy and bulky for prolonged use under field conditions, but ideal when working from a fixed hide and in poor ambient light. Even with a 2x extender, the f/2.8 lenses still offer a maximum aperture of f/5.6. The two "conventional" 250mm and 350mm TELYT-R lenses have relatively short rotary focusing movements, but they cannot be operated as fast as the follow-focus lenses, however they are still quick for their class and offer bigger maximum apertures for poorer light levels. For the occasional wildlife photographer a 2x extender on a 180mm lens gives a useful focal length, but it requires a lot of work with the wrist to keep a fast moving subject in focus. The 500mm, f/8 MR-TELYT-R may not allow fast enough shutter speeds in shady conditions, but it is so handy and light in weight that these factors might govern the choice. Finally, the 800mm, f/6.3 Telyt-S, with the option of adding extenders, is the ideal instrument for operating over long distances, such as in game parks, but it can only be used from a fixed position.

For a photo-safari in Africa a very careful selection of lenses will have to be made and a compromise reached between what is practical and what is ideal. The two problems that will have to be faced are the weight and the security of the equipment – which points to a minimum outfit. It is difficult to give advice, but a minimum choice might be a 28mm or 35mm for general habitat shots, a 60mm MACRO-ELMARIT-R, a 180mm, f/4 ELMAR-R and a 2x EXTENDER-R. High maximum apertures will not be required. A more extensive outfit would also include a 400mm, f/6.8 TELYT-R.

For birds the very long focus lens is essential if anything near a frame-filling picture is to be obtained. The two follow-focus lenses are ideal. Their smallest object fields, attainable from reasonable distances (3.5m and 6.4m respectively), allow for working with care, without a hide, whenever the nature of the subject makes this possible. The 800mm, f/6.3 TELYT-S or a 400mm APO-TELYT-R with 2x APO-EXTENDER-R is more suitable when a fixed position, probably a hide, is being used when they can be rigidly mounted; they are then perfect for observing a nest. If such long lenses are not available for observing a nest, then shorter focal lengths must be employed with the camera released from a distance by means of the Remote Control-R unit. The photographer can be hidden further away and observe through binoculars.

Flocks of birds in flight are easier to photograph than individual birds and shorter focal lengths are suitable. The working distances will be greater so focusing will not be critical. Flocks of birds in flight often make interesting patterns.

The key to successful wildlife photography is to learn as much as possible beforehand about the habits of the creatures that might be encountered. Their behaviour can then be anticipated and precautions taken to avoid disturbing or frightening them.

Sport

In sports photography we are trying to convey action, drama and excitement. We need some general shots to set the scene, but generally we need to concentrate on the individual player, or a small group of players who are involved in the action at any one time. We need to record not only their movements in a manner which will convey vigour, but also their facial expressions which emphasize the drama.

Once it has started, the amateur photographer at a professional sports event very rarely has the opportunity to move about and select the most favourable positions. He usually has to buy his ticket for a particular seat and stay there, so he must choose his seat position carefully in advance with respect to the anticipated action, position of the sun, etc., and select the right lenses to take with him.

Sports can be classified photographically into a number of categories according to the demands they make on the equipment, so the choice can be narrowed down in advance. In field games, such as football, rugby, hockey, the action takes place in a fairly small area, but the centre of action moves rapidly and unpredictably over a very large area. We need to be able to focus rapidly and follow the ball or puck in the viewfinder, because it is nearly always the centre of action. For the LEICA M this must mean the 135mm, f/2.8 ELMARIT-M, not only because we need the wide aperture to get the fastest possible shutter speed, but also for its enlarged viewfinder image. For the LEICA R the 180mm, f/2.8 ELMARIT-R may be better than the 135mm lens because it covers a smaller area and will be more selective. A 90mm, f/2 SUMMICRON-M or -R will be useful for more general shots.

If you are in a position where the lens can be manipulated without incurring the wrath of your fellow spectators, a 400mm, f/6.8 TELYT-R will be the ideal lens for really concentrated shots, particularly of faces. The foreshortened perspective of the very long focal length enhances the drama by making the players appear very close together. The floodlighting that is common at sports stadiums these days renders the small maximum aperture less of a hindrance on dull days. For the professional and the really dedicated amateur the 280mm or 400mm APO-TELYT-R lenses are the supreme sports lenses. They can be rapidly focused and the apo-quality images they yield mean that the definition in enlargements from even small portions of a negative is limited only by the film. The 400mm, f/2.8 APO-TELYT-R even has a focusing stop whereby it can be pre-focused on the nearest goal, for example, and the focus can be instantly returned to that position whenever the action moves that way. In the type of games we are discussing here the photographer will need to be further away than when using the shorter lenses, but that is an advantage because the action will take place over a smaller angle relative to him, which makes it easier to follow.

In games such as cricket and baseball most of the action takes place round fixed points in the middle of a very large field. This allows us to set up a very long focus lens on a tripod, with or without an extender. Being summer games, the light is usually going to be adequate and the aperture penalty of an extender will not be relevant.

In races the participants move at a fairly uniform speed on a predictable course. Close-up, low-angle, head-on shots are the most effective and they usually have to be achieved with long focus lenses. The distance from which the photographer has to operate is usually determined by the speed of the racers, ranging from long-distance running at one extreme to motor racing at the other. The lens should be pre-focused on a suitable marker on the course, perhaps the finishing line. A motor winder enables the release to be pressed slightly early and for a number of frames to be secured so that the zone of sharp focus is safely bracketed. The alternative way of tackling a race is from the side by panning the camera. A motor winder is a great asset here. The choice of focal length will depend entirely on the distance of the camera from the track, but it is better to be further away and use the longer lens so that the panning angle is less.

With athletic field events, discus, high-jump, etc., and sports such as golf, the action is confined to one spot and the expression on the face is more telling than the action itself. For these we need close-ups with long focus lenses, and it is better to go further away and use a longer lens so that the subject can be isolated, with the background totally out of focus.

The wide-angle lens also has a role in sports photography if you can get close enough, and this is more likely at an amateur event. Wide-angle shots need to be taken from low down looking up so that the sky becomes the background. The wide-angle perspective can give very striking pictures from low down behind the goal, or beside the finishing line, or of field athletes, providing they agree to the camera being so close.

Nature

Having already dealt with animals and birds, we are concerned here with plants, flowers, trees, insects, and so on. The macro-lenses are perfect for much of this type of work; the 100mm macro-lenses in particular because they allow a greater working distance. Many of the subjects will be fairly small but for various reasons cannot be approached very closely. This may be because getting close would damage the habitat, or disturb a butterfly or a lizard, or make it difficult to arrange flash or reflectors. It may also be that the specimen is inaccessible without risking life and limb. It is surprising how often 100mm is sufficiently long to bring it in range. On the other hand, the 60mm macro-lens is a very good general purpose lens, particularly if you want to record habitat as well, or if nature photography is part of a wider interest in landscape. It can always be used with the 2x EXTENDER-R.

If a macro lens is not available, then a conventional medium-focus lens of 90mm or 135mm will be more useful than a standard focal length. If it is an R-lens, then an ELPRO close-up attachment can be carried for the nearer distances.

With a medium long focus lens with close-up facility, macro or otherwise, as the basic lens, a longer focal length, 180mm or more, should be added to the kit for bridging longer distances.

For larger objects, such as trees or shrubs, as well as habitats a standard or wide-angle lens can be used. A particularly effective way of showing a specimen in its habitat is to use a wide-angle lens from a fairly low angle and have the specimen close-up in the foreground. It will stand out as the centre of attention but its surroundings forming the background will also be in sharp focus.

In nature photography we generally demand sharp focus and great depth of field. This means stopping down with a consequently slow shutter speed. Although flash could be used to supplement daylight, an alternative approach can also be very effective with colour. Use a wide-aperture lens, wide open, and focus carefully on one plane to bring one or more features or individuals into prominence and at the same time suppress the confusion of detail in the foreground and background. With colour film the blurred surroundings can add an interesting pattern of colour to enhance the impact of the chosen subject. If the essential subject features are distributed at various distances from the camera the focus should be panned through the whole depth of the subject, assuming a reflex camera is being used, until the image on the screen exhibits the effect that is desired. For stalking insects the ideal lens is the 100mm, f/2.8 APO-MACRO-ELMARIT-R by reason of its long and continuous focusing range, and the greater working distance it allows, which is less likely to disturb the subject.

As with animals, the key to success in nature photography is to learn as much in advance about the intended subjects as possible.

Low-light situations

Not really a subject in itself because low-light situations can occur in any of the subject areas we have discussed so far. But low lighting levels, often coupled with high contrast, are characteristic of some fields of photography and in situations where flash is inappropriate, tripods for

Leica wide-aperture lenses are designed for use in available light and are meant to be used fully open. The 80mm, f/1.4 SUMMILUX-R at full aperture shows virtually no flare from bright lights in the picture area. *Rudolf Seck*

For recording life in towns and villages 35mm or shorter is best. 35mm, f/1.4 Summilux-M.
Dennis Laney

Above: This is an example of the right equipment being a handicap. In the Camargue region in the south of France we stopped to watch a flock of flamingoes wading in a lake about 400m away. A patient bird photographer was nearby, camera and long lens rigidly mounted on a tripod. Suddenly the flock took off and headed towards us. I got off four shots with the 135mm, f/4 Tele-Elmar-M while the unfortunate bird photographer was hastily dismounting his camera, by which time the flock had gone.

Below: The longer reach of the 100mm, f/2.8 Apo-Macro-Elmarit-R, compared with its 60mm counterpart, enables small creatures to be approached with less chance of their being frightened away, or biting back *Dennis Laney*

long exposures either cannot be used or are not allowed, or fast shutter speeds are essential. Every photographer will have his own list, depending on his interests, but here are some of those situations:

Theatre	Museums	Night life	Candid portraits
Ballet	Galleries	Cafés	Indoor sports
Circus	Indoor events	Cabaret	Travel
Opera	Ceremonies	Street life	People at work
Concerts	Inside churches	Reportage	Animals at night

These days very fast films with fine grain have made such subjects much more accessible, but they are really the realm of what Leica call the "light giants", the f/1.4 SUMMILUX-R and -M lenses and the f/1 NOCTILUX-M. These lenses produce an image quality that is aesthetically much more satisfying than a flash picture. The LEICA M will often be the camera of choice in these situations because of the rapid, crisp focusing with the rangefinder in dim light, and also because of its virtually silent shutter. These lenses are remarkably free of flare, despite their very large apertures. There is no point in buying them unless they are going to be used at full aperture most of the time. They make available-light work with a LEICA very rewarding. With subjects such as those listed above bright light sources in the picture area are unavoidable. This is no problem because the lenses are quite capable of handling the large contrast differences. They are virtually free of coma so the light sources will not be distorted.

In theatres and other places where the subject is at a distance the 75mm SUMMILUX-M or the 80mm SUMMILUX-R will be needed. Where there are brilliant spotlights picking out an actor or small group a 90mm, f/2 Summicron, or even a 135mm, f/2.8 Elmarit may give a fast enough shutter speed. With modern high speed films, black-and-white and colour, there is no need to worry so much about grain. Fast lenses with fast film will enable even dimly lit scenes to be captured.

The best perspective in a theatre is obtained from the front circle, rather than from the front stalls where the view is from below, here the 180mm, f/2.8 ELMARIT-R is the appropriate lens.

For photography at closer quarters a 50mm or 35mm SUMMILUX will be called for, depending on the circumstances. If it's to be snapshots with no time for focusing, then 35mm is best. A 50mm, f/1 NOCTILUX-M with a very fast film will secure a picture from what, to the eye, is getting close to total darkness. Candle-lit photography is within reach of a hand-held camera with this lens.

5. Choosing the Right Lenses

The Leica R- and Leica M-systems have separate, distinctive, but complementary roles in professional and advanced amateur photography. Leica provide a comprehensive choice of lenses for each system that will cover virtually all eventualities appropriate to 35mm photography. The Leica R-system offers the greatest range of applications and can be used with virtually any focal length lens. It requires less skill and experience to produce good pictures with standard lenses and moderately long focus and wide-angle lenses. The screen enables the user to compose the picture and study the changes in perspective and framing as the camera position is moved or lenses changed. But it is not ideal for everything, and its weaknesses lie in the very areas where the rangefinder camera has its strengths, which is why professionals use both.

The Leica M-system offers rapid, accurate focusing in the mid-range of focal lengths, from 21mm to 135mm, whereas the reflex cameras are more difficult to focus with short focal lengths. The M camera's rangefinder will give accurate, rapid focusing in lighting conditions which would be too dim for focusing on a reflex screen, even with the split-image and microprism aids. On the other hand, the photographer with a Leica M has to be able to see his flat, two-dimensional picture in his mind's eye; the viewfinder can only show a frame superimposed on the three-dimensional scene. The absence of a mirror means that the shutter operation of a Leica M is virtually silent, so it comes into its own for quick action, unobtrusive photography, especially in poor lighting conditions and with large apertures when precise focusing is vital.

The two lens systems have been discussed in general terms in Chapter 2. In the Lens Directory at the back of the book each lens is described in detail with a summary of its applications. At first sight there is a bewildering selection of lenses and there appear to be considerable overlaps. On closer study of the two systems, however, it will be seen that each lens will be best in its focal length group for particular applications. The fact that certain applications have been highlighted for particular lenses does not mean that they are unsuitable for other employment, but alternative lenses in the focal length group might be better. Very few of us can afford to own all the lenses that would be perfect for our own photographic interests; we have to compromise.

Generally the amateur photographer will want lenses which are as universal in application as possible. As he develops special interests he will want lenses which are best fitted to those particular interests, whether in terms of focal length or maximum aperture. As a general rule, the more extreme the focal length or aperture, the less universal a lens becomes. So don't be seduced by an ultra-fast lens if you are unlikely to use it very often at maximum aperture, and your real interests lie in landscapes and close-ups of flowers. On the other hand if you enjoy recording daily life about you, by night and day, it may be just what you need.

All lenses described in this book are in current production. Leica pursue a policy of continually improving their products. With lenses this has meant major recomputations from time to time to take advantage of new glasses, usually resulting in better performance and/or reduction in weight and complexity, or redesign of lens mounts for greater convenience in use, or minor cosmetic changes either for user convenience or better manufacturing methods.

For readers who want to know more about the technical aspects of their lenses there is a paragraph for each lens described in the Directory headed "Characteristics". This lists the special qualities of each lens, and also its limitations. Both of these will be a reflection of its optical design with regard to its intended use and its focal length and maximum aperture. In lens design, coma and contrast are difficult to correct at shorter focal lengths, whereas colour aberrations are difficult to correct at longer ones; flare is inherent in wide aperture lenses, barrel distortion is a problem in wide-angle lenses, and both barrel and pincushion distortion plague zoom designs. Hence when these problems have been overcome, or reduced to an unnoticeable minimum, the resulting lens is likely to be a remarkable achievement in its class. It is in this context that the lens descriptions in the Directory section should be read. Excellent colour correction in a long-focus lens, for example, is worth remarking on, but it is taken for granted in a 50mm lens from a quality manufacturer. So it is only the unique qualities in a lens which have been highlighted in the Directory; that is, those qualities that make certain Leica lenses the best of their class in the world.

Planning an outfit

One of the original intentions when planning the first edition of this book had been in include a chapter suggesting suitable lens outfits for particular purposes. However, the more I thought about it and wrestled with what would be the likely need of the landscape photographer, the traveller, the person interested in architecture, the sports and wildlife enthusiasts, the reporter of daily like, etc., the more difficult it became to be definitive. The choice of lenses is really a very personal one and to recommend specific outfits would be impertinent. The dedicated enthusiast for a particular subject will be able to select suitable lenses readily from the information given in the previous chapters, and in the Lens Directory. But don't most of us, even when we have one abiding interest, want to use our cameras for other purposes as well? Perhaps, for instance, to record the growing-up of the children. This means we have to make compromises and depart from the ideal specification for our particular interest. We may need to include just one really fast lens so that we can cope with available light situations, even though the lens will not be used at maximum aperture to the extent that it should, and it may have to serve as the general purpose lens at that focal length.

However, here are a few general principles that can be borne in mind when selecting the next lens, or planning an outfit:

* The more extreme the focal length of a lens the more limited will be its potential for general photography.

* When circumstances or pictorial requirements demand, there is no substitute for the optimum focal length: – extreme long-focus for bridging distance and extreme wide-angle for working in confined space.

* The heavier and/or bulkier the equipment the greater the temptation to leave it at home.

* Long focal lengths, longer than 180mm, are only likely to be carried when suitable subjects are anticipated. On the other hand, an extender can always be in the pocket.

* Ultra-fast lenses are wasted if they are not frequently used at maximum aperture. If this is not to be the case it is better to buy a lens with a more modest maximum aperture and put the money saved towards another lens.

* For critical subjects demanding the highest possible image quality a prime lens will give superior results compared with a zoom, but the differences will not normally be discernible in landscapes, portraits wildlife and similar subjects.

* On the other hand, a zoom lens will teach more about framing and being selective than a number of prime lenses. It will be lighter than a set of prime lenses covering the same focal length range, but slower. There is less chance of missing a subject if lenses do not have to be changed.

Spacing of focal lengths

Whatever our photographic interests may be, and whichever part of the focal length spectrum we work in – the mid-range, the long-focus range or the wide-angle range – we generally need an evenly spaced set of focal lengths. Few people are able to buy a complete set of lenses at one time, so it is better to plan a strategy in advance rather than buy the next lens on whim when the funds become available.

Just how big a gap can be tolerated between neighbouring focal lengths in an outfit will depend on the type of photography we do and the amount of freedom we have over the camera position. A combination of a 35mm and a 90mm lens has been recommended as a minimum basic, but versatile, outfit for travel, when weight and bulk need to be kept to a minimum. The ratio between these focal lengths is 1:2.6, so if we want frame-filling pictures we will have to walk back from the subject with the 90mm, or towards it with the 35mm in order to cover the shots that might have been taken more conveniently with a 50mm or a 60mm lens. Generally the distances involved will not be very great because the subjects, such as people or buildings, will be relatively close. If, on the other hand, we habitually work at long distances such a big gap between focal lengths would be too inconvenient. We might have to walk several hundred yards for the frame-filling shot, even with our focal length ratios as close as 1:2. For example; suppose we have with us a 180mm and a 350mm and see a subject 1000m away. We find that the 350 will not cover it but the 180 leaves a lot of empty space round it. The ideal lens would be a 250mm, but in its absence we either have to fit the 180mm and go forward about 500m, or go back a similar distance with the 350mm. If we had a 135mm and a 2x Extender-R in the bag, then that would also do equally well.

Other circumstances where more closely spaced focal lengths may be essential are when the camera position is fixed, but the subject distance varies considerably, for example at public events, sports, or with wildlife. Work in confined spaces, as with interiors or architecture, may also require a variety of wide-angle lenses fairly closely spaced in order to fill the frame with the wanted subject when you cannot move back far enough for one lens to suffice.

A good plan when building an outfit is to aim at a ratio of about 1:2 between successive focal lengths for the basic outfit, and then fill in the gaps afterwards where experience has shown additional focal lengths are desirable. The precise halfway point between two lenses where the focal length of the second is twice that of the first would be provided by a third lens with a focal length 1.4 times that of the first. (Strictly speaking, 1.4142 or $\sqrt{2}$). This is why the focal lengths of many pairs of Leica lenses are in the ratio of 1:1.4 to each other. In Table 3

	19	21	24	28	35	50	60	75	80	90	100	135	180	250	280	350	400	500	560	800
15	**1.3**	**1.4**	**1.6**	**1.9**	2.3	3.3														
19		1.1	**1.3**	**1.5**	**1.8**	2.6	3.2													
21			1.1	**1.3**	**1.7**	2.4	2.9	3.6												
24				1.2	**1.4**	2.1	2.5	X	3.3											
28					**1.3**	**1.8**	2.1	2.7	2.9	3.2										
35						**1.4**	**1.7**	2.1	2.3	2.6	2.9	3.9								
50							1.2	**1.5**	**1.6**	**1.8**	**2**	2.7	3.6							
60								X	**1.3**	**1.5**	**1.7**	2.3	3							
75									X	1.2	X	**1.8**	X							
80				M-system						1.1	**1.3**	**1.7**	2.3	3.1						
90				boundaries							1.1	**1.5**	**2**	2.8	3.1					
100												**1.4**	**1.8**	2.5	2.8	3.5				
135													**1.3**	**1.9**	2.1	2.6	3			
180														**1.4**	**1.6**	**1.9**	2.2	2.8	3.1	
250															1.1	**1.4**	**1.6**	**2**	2.2	3.2
280																**1.3**	**1.4**	**1.8**	**2**	2.9
350																	1.1	**1.4**	**1.6**	2.3
400																		**1.3**	**1.4**	**2**
500																			1.1	**1.6**
560																				**1.4**

Ratios shown are for focal lengths at the top over those at the side. Thus 19mm over 15mm is 1.3. Ratios in bold are of lens combinations near the ideal of 1:1.4.

Table 3. Ratios between near-neighbour focal lengths

the ratios between near-neighbour focal lengths in the current Leica R and M systems are shown. This table can be used when planning an outfit if you want regular spacing. Zoom lenses, within their limits, overcome the problem of spacing, and the extenders give other possible focal lengths in the Leica R-system from 100mm (2x50) upwards.

Angle of view

With focal length goes angle of view. The angle of view quoted for a Leica lens is the angle subtended at the lens by the circle embracing the subject area. The normal photographic image in the camera is a rectangle, not a circle, so the angle of view is the angle subtended by the diagonal of the rectangle, as shown in the diagram. The angle that concerns the photographer is somewhat less than this. Photographers need therefore to think in terms of the angles of view to the horizontal or vertical sides of this rectangle, not its diagonal.

Focal length and perspective

Focal length and maximum aperture are the two parameters which govern the degree of control a lens will give us over picture composition. The effects of focal length and aperture can be summed up in a few simple rules:-

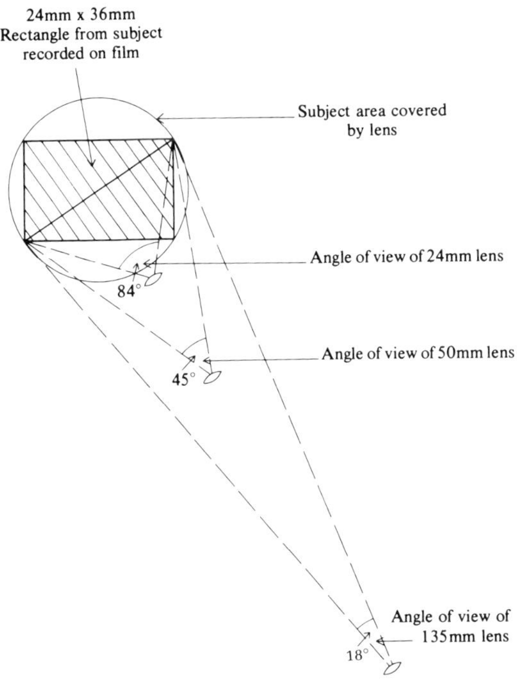

The angle of view as quoted for Leica lenses is that subtended by the diagonal of the frame.

* Wide-angle lenses exaggerate perspective. They emphasise the foreground at the expense of the background.
* Long focus lenses compress distance. They appear to foreshorten objects.
* Depth of field is greater with wide-angle lenses, and less with long-focus lenses, than it is with lenses of standard focal length.
* The smaller the aperture the greater will be the depth of field with any particular lens.

All of these statements are, to a degree, untrue! Nevertheless, they are very useful as general rules-of-thumb and in day-to-day photography they give adequate guidance. It is as well to know, though, what really controls perspective and depth of field.

The four pictures opposite page 112 sum up what is in the following three paragraphs.

Perspective is a function, not of the lens, but of the distance of the camera from the subject and the distance from which the resulting picture is viewed. If pictures of the same scene are all taken from the same spot with lenses of different focal lengths, the perspective will be identical in all the pictures. The difference between them will be the amount of the scene included in the pictures, and consequently the size of the images of the various components in the scene – trees, buildings, hills, people, etc. Individual components in the picture will be smaller with wide-angle lenses and bigger with long focus lenses than they would be with standard lenses. But they will all be the same relative size to each other.

Wide-angle lenses enable us to move in close to a subject and thus get a different perspective. This perspective tends to emphasise the foreground because we are much closer to it in relation to the background, which appears to be reduced in scale. The effect is greater the wider the angle of view; which is the same as saying the shorter the focal length. There is nothing inherently unnatural about the resulting pictures, provided we view them from the appropriate distance. This will be the distance from the print or projection screen at which the various components, tree, tower, etc., occupy the same angles at the eye as they did to the camera lens. In other words, for a picture taken with a wide-angle lens hold the print closer to the eye, or sit nearer the screen, to see the same perspective as with the 50mm lens. In the case of a 24mm lens, for example, these distances would have to be halved. In reality, of course, we view all pictures of the same overall size from the same distance. This is what enables us as photographers to select the perspective in our pictures creatively by using lenses of different focal length to give us a greater choice over camera position, knowing that our audience will view them all from the same distance.

Long focus lenses allow us to move further back to flatten the perspective and take the emphasis off the foreground. Distance becomes foreshortened, so that a train, for example, taken head-on appears to have been compressed and the carriages may appear no longer than they are tall. But if the picture is viewed from further away than a print of that size is normally seen, then a point can be found from where the train appears undistorted.

Depth of field

Depth of field is an illusion of the eye rather than a property of the lens. Strictly speaking a perfect lens has no depth of field, but because the human eye sees a circle below a certain size as a sharp point we see images which are slightly out of focus as being sharp. It is this tolerance of the human eye which is exploited in depth of field tables and depth of field scales on lenses. Again, like perspective, it depends on the picture being viewed from a normal distance.

The practical factors which govern depth of field for the photographer are:-

Depth of field increases as:

* Subject distance increases
* Focal length decreases
* Lens is stopped down

Depth of field decreases as:

* Subject distance decreases
* Focal length increases
* Lens aperture is opened up

Hence wide aperture lenses have an additional value besides their light gathering power. They can be used to isolate a subject from its background by restricting the depth of field. Similarly, long focus lenses can be used for the same purpose, in addition to their use in bridging distance.

6. LEICA Lenses in Practice

Filters

The range of filters carried in the LEICA catalogue is much smaller now than it used to be and is restricted to those in most common use. This is partly because modern black-and-white films are much better balanced for colour. Also specialist manufacturers, such as B+W and Hoya, produce filters of very high quality in great variety that Leica can safely recommend for use with their lenses. Unless a filter is of the highest possible optical grade it will degrade the performance of a lens, and screw-in mounts must also be of high quality in order not to damage the filter thread on the lens.

In certain photographic situations even the highest quality filters may cause problems. High contrast in the subject, as at sunset, bright scenes taken through an arch, shots at night with strong light sources in the picture area, etc., may cause reflections on the filter surface. Other effects may be double images, partial lightening by stray light, or general degradation of contrast. Another problem to watch out for is that built-in extensible lens hoods are less effective with filters because the filter projects in front of the lens and the effective length of the hood is reduced. Filters may also lead to inferior results with ultra-wide-angle

Some Leica long focus lenses have a slot at the bayonet end to take much smaller filters than would be necessary if they were mounted on the front. The 280mm, f/2.8 Apo-Telyt-R has recently been modified in this way and now has this special holder for Series filters.

lenses. The marginal light rays coming in from the side must travel a slightly longer path through the filter than rays from the centre of the subject. This can have an optical effect which degrades the picture quality. This is why most of these lenses now have a built-in filter turret at the bayonet end where the light beam is narrow.

Many of the long telephoto lenses have a filter slot at the bayonet end to take filters of a smaller size than would be necessary if they were fitted on the front. With some of the long APO-TELYT lenses the neutral-density (ND-1) filter provided must always be in place if no other filter is fitted because it is an integral part of the optical design. Apart from these examples it is best to avoid using filters with apo-lenses.

LEICA filter mounts are either screw-in and fit the filter thread of the lens, or they are of the "Series" type. Series filters are mounted in thin metal frames and are held in place on the lens by a separate screw-in filter ring or by the lens hood, or they fit into a filter slot in the barrel of the lens. See the Lens Directory for filter details of individual lenses.

Through-lens metering will generally look after the exposure increase required for all filters other than ND-1 and UV filters. For cameras without TTL-metering the filter factor given on the filter mount indicates by how much the exposure should be multiplied. The filter factor should not be taken as an absolute value. It depends on the colour sensitivity of the film and on the spectral content of the illumination. For critical pictures it is best to determine the right factor by test exposures: this is also a wise precaution with TTL-metering because some filters emphasize any slight differences there might be between the colour sensitivity of the meter and that of the particular film in the camera.

Filters for colour and black-and-white films

Ultra-violet – UVa. Modern LEICA lenses absorb u.v. light, so there is no need for a UVa filter in normal photography, except perhaps at very high altitudes. These days a UVa filter, because it is colourless and has a zero filter factor, is normally used to protect the front element of the lens. It is particularly important to protect the front element by the sea, where salt spray can be carried a long way inshore on the wind, or in dusty or sandy conditions with high winds. However, to get the absolute top performance from a lens omit the filter and rely on the lens cap for protection.

Skylight or haze filters should not be necessary with LEICA lenses because their colour rendering is neutral.

Polarizing filters are used to reduce or eliminate reflections. The full extinction of reflections is only possible at certain critical angles of the camera, about 37° to water, 33° to glass or 35° to polished wood. Pictures become possible taken through shop windows or museum showcases. The elimination of reflections when recording polished furniture enables the full beauty of the wood grain to be reproduced. Eliminations of reflections generally leads to higher contrast and better colour saturation, this can be of benefit in landscapes or other pictures involving foliage or grass. Polarizing filters can also dramatize the sky and clouds in landscapes because a high proportion of the light coming from a blue sky is polarized. A polarizing filter is the only means we have for darkening the sky in colour pictures. The higher the altitude the greater is the possible effect of a polarizing filter. The highest proportion of polarized light from the sky is radiated at right-angles to the direction of incidence of the sunlight, consequently when the sun is to one side a polarizing filter will have its greatest effect.

The only way reflections can be controlled from metallic surfaces is to polarize the illuminating light. This is easily done with artificial light by placing a polarizing filter in front of the light source.

LEICA R-cameras with TTL metering require circularly polarizing filters. This is because the light for the metering cell is reflected by a beam splitter which has the effect of polarizing the light and if a normal linearly polarizing filter were used it could lead to false exposure readings.

Neutral density – ND filters are grey in colour and are for the attenuation of the light entering the lens. They come in various densities indicated by the filter factor; ND-2, ND-4, etc. They are the only means for attenuating the light entering mirror lenses, such as the 500mm, f/8 MR-TELYT-R, which have no iris diaphragm. They are also used in circumstances where the exposure cannot be controlled by aperture and shutter speed alone. An example would be when a fast lens is used at maximum aperture to limit depth of field and even the fastest available shutter speed would give too long an exposure.

Colour filters for black-and-white film

These are used to enhance or suppress particular tones in black-and-white photography. They lighten their own colour and darken their complementary colour, but due regard must be paid to the colour sensitivity of the film.

Yellow-green is generally the most useful with modern films. It darkens blue skies against white clouds or buildings and improves the brilliance of landscape pictures with a lot of trees or grass by lightening greens. It can generally improve skin tones in artificial light. Filter factor 2.

Yellow is no longer as important as it once was. Its effect on skies is similar to that of yellow-green, but foliage is not lightened. It lightens skin tones and skin blemishes are slightly suppressed. A yellow filter is essential in snow scenes to enhance the contrast of the blue shadows if the picture is not to appear flat. A range of densities of yellow was offered at one time, but now the filter factor is generally 2.

Orange renders yellow and red tones very light, so it can be used to suppress skin blemishes and freckles. The main use for orange is to increase the drama in landscape subjects by rendering blue sky much darker so that white buildings stand out strongly and cloud formations look very dramatic. In distant landscape shots orange removes the bluish haze so that the view becomes much clearer and more brilliant. Filter factor 4-5.

Red has a similar effect to orange, but much stronger. It dramatizes the atmosphere in a landscape by exaggerating the contrast between cloud formations and the blue sky, which will be almost black. It is also used in architectural photography to show brilliant white buildings standing out against a very dark sky, and is even more effective than orange in penetrating haze in distant views. Very dark red is used with infra-red film to suppress most of the visible light. Filter factor around 8, depending on film, lighting, etc.

Blue is used in daylight or with flash to suppress the red sensitivity of panchromatic films. In medical photography it emphasizes blood vessels, scars or other red features. Is used in landscape pictures to preserve fog or mist.

Correction filters for colour film

These enable a colour film to be used in lighting conditions for which it was not formulated and give a reasonably faithful colour rendering. Blue is the most useful for using daylight film in tungsten lighting to remove the yellow cast. Conversion filters for using artificial light film in daylight are brownish in colour and they greatly reduce the film speed. A blue conversion filter is provided in those LEICA lenses with built-in filters.

Another type of colour correction filter is for correcting colour casts, such as that caused by the yellowish daylight which occurs near dawn and sunset. Correction filters are also available for use in fluorescent lighting which gives a greenish cast on daylight film. Considerable care is needed when using colour correction filters and to use them properly a colour temperature meter is required.

Close-up with Leica R-lenses

Close-up photography opens up a whole new world and greatly increases the scope of one's general photography, especially when it can be readily done hand-held. Very precise focusing is necessary because of the very shallow depth of field, but it can be done with practice. It is best to focus approximately with the focusing mount and then sway the body slightly to and fro until the subject jumps into focus.

For anyone intending to mix in close-ups with general photography it is best to invest in a macro-lens right from the start. The 60mm, f/2,8 MACRO-ELMARIT-R replaces the standard 50mm lens, but if a longer reach is needed for more difficult-to-approach subjects, such as wild flowers or small creatures, then the 100mm, f/2.8 APO-MACRO-ELMARIT-R or 100mm, f/4 MACRO-ELMAR-R would be the better choice, when it would replace a 90mm or 135mm. All these lenses can be used hand-held quite easily for reproductions down to 1:2 (1:3 with the 100mm, f/4). With a little more care and practice the two f/2.8 lenses can be used hand-held down to 1:1. For this you need the MACRO-ADAPTER-R in the case of the 60mm or the special ELPRO 1:2-1:1 attachment for the 100mm. The 100mm, f/4 MACRO-ELMAR goes to 1:1.6 with the MACRO-ADAPTER-R. All these macro-lenses, of course, are eminently suitable for careful, static work mounted on a tripod or repro stand.

Leica offer three different means of extending the focusing ranges of R-lenses. These are supplementary front lenses for shortening the focal length, two types of extension tubes to place between the camera and the lens to extend the focusing range, and a bellows unit for the same purpose. Extension devices permit closer focusing than supplementary lenses, but the latter are easy to use, and so is the Macro-Adapter-R from among the extension devices. The aperture of a lens as marked on the diaphragm ring applies only when the lens is focused at infinity. When the lens is extended forward to focus on nearer objects the aperture is effectively reduced. This is normally insignificant over the focusing range of the lens mount (except with macro-lenses), but in close focusing with extension devices the distance of the lens from the film plane becomes much greater and has a significant effect on exposure, which has to be increased. This is no problem with TTL-metering, provided one is aware of the fact. For example, a 50mm, f/2 lens has to be extended forward by 50mm to give a reproduction ratio of 1:1, so the distance from the lens to the film plane is 100mm instead of 50mm. This reduces the effective maximum aperture from f/2 to f/4. Supplementary lenses act by shortening the focal length, so there is no undue extension and hence no exposure penalty. On the other hand they do project forward, thus rendering built-in extensible lens hoods less effective.

ELPRO close-focusing attachments

These supplementary lenses are two-element coated achromats, specially computed to shorten the focal length of certain Leica R-lenses and improve their optical performance in the close-up range.

ELPRO attachments are two-element achromats and are the least expensive way of extending the focusing range of suitable lenses into the close-up region.

They are relatively inexpensive and take up little more room than a filter. They screw into the front of the lens and have an E55 female thread to take filters. Screwing two ELPRO attachments together to get even closer is not recommended because the overall performance of the camera lens will be degraded. Table 4 lists the four ELPRO's available and the lenses they match.

MACRO-ADAPTER-R

This is an extension ring with diaphragm linkages so that any lens with an automatic diaphragm will retain its fully automatic operation when attached to it. It can be used with any lens with an automatic pre-set diaphragm of 50mm focal length or longer, but the f/1.4 SUMMILUX lenses will not give satisfactory results because their optical design precludes the retention of image quality at such close distances. It is the ideal companion for the 60mm, f/2.8 MACRO-ELMARIT-R and the 100mm, f/4 MACRO-ELMAR-R (but *not* the 100mm APO-MACRO-ELMARIT-R). It extends

Lens	ELPRO Code No.	Distance scale at	Distance in cm Object to film	 Object to front lens	Object field in mm	Repro-duction scale
SUMMICRON-R f/2/50 mm from No. 2777651[1]) (E 55)	1 16541	∞ 0,5	50 31	41 21	184 x 276 91 x 137	1: 7.7 1: 3.8
	2 16542	∞ 0,5	30 24	21 14	94 x 141 62 x 93	1: 3.9 1: 2.6
SUMMICRON-R f/2/90 mm from No. 2770951[1]) (E 55)	3 16543	∞ 0.7	74 44	61 30	161 x 241 72 x 108	1: 6.7 1: 3.0
ELMARIT-R f/2.8/90 mm from No. 2809001[1]) (E 55)	3 16543	∞ 0.7	74 44	61 30	161 x 241 72 x 108	1: 6.7 1: 3.0
MACRO- ELMAR-R f/4/100 mm (E 55)	3 16543	∞ 0.6	75.5 41.6	61 24	145 x 218 48 x 72	1: 6 1: 2
	+ MACRO- ADAPTER-R 14256	∞ 0.6	42 37.4	24 17	49 x 73 29 x 44	1: 2 1: 1.2
	4 16544	∞ 0.6	150.5 48.6	136 31	323 x 484 61 x 92	1: 13 1: 2.5
	+ MACRO- ADAPTER-R 14256	∞ 0.6	48.8 40.4	31 20	63 x 94 34 x 51	1: 2.6 1: 1.4
APO-MACRO- ELMARIT-R f/2.8/100 mm	16545	∞ 1:2	35.4 30.5	16 10	49 x 73 22 x 33	1: 2 1.1: 1
ELMARIT-R f/2.8/135 mm from No. 2772619[1]) (E 55)	3 16543	∞ 1.5	76 58	61 42	107 x 160 66 x 99	1: 4.5 1: 2.8
	4 16544	∞ 1.5	150 84	135 68	237 x 355 106 x 159	1: 9.9 1: 4.4

Table 4. Reproduction scales available with ELPRO attachments on Leica R-lenses.

the focusing range of these two lenses down to 1:1 and 1:1.6 respectively without a break. With other R-lenses there is a break in the focusing range between the nearest focusing distance of the lens alone and the focusing distance with the Macro-Adapter and the lens set at infinity. The gap can be filled by using ELPRO attachments instead. ELPRO attachments can also be used in combination with the MACRO-ADAPTER-R to get even closer. Table 5 lists possible reproduction ratios.

1. 60mm lens at 20 paces

2. 60mm lens at 60 paces

3. 180mm lens at 20 paces

4. 180mm lens at 60 paces

Focal length, angle of view and perspective – these four shots of Brighton sum it up. Two lenses were used, with the focal length of one three times that of the other (60mm, f/2.8 MACRO-ELMARIT-R and 180mm, f/3.4 APO-TELYT-R). Two pictures were taken with each lens, the second one from three times as far as the first (20 paces and 60 paces). The distances were measured from the pavilion in the middle of the picture (it houses the lift to the beach below).

Pictures **1** and **3** exhibit the same perspective because they were both taken from the same distance. The image of the shelter on the right dwarfs that of the pavilion, although in reality the shelter is the smaller building. The 180mm lens used in **3** has simply recorded a smaller section of the scene than the 60mm lens in **1**, but everything appears to be closer because we are viewing both pictures from the same distance.

For pictures **2** and **4** the camera has been moved back three times as far, to 60 paces. In these two pictures the image of the shelter is much less significant in relation to that of the pavilion. The perspective in **4** is the same as that in **2**, but quite different from that in **1** and **3**. No difference is noticeable with the pier in the far distance, however, because it is nearly a mile away and an extra 40 paces is quite insignificant.

Note that the image of the pavilion in **4** is the same size as its image in **1**, because although the focal length of the lens by which it was photographed has been trebled, the distance of the camera from it has also been trebled and so it subtends the same angle at the lens. *Dennis Laney*

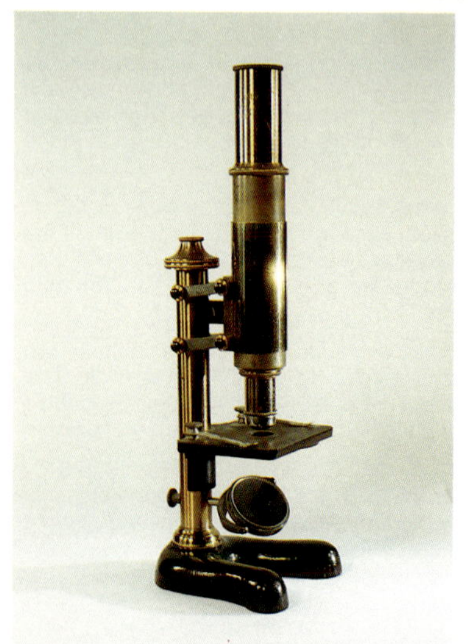

Use a macro lens to make a record of your collection or of valuables for insurance purposes. Jewellery is best photographed against a very dark background, such as black velvet. For larger objects, like clocks, porcelain, instruments, etc., a linen sheet or a large sheet of paper suspended in a curve makes a good, almost shadowless background. The bracelet was taken with a 100mm, f/2.8 APO-MACRO-ELMARIT-R, with the ELPRO 1:2-1:1 attached for 1:1 reproduction of the detail. A 60mm, f/2.8 MACRO-ELMARIT-R was used for the microscope. *Dennis Laney*

The Macro-Adapter-R is an extension tube with diaphragm linkages so that any lens with an automatic diaphragm will retain its fully automatic operation when attached to it.

Three Ring Combination

The inner ring with the male bayonet fits on the camera and the outer ring the lens. The two rings screw together to give an extension of 25mm. Insertion of the middle ring gives a further 25mm. Any number of middle rings may be used, but the risk of internal reflections, reducing

The Three-Ring Combination is more versatile, but less convenient than the Macro-Adapter-R and is more suited to specialized work.

Lens	Distance scale at (m or reproduction scale)	Distance Object to front lens in cm	Reproduction scale	Object field in mm
SUMMICRON-R f/2/50 mm	∞ 0,5	11.6 9.9	1: 1.75 1: 1.42	42 x 63 34 x 51
MACRO-ELMARIT-R f/2.8/60 mm	∞ 1:2	16 9.7	1: 2 1: 1	48 x 72 24 x 36
SUMMICRON-R f/2/90 mm ELMARIT-R f/2.8/90 mm	∞ 0.7	32 23	1: 3 1: 2	72 x 108 48 x 72
MACRO-ELMAR-R f/4/100 mm	∞ 0.6	42 25	1: 3.3 1: 1.6	80 x 120 39 x 59
ELMARIT-R f/2.8/135 mm	∞ 1.5	75 55	1: 4.5 1: 3	108 x 162 72 x 108
ELMARIT-R f/2.8/180 mm	∞ 1.8	124 78.4	1: 6 1: 3.4	144 x 216 82 x 123
APO-TELYT-R f/3.4/180 mm	∞ 2.5	133 95.6	1: 6 1: 3.9	144 x 216 95 x 142
TELYT-R f/4/250 mm	∞ 1.7	256 99.1	1: 8.4 1: 2.9	202 x 303 70 x 105
TELYT-R f/4.8/350 mm	∞ 3.0	477 178	1: 11.6 1: 4.1	278 x 417 97 x 146

Table 5. Reproduction scales available with the Macro-Adapter-R in combination with Leica R-lenses.

contrast, increases with increasing numbers of rings. Table 6 shows the reproduction ratios available with different lenses.

Focusing Bellows-R BR2

For the macro-photography specialist, and for scientific work, focusing bellows offer the most versatile means. These latest bellows from Leica are equipped with the necessary linkage to operate the automatic pre-set diaphragm of the lens, a convenience not available on the previous Universal Focusing Bellows-R. In combination with the special 100mm, f/4 Macro-Elmar-R lens-head the available scale ratio is from infinity to 1:1.1. With the 50mm, f/2 Summicron-R scale ratios range from 1:3.2 to 1:1. The unit, complete with camera and lens, can be used hand-held if it is mounted on the Universal Handgrip and Shoulder Stock, but is more likely to be rigidly supported on a tripod or the Reprovit-R copy stand. When so mounted, the whole unit can be racked back or forth in relation to the mount which greatly assists focusing and composition. Table 7 lists possible reproduction ratios.

The latest Focusing Bellows-R BR2 offer the most versatile close-up system, especially since they are equipped with the necessary linkages to operate operate automatic pre-set diaphragms.

Don't be afraid to use the focusing bellows hand-held (here the earlier Universal Focusing Bellows-R). The Universal Handgrip and Shoulder Stock is the essential extra component for a steady hold.

Lens	Distance scale at	Ring combination					
		2-part (height 25 mm) 14 158			3-part (height 50 mm) 14 159		
		Distance Object – front lens cm	Repro-duction scale	Object field mm	Distance Object to front lens cm	Repro-duction scale	Object field mm
SUMMICRON-R f/2/50 mm	∞ 0.5	13.5 11.2	1: 2.1 1: 1.6	50 x 75 38 x 58	8.1 7.5	1:1.04 1.09:1	25 x 37 22 x 33
SUMMICRON-R f/2/90 mm ELMARIT-R f/2.8/90 mm	∞ 0.7	37.6 25.2	1: 3.6 1: 2.2	86 x 130 53 x 79	21.4 17.6	1:1.8 1:1.4	43 x 65 34 x 50
ELMARIT-R f/2.8/135 mm	∞ 1.5	87.2 59.7	1: 5.4 1: 3.4	130 x 195 81 x 121	50.7 42.3	1:2.7 1:2.1	65 x 97 50 x 75
ELMARIT-R f/2.8/180 mm	∞ 1.8	146 84.9	1: 7.2 1: 3.8	172 x 258 91 x 137	81.2 61.3	1:3.6 1:2.5	86 x 129 60 x 90
APO-TELYT-R f/3.4/180 mm	∞ 2.5	154 104	1: 7.2 1: 4.4	172 x 258 106 x 159	89.4 74.0	1:3.6 1:2.7	86 x 129 66 x 99
TELYT-R f/4/250 mm	∞ 1.7	299 104	1:10.1 1: 3.2	242 x 363 76 x 114	172 85.8	1:5.0 1:2.3	121 x 181 55 x 82
TELYT-R f/4.8/350 mm	∞ 3.0	558 187	1:13.9 1: 4.4	334 x 501 105 x 157	316 153	1:7.0 1:3.2	167 x 250 76 x 114

Table 6. Reproduction scales avaiable with the Three Ring Combination and Leica R-lenses.

Photar lenses

Magnified reproduction is possible with Photar lenses and the Focusing Bellows-R BR2. These are computed for the extreme close-up range and three are available: 50mm, f/4; 25mm, f/2; 12.5mm, f/2.4. Magnifications on the film up to about 16x becomes possible, corresponding to an object

Lens	Reproduction scale	Distance Object to front lens cm	Object field mm
SUMMICRON-R f/2/50 mm	1: 1.2 - 2.9 : 1	9.1 - 4.5	29.6 x 44.4 to 8.4 x 12.5
MACRO-ELMARIT-R f/2.8/60 mm	1 : 1.5 - 2.8 : 1	12.5 - 5.7	35 x 53 to 8.5 x 12.8
SUMMICRON-R f/2/90 mm ELMARIT-R f/2.8/90 mm	1 : 2.1 - 1.8 : 1	24.5 - 10.4	51.1 x 76.6 to 13.7 x 20.6
MACRO-ELMAR® f/4/100 mm	∞ - 1 : 1	∞ - 18.7	∞ to 24.0 x 36.0
MACRO-ELMAR-R f/4/100 mm with helical focusing mount	1 : 2.4 - 1.7 : 1	32.6 - 14.7	57.1 x 85.7 to 14.2 x 21.3
ELMARIT-R f/2.8/135 mm	1 : 3.2 - 1.2 : 1	57.7 - 25.9	77.2 x 115.8 to 20.6 x 30.9
ELMARIT-R f/2.8/180 mm	1 : 4.3 - 1 : 1.09	93.5 - 36.3	102.7 x 154.0 to 26.2 x 39.4
APO-TELYT-R f/3.4/180 mm	1 : 4.3 - 1 : 1.14	101.8 - 45.3	102.7 x 154.0 to 27.4 x 41.1
TELYT-R f/4/250 mm	1 : 6 - 1 : 1.1	195.9 - 62.2	144.0 - 216.0 to 27.4 x 41.1
TELYT-R f/4.8/350 mm	1 : 8.3 - 1 : 1.6	362.0 - 107.0	199.0 x 298.0 to 38.0 x 57.0

Table 7. Possible reproduction scales with LEICA R-lenses on the Focusing Bellows.

Photar lenses, mounted on the focusing bellows, extend the reproduction scale beyond 1:1 into the realm of magnification up to 15.5:1.

Lens	Code No.	short bellows extension		long bellows extension	
		repr. scale	free working distance	repr. scale	free working distance
PHOTAR 1:2.4/12.5 mm	549025	7.5:1	8 mm	15.5:1	7 mm
PHOTAR 1:2 /25 mm	549026	3:1	22 mm	7:1	17 mm
PHOTAR 1:4 /50 mm	549027	1.2:1	88 mm	3.2:1	59 mm
All values rounded off. The free working distance is the distance between the object and the lens mount.					

Table 8. Magnification ratios available with Photar lenses mounted on the Focusing Bellows.

size of 1.5x2.3mm. Considerable skill is needed in working at such close distances, not least that being concerned with the problem of lighting. Adapter [14259] is needed to mount PHOTAR lenses on the bellows. Achievable reproduction ratios are given in Table 8.

The right focusing screen for the lens

For those LEICA R-cameras which accept interchangeable focusing screens (R4 and later) it is of benefit to select the best screen for the particular lens in use. The Universal screen [14303] is the best general purpose screen when no other is available. However, it is not easy to use in poor light and one half of the split-image aid may black out when the lens is stopped down or the effective aperture with extension tubes or bellows is f/5.6 or smaller. The 2mm wide microprism collar is better for focusing wide-angle lenses, or for subjects without strong vertical lines, or in low-light conditions for lenses up to medium focal lengths. The surrounding matt screen should be used for focusing long focal lengths.

For wide-angle lenses the Microprism screen [14305], similar to the Universal screen but without the split-image aid, is better. The central microprism disc gives good differentiation between sharp and unsharp zones, even with slow telephoto lenses. Use the Universal Ground-glass screen [14304] for focusing lenses of 350mm and longer and also for extreme close-up work. Some photographers also prefer it for very fast lenses. The Ground-glass screen with grid divisions [14306], designed for architectural and similar work requiring precise alignment, will be a useful adjunct to the shift lenses.

Care of lenses

The exposed front and rear elements of a lens should always be protected by the front and back caps when not in use. The lens-hood helps to protect the front element from rain or spray and accidental knocks, and is worth keeping in place for this purpose, even if the lighting conditions do not demand a hood. The back cap on LEICA R-lenses also protects the cams and diaphragm operating levers; these are recessed in Leica lenses, which makes them less vulnerable to damage, but one must still be aware of their presence and take appropriate care.

If it is necessary to clean a lens it must be done very carefully. First remove loose dust with a blower (a rubber bulb with a soft rubber nozzle is best) or with a soft camel-hair brush. Then remove any grease or finger prints with a clean, well washed cotton cloth, such as a good quality handkerchief, after first breathing on the lens surface. Water and rain-drops should be wiped off as soon as possible with a cloth. Only use the cloth once, and then wash it again. Never use spectacle-lens cleaning tissues because they are often impregnated with chemicals that, although harmless to spectacle lenses, can damage the optical glass used in camera lenses.

A small scratch on a lens surface will not affect its performance to a perceptible extent, but if the surface is more severely damaged the lens should be returned to the factory for repolishing. Never attempt to take a lens apart yourself. Not only are special tools used in the factory, many of them of wood to avoid damage to glass components, but lens assembly is a highly skilled job requiring the use of a precision optical bench for alignment.

LEICA Lens Directory

This directory section describing every current Leica R- and Leica M-lens has been laid out for easy reference, to assist readers in the selection of a new lens, to allow comparison of one lens with another, and to give guidance on the capabilities of each lens.

Under "Applications" are listed the types of photography and subject for which a lens is best suited. Experienced and creative photographers will not be limited by this and will find many more uses.

Under "Characteristics" will be found comments on the optical strengths of the lens, bearing in mind its type, focal length and maximum aperture. The strengths will reflect the designer's intentions. However, the designer in striving for the best possible performance in one type of use, say in poor lighting conditions, has had to make decisions on what optical characteristics are the most important for the purposes for which the lens is intended. This means that other aspects of its performance may have to be compromised. In these cases the types of photography for which a particular lens might be less than suitable are also given. Particular strengths have been emphasized when they are exceptional for that type of lens. Thus excellent colour correction is remarkable in a very long focus lens, but it is to be expected in a 50mm lens from any good maker.

It is inevitable that with several new products coming out in a year, a directory such as this will appear to be out of date within a short time. But this is not strictly true. New lenses from Leica have varying degrees of novelty. Occasionally a completely new lens is added to the range which has had no antecedents at all, such as the 400mm, f/2.8 Apo-Telyt-R. More usually an existing lens is redesigned optically, so the comments on applications remain valid, and its listed strengths are improved. On other occasions the optical design remains unchanged but the mount is redesigned, usually to make handling more convenient, by replacing a separate lens hood by a built-in retractable one, for example. In such cases all comments in the Directory remain valid, but there might have been a change in filter size and other dimensions.

Note: Cams 1 and 2 for coupling to the metering of Leicaflex, and in some cases Leicaflex SL and SL2 cameras, are no longer fitted to the more common new lenses, or redesigned older ones. Leica Service Centres can fit the necessary cams in some cases. There are plenty of older versions of these lenses with the additional cams on the second-hand market.

15mm, f/3.5 SUPER-ELMAR-R

Applications

This is the most extreme of the wide-angle lenses. It is not a fisheye; it yields a normal rectilinear image. It can be used for landscapes, townscapes, architectural work, and really close-in candid portraiture. Unusual effects can be obtained by exploiting the opportunity it affords for exaggerated close-up perspective. For these reasons it is much used in advertising. On the other hand, very realistic perspective shots of architectural and other models can be obtained to give an impression of the full-sized building or other object. It finds many other specialist and technical applications, such as the recording of instrument panels in confined spaces, like aircraft cockpits. For LEICA R and LEICAFLEX SL2 cameras only.

Characteristics

For a lens of this type the correction of optical errors is very good, with only minimal fall-off in illumination towards the corners, provided it is

Construction: 13 elements in 12 groups, floating elements	Diaphragm: automatic, pre-set
Lens hood: see above	Angle of view: 110°
Filters: built-in	Smallest aperture: f/22
Weight: 910g	Closest focusing distance: 16cm, 6.3in.
Length: 92.5mm	Smallest object area: 70 x 106mm, 2.8 x 4.1in.

15mm, f/3.5 SUPER-ELMAR-R *(continued)*

stopped down slightly. It maintains its high resolution at close range. A filter turret is built-in which houses UVa, yellow and orange filters, as well as a blue correction filter for using daylight film in tungsten lighting. The UVa should be selected for normal photography. A vestigial lens hood protects the front element; a properly sized hood would be too big and impracticable. With strong side lighting or back lighting the lens should be shaded, taking care not to intrude on the very wide angle of view. With this lens it is better to keep the shutter speed on the high side to avoid camera shake.

16mm, f/2.8 FISHEYE-ELMARIT-R

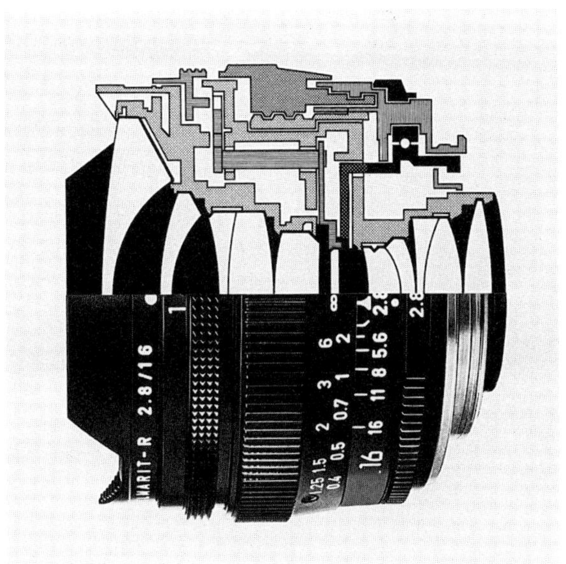

Applications

This lens fills the complete frame, it is not the type of fisheye which produces a circular image within the 24x36mm format. It is the only possible lens for technical applications where the 180° coverage is the overriding consideration. It is an exciting lens for creative pictorial photography, for panoramas and for exploring familiar objects and places and presenting them in an unfamiliar way. Straight lines passing through the lens axis, the horizon for example, are reproduced straight and pictures may be composed by careful selection of subject and camera position which do not betray that they were taken with a fisheye. Such pictures have powerful emphasis on the foreground and tremendous depth of field. A fisheye lens requires more skill on the part of the photographer than any other lens if attractive and lasting pictures are to be produced rather than gimmicks. For LEICA R and

Construction: 11 elements in 8 groups
Lens hood: see above
Filters: built-in
Weight: 470g
Length: 60mm
Angle of view: 180°

Smallest aperture: f/16
Diaphragm: automatic, pre-set
Closest focusing distance: 30cm, 12in
Smallest object area: 401 x 601mm, 15.8 x 23.8in

Extreme Wide-angle Group

16mm, f/2.8 FISHEYE-ELMARIT-R *(continued)*

LEICAFLEX SL2 cameras only, preferably with aperture priority or manual mode (see below).

Characteristics

The lens has good contrast and definition, with no vignetting. It fills the frame in the fisheye manner, in that straight lines in the image become progressively more curved the further they are from the lens axis. Depth of field at 2m (6.5ft) at f/2.8 stretches from 1m to infinity; stopping down increases this considerably. A built-in filter turret has UVa, yellow and orange filters, together with a blue tungsten-light correction filter. Vestigial lens hood to protect front element: lens should be shaded whenever the light is from anywhere other than from behind the photographer. Viewfinder symbols for shutter priority and program modes in LEICA R cameras may continue to flash even when lens is set to smallest aperture.

19mm, f/2.8 ELMARIT-R

Optical redesign 1991

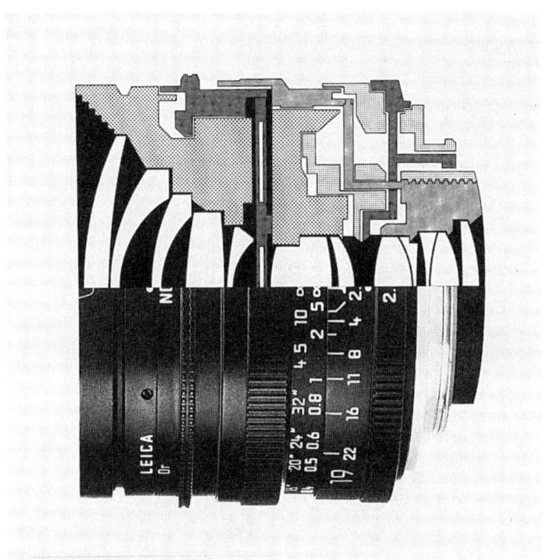

Applications

Now much more compact than its 19mm predecessor with the same aperture, this lens is even better for snapshots and photo-journalism than before. Its other applications are very similar to those of the 21mm SUPER-ANGULON-R on the next page, ie, all work in limited space, interior and exterior architectural photography and as a creative tool for landscape, advertising and industrial photography, but it offers a slightly wider angle of view and twice the speed. The very great depth of field when stopped down and preservation of the optical performance at close range can be used to produce striking perspective effects with close-ups of small models, etc. For LEICA R and LEICAFLEX SL2 cameras only.

Construction: 12 elements in 10 groups

Lens hood: Rectangular [12546] supplied with lens,together with cap [14302] which fits over hood.Filters: built-in

Weight: 500g

Length: 60mm

Diaphragm: automatic, pre-set

Angle of view: 96°

Smallest aperture: f/22

Closest focusing distance: 30cm, 12in

Smallest object area: 264 x 396mm, 10.4 x 15.6in

Extreme Wide-Angle Group

19mm, f/2.8 ELMARIT-R *(continued)*

Characteristics

Internal focusing by rear group only and 17mm slimmer than previous 19mm ELMARIT. Greatly improved contrast and flatness of field due to new design. Slight loss of definition at extreme corners at full aperture improved by stopping down. Vignetting only apparent when a uniformly bright area, such as a wall or the sky, is slightly underexposed. Because only the rear group of elements move during focusing the overall length of the lens remains constant. Thanks to the internal focusing the optical performance is preserved right to the close-up range. Filter turret built-in, with yellow/green, orange, KB12 for colour film in artificial light, and neutral density NDx1 which remains in the light path if none of the others is selected. A red ring on the lens mount warns if a filter is not fitted exactly in the light path.

21mm, f/4 SUPER-ANGULON-R

Applications

The lightest-weight, extreme-wide-angle lens, and therefore convenient when travelling. It give dramatic pictorial effects with monumental foregrounds, strongly receding backgrounds and wide horizons. It is suitable for landscapes, architecture, interiors, and specialized uses such as the photography of architect's models for assessment of townscapes, stage sets, etc. The perspective of such models taken from the minimum focusing distance of 20cm corresponds to the normal human view when looking at life-sized buildings, etc. For LEICA R and LEICAFLEX SL and SL2 cameras.

Characteristics

Focuses closer than the 19mm ELMARIT. It has excellent sharpness when stopped down to f/8 and good illumination of the entire picture area. It yields excellent close-ups down to 20cm (8in) with low distortion in the corners when well stopped down. Polarizing filters are difficult to use with these extremely short focal lengths because the light passes through the lens at such an oblique angle that the properties of the filter are negated to some extent. Bayonet fitting for lens hood, which should always be left in position because of the prominent front element.

Construction: 10 elements in 8 groups	Diaphragm: automatic, pre-set
Lens hood: [12506] supplied with lens	Angle of view: 92°
Filters: Series 8.5	Smallest aperture: f/22
Weight: 410g	Closest focusing distance: 20cm, 8in
Length: 43.5mm	Smallest object area: 148 x 221mm, 6 x 8.8in

Extreme Wide-Angle Group

24mm, f/2.8 ELMARIT-R

Applications

The most versatile ultra-wide-angle lens. Its compactness makes it suitable for travel and it is very popular with photo-journalists. It is excellent for pictures in confined spaces, as in architecture and snapshots. One can obtain pictures with interesting perspective without its being obvious that an ultra-wide-angle lens was used. A useful lens to combine with a 35mm and a 90mm for a minimum outfit. For LEICA R and LEICAFLEX SL2 cameras only.

Characteristics

Yields excellent image quality over the entire focusing range. It exhibits low vignetting for such a combination of wide angle and high aperture. Optical performance is also excellent at full aperture. Flatness of field and contrast rendering are very good over the entire focusing range, which gives it a good close-up performance too. The back focus distance is less than with most other lenses, which makes it unsuitable for earlier LEICAFLEX cameras. Bayonet fitting for lens hood.

Construction: 9 elements in 7 groups, floating elements	Diaphragm: automatic, pre-set
Lens hood: [12523] supplied with lens	Angle of view: 84°
Filters: Series 8	Smallest aperture: f/22
Weight: 420g	Closest focusing distance: 30cm, 12in
Length: 48.5mm	Smallest object area: 250 x 374mm, 9.9 x 14.8in

28mm, f/2.8 ELMARIT-R

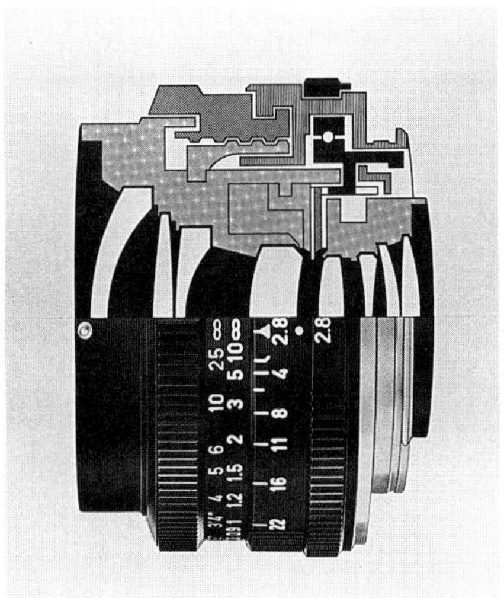

Applications

This is the lightest-weight moderate wide-angle lens for LEICA R cameras. It is the lens of choice when an extreme wide-angle is not required but 35mm does not give sufficient coverage. It is very useful for wide-angle pictures of architecture, townscapes, landscapes, groups, etc., when space is limited and a normal well-balanced perspective without undue exaggeration is wanted. It is also excellent for snapshots in reasonable available light and for shots with bright light sources in the image field. It is the ideal, general purpose, wide-angle lens; partner it with a 50mm SUMMICRON and a 90mm ELMARIT to make a very versatile and light-weight travelling outfit. The angle of view of a 28mm lens is usually the widest that can be covered by modern flashguns. For LEICA R cameras only.

Characteristics

Exceptionally light-weight and compact. From 1.5m (5ft) to infinity it is distinguished by its high contrast and good rendering of detail, virtual

Construction: 8 elements, none cemented	Diaphragm: automatic, pre-set
Lens hood: [12509] supplied with lens	Angle of view: 76°
Filters: Series 7	Smallest aperture: f/22
Weight: 275g	Closest focusing distance: 30cm, 12in
Length: 40mm	Smallest object area: 188 x 282mm, 7.4 x 11.1in

28mm, f/2.8 ELMARIT-R *(continued)*

freedom from flare and from vignetting and may be confidently used at full aperture on average subjects (people, landscape, etc.). However, the lens gives its best performance in this range when stopped down to f/5.6 or f/8. For subjects nearer than about 1m (40in) it should be stopped down further to f/8 or even f/11 if maximum sharpness right into the corners is needed. The lens hood is fitted with a knob which engages with the edge of a polarizing filter thus enabling the filter to be rotated whilst observing the effect in the viewfinder. Bayonet fitting for lens hood.

28mm, f/2.8 PC-SUPER-ANGULON-R

New lens 1988

Applications

A specialist lens primarily intended for architectural and product photography. It enables views to be taken with the camera remaining parallel to the plane of the subject that would normally require the camera to be tilted to encompass the subject. The most obvious use is in avoiding converging verticals that would occur by tilting the camera upwards to get in a tall building, or in shooting products or packaging from above. Such applications require use of a tripod, but interesting pictorial effects can be achieved with shift lenses hand-held: sideways shift gives an ability to "look round corners", and an up or down shift gives the impression that the camera position was higher or lower than it actually was. A downward shift in land-

Construction: 12 elements in 10 groups, floating elements

Lens hood: [12540] screw-in, supplied with lens

Filters: 67 EW, held in lens hood

Weight: 565g

Length: 84mm

Diaphragm: preselector

Angle of view: 73°(93° max)

Smallest aperture: f/22

Closest focusing distance: 30cm, 12in

Smallest object area: 219 x 146mm, 10 x 5.8in

28mm, f/2.8 PC-SUPER-ANGULON-R *(continued)*

scape photography will emphasize the wide-angle perspective even more by putting even stronger emphasis on the foreground. Panoramic view (see Chapter 2) of 93°. See also applications for 35mm, f/4 PA-CURTAGON-R. For LEICA R (aperture priority and manual modes only) and LEICAFLEX SL and SL2 cameras.

Characteristics

Usable circle of sharp definition is 62mm, enabling a shift of 11mm in the horizontal and vertical directions and 9.5mm diagonally. Optical system shifted in dovetail guide by micrometer drive with mm scale. Click-stops at zero and 9.5 positions. Assembly can be rotated up to 45° to the left and 90° to the right (click-stops at 45° and 90°) enabling shift to be in any direction. Flat image field and good sharpness in zero position at full aperture, contrast improved by stopping down to f/4 or f/5.6. When system is shifted, it is necessary to stop down further for best image quality – to f/11 at 11mm shift. Very slight barrel distortion increases a little on displacement. Vignetting at full aperture, noticeable on uniformly lit plain subjects improves on stopping down.

The dove-tailed slide assembly, with micrometer screw, rotates about the knurled ring adjacent to the bayonet, thus allowing shift in any direction.

35mm, f/1.4 SUMMILUX-R

Applications

The ultra-fast wide-angle lens for available-light photography. This is the perfect snapshot lens for snatching a picture in the most adverse conditions. It is ideal for reportage, photo-journalism, indoor events, etc., especially as it is very good in high-contrast situations, as in artificially-lit scenes and when shooting against the light, when many rival fast wide-angle lenses show too much flare. Although of high speed, the lens is also perfectly suitable as a general 35mm lens, except for the most critical work when the 35mm, f/2 Summicron or the 35mm, f/2.8 Elmarit would be better. For Leica-R and Leicaflex SL2 cameras only.

Characteristics

Distortion has been reduced to a very low value. Even in the near range, when stopped down to f/5.6 subjects are sharp right into the edges of the frame. For very close-up shots requiring an extension it is better to change to a more suitable lens, such as the 35mm Elmarit. Light sources in the picture area do not produce flare, and coma has been virtually eliminated. The lens has been corrected for maximum contrast for low lighting levels, which means that there is some cost in resolution. Resolution, and contrast, improve on stopping down. A circular polarizing filter is not recommended because of vignetting, characteristic of fast, wide-angle lenses, which can be improved on stopping down.

Construction: 10 elements in 9 groups, floating elements

Lens hood: built-in, extensible

Filters: E67

Weight: 660g

Length: 76mm

Diaphragm: automatic, pre-set

Angle of view: 64°

Smallest aperture: f/16

Closest focusing distance: 50cm, 20in

Smallest object area: 266 x 399mm, 10.4 x 15.7in

Wide-Angle Group

35mm, f/2 SUMMICRON-R

Applications

The wide-angle equivalent of the 50mm, f/2 SUMMICRON-R and having all its qualities. It is used for general wide-angle applications such as landscape, architecture, interiors, etc., and is also ideal as a snapshot lens, especially in available light. Typical wide-angle perspective is not very apparent at 35mm and the lens is preferred by many photographers as their standard lens, particularly if they do a lot of work in confined spaces, as in city streets. Combined with the 90mm, f/2 SUMMICRON-R it makes a good versatile basic outfit, omitting a standard lens, with more scope for available-light work than a similar outfit based on ELMARITS. For all LEICA-R and LEICAFLEX models.

Characteristics

The overall correction has been designed for the focusing range from infinity to 1.4m (56in) because high-speed wide-angle lenses are often used for snapshots in poor lighting conditions. Definition is excellent; even at full aperture the lens gives a good contrasty image. Stopping down enhances image quality further over the entire picture area through increased definition and low field curvature. Performance is still good in the near-focusing range. Gives very good colour saturation in poor weather and other bad lighting conditions.

Construction: 6 elements, none cemented	Angle of view: 64°
Lens hood: built-in, extensible	Smallest aperture: f/16
Filters: E55	Closest focusing distance: 30cm, 12in
Weight: 422g	Smallest object area: 140 x 210mm, 5.5 x 8.3in
Length: 54mm	
Diaphragm: automatic, pre-set	

35mm, f/2.8 ELMARIT-R

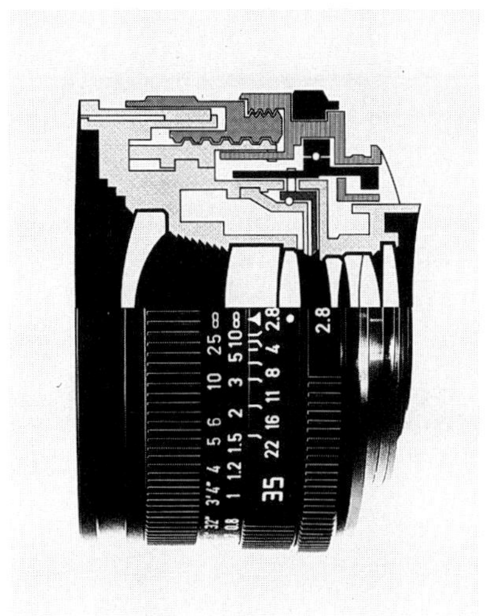

Applications

Good for travel because of its light weight and compact design, it is ideal to pair with the 90mm, f/2.8 ELMARIT-R to form a compact, reasonably priced basic outfit, omitting a standard lens. It is suitable for all moderately wide-angle work where large apertures are not needed, such as architecture or interior views when stopping down is necessary to get an adequate depth of field. It can also be used for unobtrusive candid snapshots with the camera at waist level when lighting levels are adequate. For LEICA-R cameras only.

Characteristics

High contrast, excellent resolution and good flatness of field at full aperture. Slight improvement on stopping down, with optimum performance reached at f/5.6. For exacting work below 1.5m stop down further. Below 1m (40in) the performance characteristics change a little and the lens should be stopped down to f/8 or f/11 if maximum sharpness extending right into the corners is required.

Construction: 7 elements in 6 groups
Lens hood: built-in, extensible
Filters: E55
Weight: 340g
Length: 41.5mm
Diaphragm: automatic, pre-set

Angle of view: 64°
Smallest aperture: f/22
Closest focusing distance: 30cm, 12in
Smallest object area: 140 x 210mm, 5.2 x 8.5in

35mm, f/4 PA-CURTAGON-R

Applications

Primarily intended for architectural and landscape photography in order to avoid having to tilt the camera to get in all the subject, which would result in converging verticals, or to avoid large areas of foreground which are irrelevant to the picture. It is also used to photograph architectural details, paintings, etc., which are above eye level or to "look round the corner" to avoid obstacles such as pillars or trees. It can be used to vary the perspective of subjects relative to the background, as in advertising, catalogue or industrial photography. It is also suitable in the close-up range, e.g. to photograph technical models and retain the natural perspective. Creative effects, particularly in colour photography, can be obtained by moving the lens, via the shift control, during a long exposure. For LEICA R models (aperture priority or manual mode) and LEICAFLEX SL or SL2.

Construction: 7 elements in 6 groups	Diaphragm: manual
Lens hood: [12514] supplied with lens	Angle of view: 64° (78° max)
Filters: Series 8	Smallest aperture: f/22
Weight: 290g	Closest focusing distance: 30cm, 12in
Length: 51mm	Smallest object area: 140 x 210mm, 5.5 x 8.3in

35mm, f/4 PA-CURTAGON-R *(continued)*

Characteristics

Perspective adjustment (PA) lens manufactured by Schneider to a LEICA specification. Up to 7mm of shift is available in any direction. Image circle diameter is 57mm compared with 43mm of the standard 35mm format. Exposure has to be determined at working aperture because an automatic diaphragm cannot be incorporated in this type of lens. When possible use screen [14306] because the grid lines assist in alignment. When set at maximum shift it should be stopped down to f/8 or f/11, but in any case a medium aperture should be used to minimise vignetting which is unavoidable in such a system. Panoramic view (see Chapter 2) of 78°. Very light weight for a shift lens. Bayonet fitting for lens hood.

The shift on the PA-CURTAGON is operated by turning the ring with the numbered scale adjacent to the bayonet.

Standard Focal-Length Group

50mm, f/1.4 SUMMILUX-R

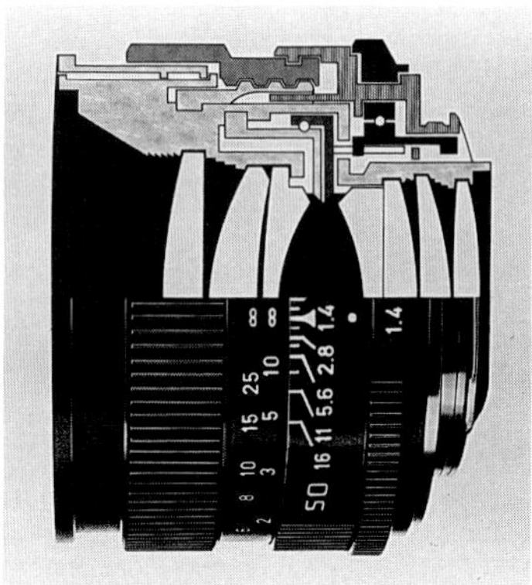

Applications

The fastest standard lens for the R-system. It is ideal for reportage, sport, photo-journalism, candid photography at close quarters in available light, and for all hand-held work in poor light, e.g: in museums, galleries, theatres, etc., especially when slow colour film is being used. It can be used for creative effects by exploiting the wide aperture to limit the depth of field. Its excellent optical performance makes it a good standard lens for general photography, but heavier and more expensive than the 50mm SUMMICRON and not quite matching that lens if maximum possible definition is needed. For LEICA-R cameras only.

Characteristics

Offers extremely high correction, with coma and flare, often a disadvantage with high speed lenses, being virtually eliminated. Image quality is extremely good over the entire focusing range with the lens corrected for maximum contrast. Image contrast improves slightly on stopping down to f/2, and overall image quality continues to improve slightly down to f/5.6. Performance remains excellent throughout the focusing range (down to 50cm), but it is not suitable for macro work because of vignetting, especially with ELPRO supplementary lenses. The freedom from flare means that even strong light sources in the subject itself cause neither ghost images nor loss of background detail. At maximum aperture the depth of field is very restricted. Despite the greater back focus required to clear the mirror system in the camera body, the definition at full aperture is comparable with that of the 50mm SUMMILUX-M.

Construction: 7 elements in 6 groups

Lens hood: built-in, extensible

Filters: E55

Weight: 395g

Length: 50.6mm

Diaphragm: automatic, pre-set

Angle of view: 45°

Smallest aperture: f/16

Closest focusing distance: 50cm, 20in

Smallest object area: 180 x 270mm, 7.1 x 10.6in

50mm, f/2 SUMMICRON-R

Applications

A light-weight, compact universal lens for all types of photography, fast enough for most purposes, and the cheapest lens in the LEICA-R range. It is excellent for all subject distances from infinity down to 50cm (20in), and for closer distances with ELPRO attachments 1 and 2. With the latter, the smallest subject area covered is 63 x 93mm (approx 2.5 x 3in). If you always carry a camera wherever you go on the chance that you might see a picture, then this is the lens to have. For LEICA-R cameras only.

Characteristics

Regarded as the world standard in optical performance for a 50mm lens. Even at maximum aperture the definition and optical correction are outstandingly good. When focused at infinity, and at full aperture of f/2, the flatness of field is outstanding, and at shorter subject distances distortion is extremely low, making it also an excellent lens for the near focusing range. The ELPRO close-up attachments maintain the optical qualities of the lens right into the macro range.

Construction: 6 elements in 4 groups

Lens hood: built-in, extensible

Filters: E55

Weight: 300g

Length: 41mm

Diaphragm: automatic, pre-set

Angle of view: 45°

Smallest aperture: f/16

Closest focusing distance: 50cm, 20in

Smallest object area: 180 x 270mm, 7.5 x 10.8in

Standard Focal-Length Group

60mm, f/2.8 MACRO-ELMARIT-R

Applications

For hand-held, available-light close-up photography. It is an ideal lens for exploring the miniature world of nature whilst at the same time being able to undertake general photography with the same lens. It is advantageous in any situation when the shots required are continually alternating from general views to close-ups. It is equally good for copying, reproduction and specialist and scientific work. With the MACRO-ADAPTER-R and ELPRO near-focusing attachment No.3 it can be used to make frame-filling copies of mounted slides without including any of the mount. This is an excellent standard lens, provided high speed is not of paramount importance. For LEICA-R cameras only.

Construction: 6 elements in 5 groups
Lens hood: built-in, fixed
Filters: E55
Weight: 390g
Length: 62.3mm
Diaphragm: automatic, pre-set
Angle of view: 39°

Smallest aperture: f/22
Closest focusing distance: 27cm, 10.8in
Smallest object area: 48 x 72mm, 1.9 x 2.9in with Macro-adapter-R: 24 x 36mm, 0.95 x 1.5in

60mm, f/2.8 MACRO-ELMARIT-R *(continued)*

Characteristics

It has been computed to give the highest possible image quality in the near and close-up range. Its resolution is outstanding and its image contrast at f/4 is comparable to that of the 50mm SUMMICRON. Even at infinity settings the performance matches that of other LEICA-R lenses if it is stopped down to f/5.6 or f/8. Optimum performance is at reproduction ratios between 1:20 and 1:10. The lens alone focuses down to a reproduction ratio of 1:2, and with the MACRO-ADAPTER-R continuously from 1:2 to 1:1. The deeply recessed front element is well protected from dirt, rain, and physical damage when pushed close up to a subject. The mount also acts as the lens hood.

MACRO-ADAPTOR-R

Moderate Long-Focus Group

80mm, f/1.4 SUMMILUX-R

Applications

An excellent lens for reportage-style pictures in low available light, especially in conjunction with high-speed film, for the roving reporter or amateur interested in recording life around him without being too intrusive. It is particularly good in high-contrast lighting conditions, such as the theatre, circus, cabaret, cafés, indoor sports arenas, etc. Its low bulk and weight for its speed make it very handy. Compared with the 90mm SUMMICRON its shorter focal length takes in only an extra 3° angle of view, but the viewfinder image is much brighter and the lens is only a little larger. The small depth of field at full aperture can be used to isolate the subject from the background. The subject snaps in and out focus in a very satisfying way, making focusing easy, especially if the uniform ground-glass screen [14304] is used and provided the correct eyesight correction lens is fitted, if one is necessary. For LEICA-R models only.

Construction: 7 elements in 5 groups	Diaphragm: automatic, pre-set
Lens hood: built-in, extensible	Angle of view: 30°
Filters: E67	Smallest aperture: f/16
Weight: 670g	Closest focusing distance: 80cm, 32in
Length: 69mm	Smallest object area: 192 x 288mm, 7.5 x 11.2in

80mm, f/1.4 SUMMILUX-R *(continued)*

Characteristics

The focal length of 80mm was chosen to give the pictorial characteristics of a 90mm lens, but to keep down weight and bulk. Contrast transfer is very good at all apertures. Performance is improved slightly on stopping down to f/2. It is outstanding in its reproduction of point light sources in the picture, with freedom from internal reflections and practically no signs of coma at full aperture. Noted for the way it reproduces graduated tonal values within highlights and shadows. At full aperture there is a slight fall-off in brightness towards the edges of the picture, which is not normally noticeable, but illumination becomes uniform with only modest stopping down. The lens performs best at fairly long range; from distances nearer than 1.5m (5ft) it should be stopped down to a medium aperture if maximum sharpness is important.

R

Moderate Long-Focus Group

90mm, f/2 SUMMICRON-R

Applications

This is the universal lens for portraits, landscapes and press work, and a reasonably fast lens for poor lighting conditions. It is useful for candid portraits without supplementary lighting. It comes into its own at dusk or in the rain when the subject contrast has dwindled to such an extent that the eye has difficulty in distinguishing detail but when the SUMMICRON will still exhibit remarkable resolution. The limited depth of field at maximum aperture can be exploited pictorially. For LEICA-R models only.

Characteristics

Very compact for its focal length and aperture. The focusing range can be extended below its limit of 70cm by use of the various close-focusing attachments. Image contrast and resolution are remarkably good, even under poor lighting conditions and at maximum aperture. Distortion is extremely small within the entire working range. In the near-focusing region below 1.5m (5ft) it should be stopped down to f/5.6 or f/8 if the highest possible quality is required.

Construction: 5 elements in 4 groups	Diaphragm: automatic, pre-set
Lens hood: built-in, extensible	Angle of view: 27°
Filters: E55	Smallest aperture: f/16
Weight: 560g	Closest focusing distance: 70cm, 28in
Length: 61mm	Smallest object area: 140 x 210mm, 5.5 x 8.3in

90mm, f/2.8 ELMARIT-R

Applications

An excellent light and handy general-purpose lens of moderate focal length, it is particularly suitable for landscapes and portraits. It makes a good travelling lens when partnered with the 35mm ELMARIT. It is equally suitable for close-ups, both within its own large focusing range and with any of the LEICA close-up attachments. Flat objects, such as maps or pictures, can be copied because of the flat field. It is used by some photographers as their standard lens because at this focal length the 35mm SLR camera begins to come into its own; faster critical focusing is possible than with shorter focal lengths. For LEICA-R cameras only.

Characteristics

This lens has been corrected for its entire focusing range at full aperture, with very high contrast and excellent rendition of detail. Stopping down to f/4 produces optimum image quality. It has excellent image flatness, even at full aperture the image is sharp to the corners. It is practically free from coma. Quality of reproduction remains virtually unchanged at and near the closest focusing distance, and with close-focusing attachments such as ELPRO 3 or the MACRO-ADAPTER-R, when stopped down to f/5.6.

Construction: 4 elements, none cemented	Diaphragm: automatic, pre-set
Lens hood: built-in, extensible	Angle of view: 27°
Filters: E55	Smallest aperture: f/22
Weight: 475g	Closest focusing distance: 70cm
Length: 57mm	Smallest object area: 140 x 210mm, 5.5 x 8.3in

Moderate Long-Focus Group

100mm, f/2.8 APO-MACRO-ELMARIT-R

New lens 1988

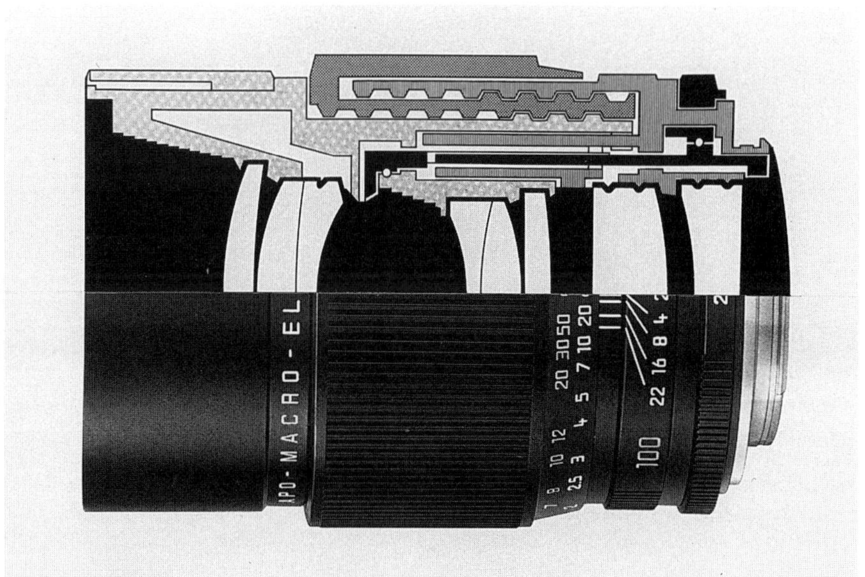

Applications

This is an outstanding lens, offering continuous focusing down to 1:2. It is intended for landscape, portrait, still-life, and nature photography. Besides taking a normal portrait, with this lens it is possible to close in so the eye can fill the entire frame. Its longer focal length compared with the 60mm MACRO-ELMARIT gives a larger working distance from the subject at the same image scale. This means that insects and other small creatures are less likely to be frightened away, and there is also more room for arranging lighting. The dedicated ELPRO 1:2-1:1 attachment extends the range down to 1:1. Tripod Adapter STA-1 keeps the assembly balanced when mounted on a

Construction: 8 elements in 6 groups, rear two fixed

Elpro attachment: 3 elements

Lens hood: built-in, extensible; separate hood supplied with Elpro

Filters: E60

Weight: 840g

Length: 104.5mm

Diaphragm: automatic, pre-set

Angle of view: 25°

Smallest aperture: f/22

Closest focusing distance: 45cm, 17.8in

Free working distance (1:2): 22cm, 8.7in with ELPRO 1:2-1:1 (1.1:1): 7.2cm, 2.9in

Smallest object area (1:2): 48 x 72mm, 1.9 x 2.9in with ELPRO 1:2-1:1 (1.1:1): 22 x 33mm, 0.9 x 1.2in tripod or shoulder stock. Extension rings or the 2x Extender-R are not recommended because they will degrade the performance, and the 1.4x APO-EXTENDER-R will cause physical damage. Only the 2x APO-EXTENDER-R may be used. For LEICA R and LEICAFLEX SL and SL2 cameras.

Characteristics

Apochromatic correction means colour correction is complete for the visible spectral range and extends into the infra-red. There are no residual traces of coma, field curvature, astigmatism or colour fringing. Neither is there any loss of image contrast, at any aperture, between infinity and the closest focusing distance of 45cm. Two elements at the rear are fixed and do not move during focusing. Because of this construction, extension devices are unsuitable and the specially designed three-element ELPRO 1:2-1:1 is offered instead. Despite being a macro-lens, because of its outstanding overall correction it delivers exceptional resolution of fine detail and high contrast at full aperture right through the focusing range. Only a slight improvement is brought about by stopping down to f/4. No focusing adjustment is necessary for infra-red photography. Optical performance is largely retained when the lens is used in conjunction with the special ELPRO attachment, but for critical copying work when sharpness must extend to the corners of the frame it should be stopped down one or two stops. There is no further improvement beyond f/8, and smaller apertures may result in slight loss of resolution due to scatter at the diaphragm.

ELPRO 1:2-1:1 attachment

Moderate Long-Focus Group

100mm, f/4 MACRO-ELMAR-R

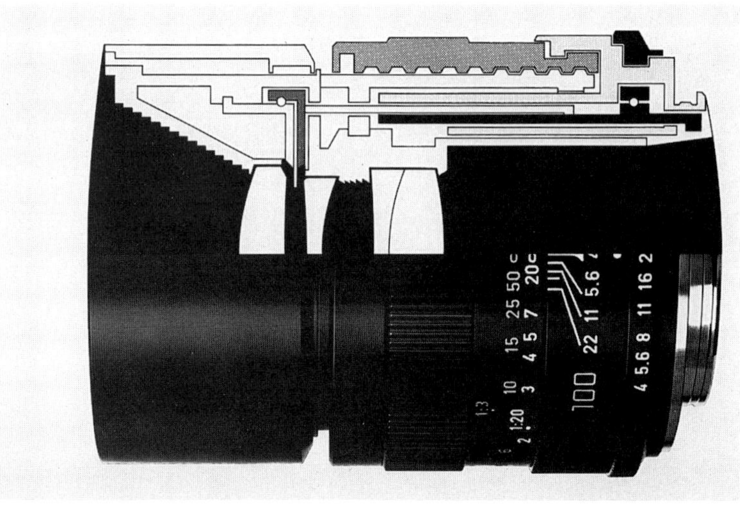

Applications

The applications of this lens are similar to those of the 100mm, f/2.8 Apo-Macro-Elmarit-R. It is one stop slower and lacks the apochromatic correction. Focuses down to a reproduction ratio of 1:3. For LEICA R and LEICAFLEX SL and SL2 cameras.

The optical unit only, without focusing mount, is available for use with the Focusing Bellows-R or Focusing Bellows-R BR2 for continuous focusing from infinity to 1:1.

Characteristics

Corrected to give its optimum performance in the range from 1:5 to 1:10. It yields its highest contrast and definition when the diaphragm is closed by one stop. At its closest focusing distance it gives a reproduction ratio of 1:3, or 1:1.6 with the MACRO-ADAPTER-R. ELPRO close-up attachments may be used alone or in conjunction with the MACRO-ADAPTER-R or the Extension Rings.

Construction: 4 elements in 3 groups

Lens hood: built-in, extensible

Filters: E55

Weight: 540g

Length: 90mm

Diaphragm: automatic, pre-set

Angle of view: 25°

Smallest aperture: f/22

Closest focusing distance: 60cm, 24in

Smallest object area: 72 x 108mm, 2.8 x 4.3in.

135mm, f/2.8 ELMARIT-R

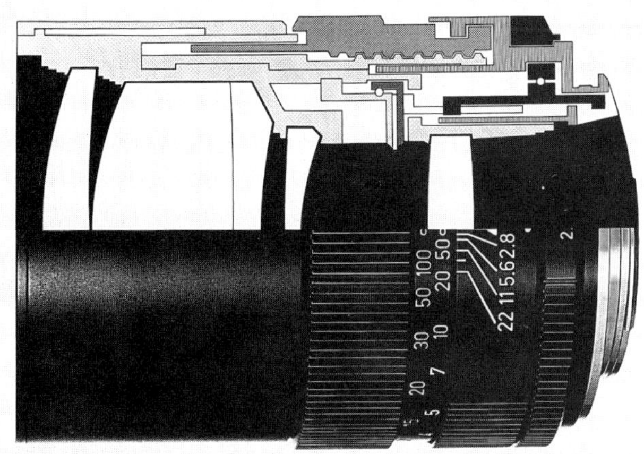

Applications

An alternative choice to the 90mm ELMARIT, but heavier, especially if the 60mm MACRO-ELMARIT has been selected as a standard lens. It is ideal for frame-filling character studies in portraiture. In landscape work it compresses the subject and reduces apparent distance somewhat more than the 90mm lens. This focal length starts to be useful for distant subjects, e.g: at functions where the photographer may not be able to get in close. The near range can be extended with ELPRO near focusing attachments to a reproduction ratio of 1:2.8, when the relatively long working distance helps in the photography of small animals. For all LEICA-R and LEICAFLEX models.

Characteristics

At full aperture it has above average resolving power and high contrast in the distant range. Optimum performance is reached at f/4. In the near focusing range the best detail rendering is produced by stopping down to f/5.6 or f/8. Optically it is identical to the 136mm, f/2.8 ELMARIT-M.

Construction: 5 elements in 4 groups	Diaphragm: automatic, pre-set
Lens hood: built-in, extensible	Angle of view: 18°
Filters: E55	Smallest aperture: f/22
Weight: 730g	Closest focusing distance: 1.5m, 5ft
Length: 93mm	Smallest object area: 220 x 330mm, 8.7 x 13in

Moderate Long-Focus Group

180mm, f/2.8 ELMARIT-R

Applications

For quick, critical focusing in poor light; combined with fast film it can secure pictures in bad lighting conditions, e.g: for reportage, sports, unobtrusive photography from a distance with available light. It is good for portraits from a greater distance than normal, particularly the unposed ones, and for isolating a head from an out-of-focus background. Whenever fast shutter speeds are essential in good light it is the best choice. It is also valuable for architectural detail, especially when the camera must be hand-held. For all LEICA-R and LEICAFLEX models.

Characteristics

A fast telephoto lens always noted for its outstanding contrast and flatness of field. Freedom from flare and internal reflections are excellent. Colour rendering is almost perfectly neutral and transmission efficiency in the relevant spectral region is very high. Optimum image quality is achieved at f/4. In the near focusing range there is a slight fall-off towards the corners due to field curvature.

Construction: 5 elements in 4 groups	Diaphragm: automatic, pre-set
Lens hood: built-in, extensible	Angle of view: 14°
Filters: E67	Smallest aperture: f/22
Weight: 825g	Closest focusing distance: 1.8m, 6ft
Length: 121mm	Smallest object area: 193 x 290mm, 7.6 x 11.4in

180mm, f/3.4 APO-TELYT-R

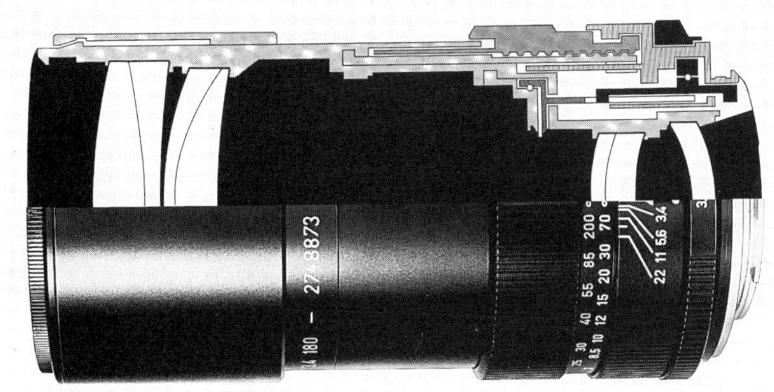

Applications

This is the "180" to choose whenever the recording of fine detail and/or accurate colour rendering is essential, especially when extreme part enlargements are to be made from the negative or slide. Focusing for infra-red photography can be carried out without the filter in place and no further correction to focus is necessary. It is also used for technical applications for subjects with much fine detail, such as process supervision or control, surveillance, inspection of buildings, etc.. It gives its superior performance with subjects at infinity and at large apertures: closest focusing distance is limited to 2.5m. The further the lens is stopped down from f/3.4 the less will be the discernible difference from the other two 180mm lenses. For all LEICA-R and LEICAFLEX models.

Characteristics

Fully apochromatically corrected, i.e: all colours, including infra-red, are brought to focus at the same point. It approaches the theoretical limits of resolution for a lens of this focal length, with outstanding contrast and edge sharpness. Optimum performance is already available at maximum aper-

Construction: 7 elements in 4 groups	Diaphragm: automatic, pre-set
Lens hood: built-in, extensible	Angle of view: 14°
Filters: E60	Smallest aperture: f/22
Weight: 750g	Closest focusing distance: 2.5m, 8.3ft
Length: 135mm	Smallest object area: 276 x 414mm, 10.9 x 16.3in

180mm, f/3.4 APO-TELYT-R *(continued)*

ture and best performance is given in the distant focusing range. Critical exposure measurement is important at full aperture for subjects with uniform brightness to avoid the falling-off in brightness at the corners which is inherent in the design; it can be improved by a slight increase in exposure of about half a light value. It can only be fully exploited with the finest high-resolution film and careful printing of the enlargements.

180mm, f/4 ELMAR-R

Applications

The "180" for travellers, hikers, climbers, back-packers and all those who need light weight and compactness rather than high speed. With a 2x Extender-R it makes a very light and compact 360mm telephoto. E55 filter mount means that the same filters and ELPRO attachments 3 and 4 can be used with shorter lenses in the outfit, thus keeping to a minimum the accessories that need to be carried. Its applications are similar to those of the 180mm ELMARIT, except when restricted by the lower speed. For all LEICA-R and LEICAFLEX models.

Characteristics

Shows optimum optical performance at full aperture nearly equal to that of the 180mm, f/2.8 ELMARIT. In the near range below 3m (10ft) stopping down to f/5.6 or f/8 leads to a slightly improved performance. At its nearest

Construction: 5 elements in 4 groups

Lens hood: built-in, extensible

Filters: E55

Weight: 540g

Length: 100mm

Diaphragm: automatic, pre-set

Angle of view: 14°

Smallest aperture: f/22

Closest focusing distance: 1.8m, 6ft

Smallest object area: 175 x 262mm, 6.9 x 10.3in

180mm, f/4 ELMAR-R *(continued)*

focusing distance of 1.8m (5.8ft) the object field covered is smaller than that of the ELMARIT. This is due to the optical design. With ELPRO attachments 3 and 4 a continuous range of reproduction ratios down to 1:2 is available. It should not be used, however, for reproduction or similar applications where the highest possible optical performance at close range is demanded over the whole image area.

250mm, f/4 TELYT-R

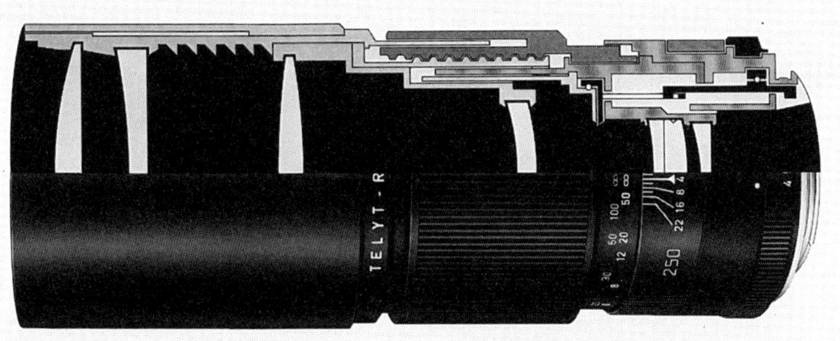

Applications

For photo-journalism, landscape, wildlife, sport; the lens is quite fast for its focal length and reasonably fast in focusing, with a short focusing travel. Subjects in the middle distance can fill the picture area but be photographed unobtrusively. The short close-focusing distance allows close-ups from a distance, e.g: of small shy creatures or inaccessible flowers. The tripod bush is mounted on a rotatable carrier, making it easy to switch between horizontal and vertical formats on a tripod. This is the shortest focal length R-lens with this feature. Relatively slow shutter speeds for the focal length are possible with the Universal Handgrip and Shoulder Stock [14239]; just how slow will depend on the photographer and practice. For LEICA-R and LEICAFLEX SL and SL2 cameras.

Characteristics

Rendering of detail and contrast are very good, even at full aperture, although contrast is at a maximum when stopped down to f/5.6. Residual chromatic aberration in extreme corners of the image, characteristic of long focal length lenses, is practically unnoticeable. In the near focusing range stopping down to f/5.6 or f/8 is advisable. During focusing the front group of four elements moves internally in relation to the rear group: a system that requires only a very short focusing travel. The short closest focusing distance allows a reproduction ratio of 1:5.2. For LEICA-R and LEICAFLEX SL and SL2 cameras.

Construction: 7 elements in 6 groups

Lens hood: built-in, extensible

Filters: E67

Weight: 1230g

Length: 195mm

Diaphragm: automatic, pre-set

Angle of view: 10°

Smallest aperture: f/22

Closest focusing distance: 1.2m, 5.7ft

Smallest object area: 124 x 186mm, 4.9 x 7.3in

Extreme Long-Focus Group

280mm, f/2.8 APO-TELYT-R

New mount with filter slot 1992

Applications

Designed primarily for sports and wildlife photographers and for whenever the recording of fine detail and/or accurate colour rendering is essential, especially when extreme part enlargements are needed. Has application also in portraits, fashion and advertising for its abilities in hand-held, poor light telephotography, or for its very limited depth of field at full aperture to isolate an image in a dramatic way, or for its slightly softer image at full aperture at the closest focusing distance. The special palm grip and the Shoulder stock [14239], together with a very short travel of the focusing ring, allow rapid, hand-held work. For Leica-R and Leicaflex SL and SL2 cameras.

Characteristics

Apochromatically corrected; contrast and resolution extraordinarily good, even at full aperture. Field is flat so that sharpness is maintained right into the corners, even at f/2.8. Chromatic aberrations, normal with very long lenses, have been reduced to a level at which they can be ignored, and infra-

Construction: 8 elements in 7 groups
Lens hood: built-in, extensible
Filters: Series 5.5
Weight: 2.75kg
Length: 261mm

Diaphragm: automatic, pre-set
Angle of view: 8.5°
Smallest aperture: f/22
Closest focusing distance: 2.5m, 6.2ft
Smallest object area: 195 x 293mm, 7.7 x 11.5in

280mm, f/2.8 APO-TELYT-R *(continued)*

red photography requires no correction of focus. Very careful focusing is necessary. Designed for use primarily at long distances, so at near ranges it needs to be stopped down to medium apertures for best performance. Focusing is internal, which means the length of the lens remains constant but the focal length and aperture change slightly during focusing. At 2.5m the maximum aperture corresponds to about f/2.2. Supplied with a shoulder strap which fits two lugs on the barrel; the camera should not be carried by its own strap when this lens is mounted. The new, improved version of this lens now has a removable filter holder which takes Series 5.5 filters: for optical reasons the NDx1 filter supplied must always be in place if no other filter is in use. A special circular polarizing filter also fits in the filter slot in place of the filter holder.

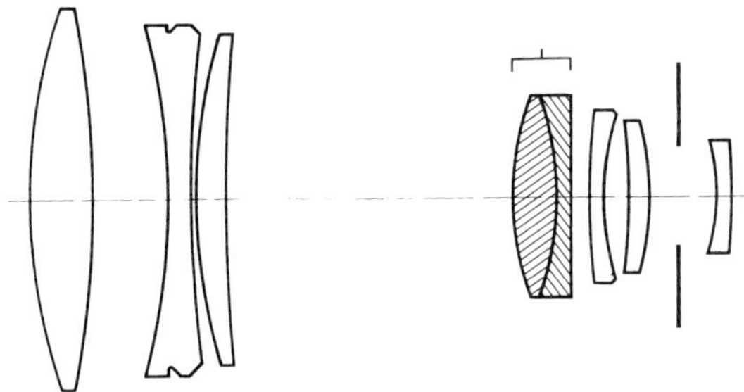

Only the shaded component moves during focusing.

Extreme Long-Focus Group

350mm, f/4.8 TELYT-R

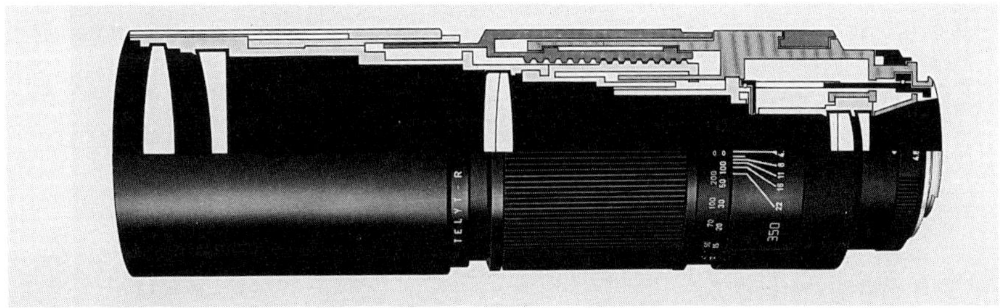

Applications

Similar to the 250mm, f/4 TELYT-R for applications in photo-journalism, landscape, wildlife, sport, etc., with the same fast focusing, but with a 40% greater reach. Its short close-focusing distance allows close-ups of small creatures, etc. Used with the Universal Handgrip and Shoulder Stock [14239] it allows, with practice, relatively slow shutter speeds for the focal length. For LEICA-R and LEICAFLEX SL and SL2 cameras.

Characteristics

Excellent definition of detail and high contrast facilitate focusing in poor light. Residual chromatic aberration, to be expected at this focal length in a non-apochromatic lens, has been reduced to such an extent, even at the edges, that it is only noticeable in extreme conditions. During focusing, as with the 250mm TELYT-R, the front group of four elements moves internally in relation to the rear group. The resulting short focusing travel gives a rapid focusing action. In the near focusing range optimum resolution will be obtained by stopping down to f/8. The short near-focusing distance allows a reproduction ratio of 1:7.1. Vignetting is inherent in the system, therefore extreme care in exposure determination is necessary for critical subjects.

Construction: 7 elements in 5 groups	Diaphragm: automatic, pre-set
Lens hood: built-in, extensible	Angle of view: 7°
Filters: E77	Smallest aperture: f/22
Weight: 1.82kg	Closest focusing distance: 3m, 10ft
Length: 286mm	Smallest object area: 171 x 257mm, 6.7 x 10.1in

400mm, f/2.8 APO-TELYT-R

New lens 1992

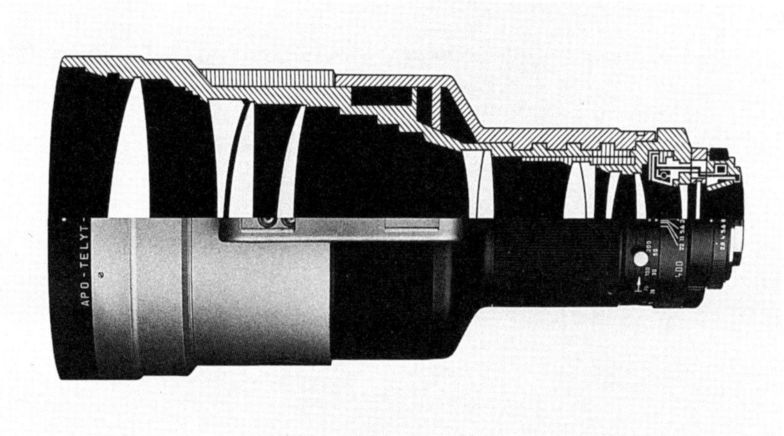

The lens is provided with a carrying handle and a very strong tripod support cradle.

Applications

The star Leica telephoto lens and the longest focal length available with an automatic, pre-set diaphragm. Applications are similar to those of the 280mm APO-TELYT, sports, wildlife, fashion, advertising, but with a 40% longer reach. The lens would normally be mounted on a tripod or monopod and a rotating camera mount allows easy switching from horizontal to vertical format. The large diameter focusing ring permits very precise, rapid focusing. It has an adjustable stop which sets a limit to the closest focusing distance. This enables the photographer, for example at a football match, to pre-focus on the nearer goal and set the catch at that point. He can then follow the action in the field but instantly flick to the goal mouth when necessary. For LEICA-R and LEICAFLEX SL and SL2 cameras.

Characteristics

Production models of this lens differ from the prototypes, which were issued to selected photographers four years before, in being lighter in weight, better

Construction: 11 elements in 9 groups

Lens hood: bayonet fitting, reversible for transport and protection of front element

Filters: Series 5.5, one must be in place

Weight: 5.53kg

Length: 365mm

Diaphragm: automatic, pre-set

Angle of view: 6°

Smallest aperture: f/22

Closest focusing distance: 4.7m, 15.4ft

Smallest object area: 280 x 420mm, 11 x 16.5in

Extreme Long-Focus Group

400mm, f/2.8 APO-TELYT-R *(continued)*

balanced and yielding an even better optical performance. The lens is fully apochromatically corrected, with outstanding contrast and rendition of detail. The image field is exceptionally flat and sharpness is maintained right into the corners of the frame at full aperture, with only a slight improvement on stopping down. Chromatic errors are of a very low order. Vignetting is so infinitesimal it can be ignored. No focusing correction is needed for infra-red work. The lens has been corrected to perform best from medium distances to infinity. For distances less than 10m it is necessary to stop down by at least one stop if maximum definition is required. Focusing is internal which causes a slight change in focal length, so at 4.7m the focal length is 321mm and the effective maximum aperture f/2.1. A slot in front of the bayonet mount houses a filter holder or a special circular polarizing filter. The 1xND filter provided must be in position if no other filter is in use.

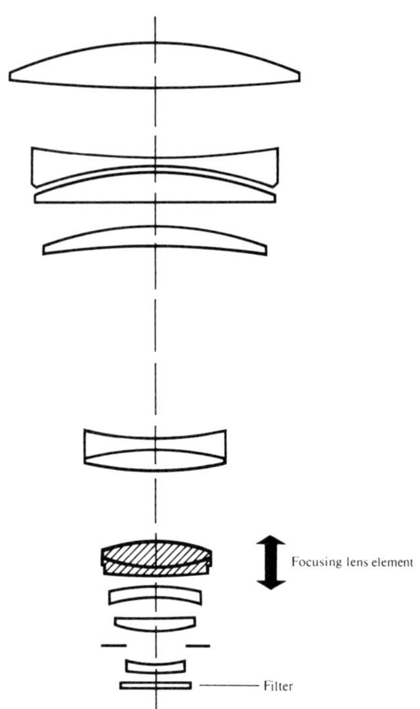

400mm, f/6.8 (Follow Focus) TELYT-R
560mm, f/6.8 (Follow Focus) TELYT-R

400mm

Applications

This is a lens system which is unique to Leica and has been part of the LEICA system in one form or another since 1966. The lenses are light-weight, for the focal length, and in rapid-focusing mounts for sports, nature and wildlife photography, as well as photojournalism. They are designed for use on a shoulder stock [14239], but they can, with care, be used without. The lenses illustrated on this page focus by sliding the barrel with the hand which supports the lens, rather than by rotating a focusing ring. This makes it easy to follow, and keep in focus, subjects moving rapidly towards or away from the camera. The lenses dismantle into two parts for transport; the lens heads themselves in their sliding focusing mounts, and the lens tube which is common to both lenses. With the special 60mm extension tube [14182] the focusing range can be extended down to give a reproduction ratio of 1:3.3 with the 400mm lens and 1:4.7 with the 560mm lens. This means the lenses are particularly suitable for use by the naturalist or photographer for small difficult-to-approach creatures such as butterflies. For LEICA R (aperture priority or manual mode) and LEICAFLEX SL and SL2 cameras.

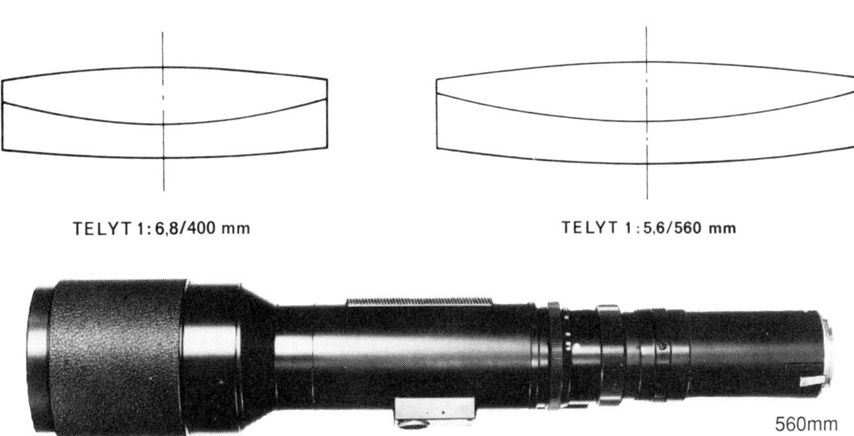
TELYT 1:6,8/400 mm

TELYT 1:5,6/560 mm

560mm

400mm, f/6.8 (Follow Focus) TELYT-R
560mm, f/6.8 (Follow Focus) TELYT-R *(continued)*

NOVOFLEX SYSTEM

Alternative mount 1990

This mount by the NOVOFLEX company is also available from Leica for these two lenses. It takes the two lens heads, which have been fitted with a special bayonet lock, complete with the familiar red dot location mark. The rear handgrip of the NOVOFLEX mount is in two parts which can be squeezed together in a trigger action. Either lens head, when on the mount, is spring-set at its closest focusing distance. Squeezing the trigger causes the lens head to move backwards towards the infinity position. This system ensures rapid and certain focusing, although it takes a little getting used to because the natural impulse is to squeeze to focus more closely (whereas with the sliding mount described above you know you have to push the lens outwards to focus more closely). By means of the locking disc on top of the mount the focus setting can be locked in position. This can readily be done by sliding the ball of the thumb of the free hand against the disc. The NOVOFLEX device has a built-in extension tube which can be pulled out to a maximum of 80mm and locked at any intermediate position. At full extension the 400mm lens gives a reproduction ratio of 1:3.8 and the 560mm lens 1:5.2. The detachable universal stock can be adapted as a shoulder stock or as a chest pod.

Both systems

Construction: single 2-element group

Lens hood: built-in, extensible

Diaphragm: manual, with click stops

Angle of view 400mm: 6°
560mm: 4.3°

Smallest aperture: f/32

400mm, f/6.8 (Follow Focus) TELYT-R
560mm, f/6.8 (Follow Focus) TELYT-R *(continued)*

Characteristics

These lenses are not of telephoto construction, so their total length is roughly the same as their focal length. They are well corrected achromats, consisting of only two cemented elements, which accounts for the light weight and brilliant image. Since there are only two air/glass surfaces light transmission losses and internal reflections are of a very low order and you can expect the exposure meter to give a reading about half a stop higher than would normally be expected with a lens of similar maximum aperture. Both lenses have high resolving power and very good colour correction. They both display curvature of field, which is characteristic of this type of achromat construction. It has the effect of moving the plane of focus at the margins of the picture nearer to the camera. In the types of photography over long distances for which these lenses are intended this can be an advantage in extending the apparent depth of field to include, for example, some of the ground in front of the subject.

LEICA SYSTEM		
Filters: Series 7 in slot in lens tube		
Weight	400mm:	1.83kg with shoulder stock
	560mm:	2.33kg with shoulder stock
Length	400mm:	384mm without stock
	560mm:	530mm without stock
Closest focusing distance	400mm:	3.6m, 12ft
	560mm:	6.4m, 21ft
with tube [14182]	400mm:	2.26m, 7.4ft
	560mm:	3.96m, 13ft
Smallest object area	400mm:	158 x 236mm, 6.5 x 9.5in
	560mm:	224 x 336mm, 8.8 x 13.3in
with tube [14182]	400mm:	80 x 120mm, 3.1 x 4.8in
	560mm:	110 x 160mm, 4.4 x 6.3in
NOVOFLEX SYSTEM		
Filters: special Novoflex or Helioplan filters in slot		
Weight	400mm:	2.93kg
	560mm:	3.2kg
Length	400mm:	406mm
	560mm:	534mm
Closest focusing distance	400mm:	7.5m, 24.5ft
	560mm:	13m, 42.5ft
with near focusing tube	400mm:	2.4m, 8ft
	560mm:	4.15m, 13.5ft
Smallest object area	400mm:	377 x 566mm, 14.7 x 22in
	560mm:	512 x 768mm, 20 x 30in
with near focusing tube	400mm:	90 x 135mm, 3.5 x 5.3in
	560mm:	124 x 187mm, 4.8 x 7.3in

Extreme Long-Focus Group

500mm, f/8 MR-TELYT-R

Applications

The long focus lens for when small volume and light weight are of paramount consideration and high maximum aperture is not, such as in air travel, back-packing or mountaineering. The lens is easily supported by the hand. The screen image is somewhat dim for focusing and the plain focusing screen [14304] is best. It cannot be stopped down, hence the depth of field cannot be influenced, but a neutral density filter is provided for conditions when over-exposure would result with even the fastest shutter speed. Generally a high speed film should be used to ensure fast enough shutter speeds for hand-holding. It is the only lens above 250mm not to have a rotating collar

Construction: 5 elements, two of them back mirror-coated	Diaphragm: none
Lens hood: fixed, but can be unscrewed	Angle of view: 5°
Filters: 5 provided	Smallest aperture: f/8; light can be attenuated to 25% by 4xND filter
Weight: 750g	Closest focusing distance: 4m, 13ft
Length: 121mm	Smallest object area: 180 x 270mm, 7.1 x 10.5in

500mm, f/8 MR-TELYT-R (continued)

for use on a tripod. For LEICA R (aperture priority or manual mode) and LEICAFLEX SL and SL2 cameras.

Characteristics

Of catadioptric construction; that is it has internal mirror surfaces which, besides focusing the image, also fold the light path, thus enabling a very short lens to be made for the focal length. It is impossible to fit a diaphragm to this type of lens, which means that all exposures have to be made at full aperture, although the 4x grey (ND) filter provided can be used to attenuate the light if necessary to give an effective aperture of f/16, but without any effect on the depth of field. It has excellent contrast rendering and definition, and is largely free of chromatic aberration. No focusing correction is needed for infra-red photography. It exhibits the "doughnut" distortion of out-of-focus point-light sources or highlights in the picture area, characteristic of mirror lenses. Five filters are provided, size M32 x 0.5, UVa, 4xND, yellow, orange and red. E77 filters with an M77 x 0.75 thread can, if necessary, be screwed onto the front of the lens in place of the lens hood.

Extreme Long-Focus Group

800MM, F/6.3 TELYT-S

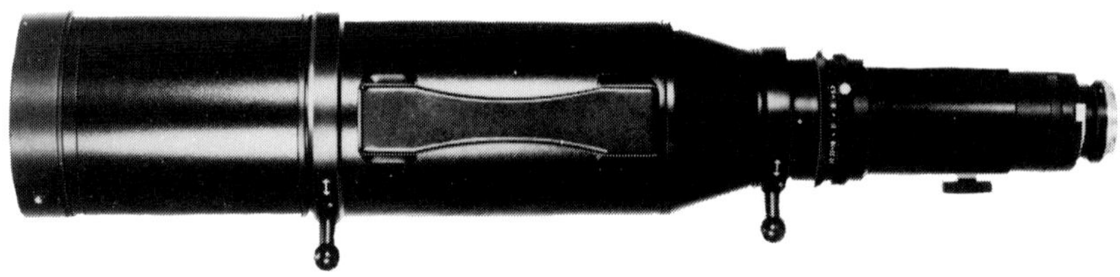

Applications

A specialist's lens, which must be used from a tripod. It is used for reportage, sports or wildlife when the subject is of necessity remote, and a static position is not a handicap: for record or inspection photography of inaccessible subjects, such as details of buildings, bridges and other engineering constructions: for long distance architectural photography, such as tall buildings which may not be readily photographed close-to but may be from a distance, perhaps from a neighbouring hill. At the other extreme it is used for close-up photography of dangerous processes from a safe distance, or of small animals or sitting birds.

Characteristics

Gives an image quality superior to that of most lenses of this focal length. Special glass, and the achromat construction (three cemented elements, only two air/glass surfaces), yield an outstandingly high reproduction of detail and colour qualities, close to apochromatic standards. The tripod bush is at the point of balance. A second tripod bush for a monopod, to give more rigid support, is provided on a rotating support ring which can be inserted between the front of the lens mount and the lens hood. The bayonet mount for the camera can be rotated through 90° for horizontal or vertical shots. A post and notch "gun-sight" is incorporated in the carrying handle to align the lens on the target. A swing-out holder in the lens mount accepts Series 7 filters. The lens can be disassembled into five components easily and quickly for stowage in its own fitted aluminium case. It is just as easily reassembled. For LEICA R (aperture priority or manual mode) and LEICAFLEX SL and SL2 cameras.

Construction: single 3-element group

Lens hood: detachable and lockable

Filters: Series 7

Weight: 6.86kg

Length: 790mm

Diaphragm: pre-set

Angle of view: 3°

Smallest aperture: f/32

Closest focusing distance: 12.5m, 41ft

Smallest object area: 320 x 480mm, 12.5 x 18.8in

28-70mm, f/3.5-4.5 VARIO-ELMAR-R

New lens 1990

Applications

This is an inexpensive lens by Leica standards, costing only half as much as the 35-70mm, f/3.5 zoom and about 50% more than the 50mm Summicron. It is an excellent light-weight general purpose lens for the amateur and travel photographer for landscapes, family pictures and events. It covers the most useful range for these purposes, from the true wide-angle to a modest longer focal length. It also focuses down to 0.5m, adding an attractive close-up facility. For LEICA R and LEICAFLEX SL and SL2 cameras.

Characteristics

The compact dimensions were achieved in part by allowing the lens speed to vary with focal length. At 28mm the maximum aperture is f/3.5 and gradually changes to f/4.5 at f/22. The engraved apertures apply to the 28mm setting. The camera's metering system will set the correct shutter speed for the true aperture. Separate control rings for focusing and setting the focal

Construction: 11 elements in 8 groups	Angle of view: 76° to 34°
Lens hood: built-in, extensible	Smallest aperture: f/22
Filters: E60	Closest focusing distance: 50cm, 20in
Weight: 468g	Smallest object area at 28mm: 336 x 504mm, 13.2 x 19.8in at 70mm: 114 x 216mm, 4.5 x 8.5in
Length: 84mm	
Diaphragm: automatic, pre-set	

28-70mm, f/3.5-4.5 VARIO-ELMAR-R *(continued)*

length. The lens yields good image contrast and fine resolution of detail at full aperture, improving slightly on stopping down one or two stops. Best performance is from medium distances to infinity. There is a slight fall-off in resolution at the corners when used close-up, improved by adequate stopping down. Like most short focus zooms, it exhibits a small amount of barrel distortion at the short end and pin-cushion distortion at the long end, and is virtually free of distortion at about 50mm. None of this matters in pictorial photography. There is some vignetting, particularly at the short end, reduced by stopping down to f/5.6 or f/8. Besides having an extensible lens hood, the front lens element retracts into the barrel as focal length increases, thus preserving the efficiency of the hood. Use of polarizing filters is not recommended because of this retraction, as well as rotation of the front element in focusing, and possible vignetting.

35-70mm, f/3.5 VARIO-ELMAR-R

Redesigned mount 1988

Applications

A relatively small and light-weight general purpose lens for pictorial photography and reportage when high maximum aperture is not of consequence. The lens has been redesigned and the front barrel no longer rotates during focusing. This means that polarizing filters, graduated filters, etc., can be used as conveniently as with other LEICA R lenses because the filter does not rotate with change of focus. For LEICA R and LEICAFLEX SL and SL2 cameras.

Characteristics

Separate control rings for focus and focal length. The plane of focus and effective aperture remain constant throughout the zooming range. Contrast and rendering of detail is good at full aperture, and improved slightly on stopping down to f/5.6 or f/8. The barrel distortion at short focal lengths and pin-cushion at long, characteristic of zoom lenses, are hardly noticeable. Optimum performance is at medium to long distances; at short distances curvature of field occurs, which is not apparent in pictorial photography but would be in pictures of plane surfaces, such as a wall, unless the lens is stopped down to f/8 or f/11. There is a certain amount of vignetting, but again, stopping down to medium apertures will eliminate it in situations where it would be apparent.

Construction: 8 elements in 7 groups	Angle of view: 64° to 35°
Lens hood: built-in, extensible	Smallest aperture: f/22
Filters: E67	Closest focusing distance: 1m, 40in
Weight: 450g	Smallest object area at 35mm: 632 x 947mm, 24.9 x 37.3in at 70mm: 338 x 507mm, 13.3 x 20in
Length: 66.5mm	
Diaphragm: automatic, pre-set	

Zoom Group

70-210mm, f/4 VARIO-ELMAR-R

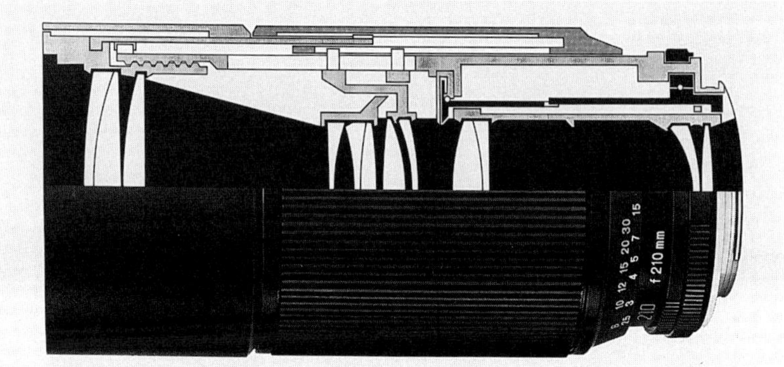

Applications

For whenever the convenience of a single lens outweighs the optical advantages of the five prime lenses whose focal lengths come within its very wide zooming range of 3:1. It also finds application in technical and scientific work when the camera position cannot easily be changed, as in an operating theatre. The single wide sleeve for focusing and zooming makes possible interesting creative effects, such as zooming during exposure to produce "streaking". Because the front barrel rotates during focusing, use of polarizing, graduated and some effects filters is less convenient than with other R-lenses. The filter has to be adjusted after focusing. For LEICA R and LEICAFLEX SL and SL2 cameras.

Characteristics

Focus and zoom controls are by a single large sleeve which rotates for focusing and slides back and forth for zooming. Optical performance is of a very high standard for a modern zoom lens. Contrast and resolution of detail meet most practical demands at full aperture and can be improved further by stopping down to f/5.6 or f/8, which also eliminates the effects of vignetting. Best performance is at medium to long distances. With near subjects, especially at the longer focal lengths, the image aberrations characteristic of zoom lenses (slightly out-of-focus areas at the edges and corners of reproductions of flat objects) can be decreased by stopping down and are scarcely noticeable in normal photographic situations. The normal barrel and pincushion distortion of zoom lenses are so minimal that they can be disregarded in most applications. The lens is practically unaffected by stray light.

Construction: 12 elements in 9 groups
Lens hood: built-in, extensible
Filters: E60
Weight: 720g
Length: 157mm
Diaphragm: automatic, pre-set

Angle of view: 35° to 12°
Smallest aperture: f/22
Closest focusing distance: 1.1m
Smallest object area at 7
100mm: 264 x 396mm, 10.4 x 15.6in at
210mm:96 x 144mm, 3.8 x 5.7in

EXTENDER-R 2X

Applications

Can be used to double the focal length of all LEICA R-lenses of focal length 50mm or longer and maximum aperture f/2 or smaller (i.e: it cannot be used with f/1.4 lenses). It makes a compact, lightweight accessory lens for travel because it doubles the number of available focal lengths in an outfit, or alternatively halves the number of longer focal lengths it is necessary to take on a trip, provided large apertures are not essential. An extender is the only means to achieve a focal length greater than 800mm and it increases the reach of all ultra-long lenses. It is suitable for the photographer with only one or two lenses of 50mm or longer who has only occasional use for intermediate or longer focal lengths. It is ideal for portraits and sport, but is less likely to be successful with distant landscape with haze. For LEICA R models only, preferably with aperture priority or manual mode.

Characteristics

The negative effects normally associated with tele-extenders have been reduced to a minimum. It reduces the aperture of the LEICA R-lens by two stops. It is designed to operate with lens apertures in the range f/2 to f/22, which becomes f/4 to f/44 with the Extender. Exposures measured by the camera's metering system will be about one third longer than expected because of the additional light absorption caused by the lens elements in the Extender. Image quality is very good at full aperture, but optimum sharpness is achieved by stopping down f/2 lenses by two stops and f/2.8 lenses by one stop. With 400mm and longer focal lengths, but not with the 500mm MR-TELYT-R, there is slight vignetting at the corners (normally hidden by the mask in the case of slides), which becomes more apparent on near focusing or stopping down. It is mounted between the lens and the camera and contains the necessary linkages to operate the automatic diaphragm.

Construction: 5 elements in 5 groups	Weight: 180g
Aperture range: f/2 to f/22	Length: 30mm

Extenders

APO-EXTENDER-R 1.4x

New lens 1986

Applications

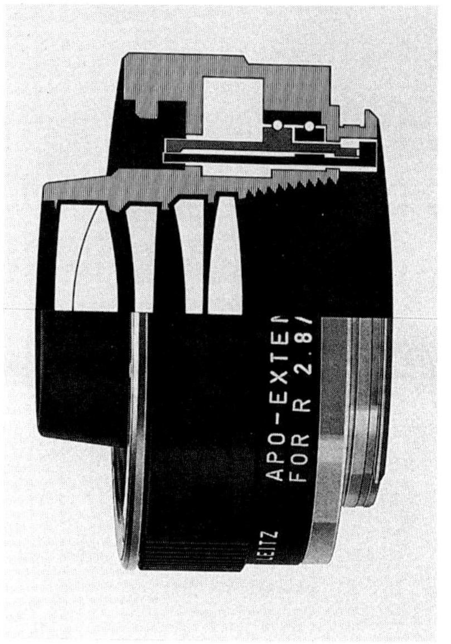

See Extender-R 2x for general applications. Designed specifically for the 280mm and 400mm f/2.8 APO-TELYT-R lenses, converting them to 400mm and 560mm, f/4 respectively. Unlike the EXTENDER-R 2x, all the camera's exposure modes are available. The APO-EXTENDER-R 1.4x is recommended by Leica for use only on the above two lenses. However, it has been used with a few other lenses, and with good optical performance, but because the front of the extender projects forward from the mount it would damage many of the LEICA R-lenses even when it is possible to fit it. The following lenses have been reported as giving satisfactory results with this extender:

100mm, f/4 ELMAR-R = 140mm f/5.6 (AM)

180mm, f/2.8 ELMARIT-R = 250mm, f/4 (ASPM)

400mm f/6.8 TELYT-R = 560mm, f/9.5 (AM)

560mm, f/6.8 TELYT-R= 800mm, f/9.5 (AM)

800mm, f/6.3 TELYT-S = 1120mm, f/8.8 (AM)

A = aperture priority, S = shutter priority, P = program, M = manual modes.

For Leica R models only.

Characteristics

Image contrast and resolution of fine detail with the lens/extender combination focused at infinity is excellent at full aperture and there is nothing to be gained by stopping down, except depth of field. Below 10m some softness appears and maximum sharpness will be achieved by stopping down by one stop, or two stops if below 5m. Complete transmission of all diaphragm control functions between lens and camera body when employed with the 280mm and 400mm APO-TELYT-R lenses.

Construction: 5 elements in 4 groups	Weight 220g
Aperture range: f/2.8 to f/22	Length: 36m

APO-EXTENDER-R 2x

New lens 1992

Applications

See Extender-R 2x for general applications. A 2x extender matched to the apo-lenses in the LEICA R-system to maintain their apochromatic qualities: these are the 100mm, f/2.8 Apo-MACRO-ELMARIT-R; 180mm, f/3.4 APO-TELYT-R; 280mm, f/2.8 Apo-TELYT-R and 400mm, f/2.8 APO-TELYT-R. In addition it is suitable for all other LEICA R-lenses of focal length 50mm or more and maximum aperture f/2 or smaller. Its automatic spring-back diaphragm transfer mechanism ensures that it can be used without restriction in aperture priority and manual modes. For LEICA R-models only.

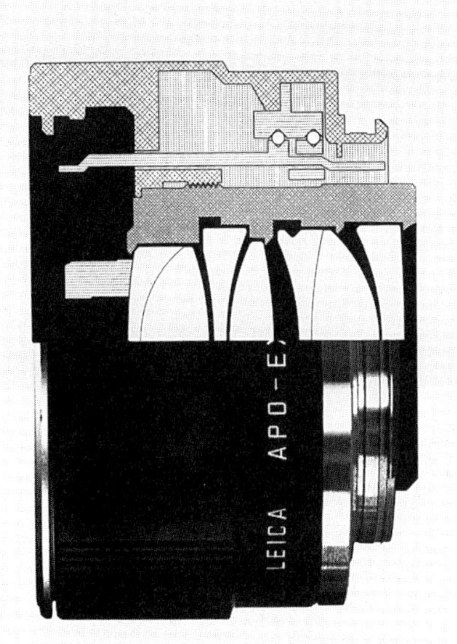

Characteristics

A highly corrected optical system employing glasses of high refractive index. Optical performance is remarkably good with the aperture of the prime lens fully open.

Construction:7 elements in 5 groups	Length: 35.4mm
Weight: 245g	

TELESCOPE OCULAR TO-R

New lens 1992

This attachment revives an idea from the 1950's when Leitz sold the OSBLO eyepiece for screw lenses to convert them to a telescope. The TO-R, however, is a much more refined instrument. It is attached to the lens bayonet and is suitable for use with any LEICA R-lens with a focal length of 50mm or longer. It may also be used with VISOFLEX lenses via adapter [14167] or lens heads alone together with the bellows. The combination produces a high quality telescope with a right-way-round image due to the Schmidt-Pechan-type prism in the ocular. Magnification depends on the focal length of the lens and may be calculated by dividing the lens focal length by the ocular focal length (12.5mm). Thus a 50mm lens gives 4x magnification and the 800mm TELYT-S gives 64x. Extenders may also be added to increase the magnification by a further 1.4x or 2x, but remember the restrictions on fitting the 1.4x APO-EXTENDER-R to certain lenses.

There is a dioptric compensation feature enabling the user to adjust the ocular to his eyesight by up to +/- 3 dioptres. Spectacle wearers may prefer to fold back the rubber eyecup instead in order to be able to observe the entire field. The back focus of 12.7mm is adequate for spectacle wearers. The lens aperture has to be set wide open for maximum light transmission because the diaphragm blades do not open automatically when the ocular is attached (unlike when a camera is attached). In practice the prism limits the effective aperture to f/3.3.

Construction: 3 elements in 2 groups with Schmidt-Pechan image-reversal system.	Max. diameter of exit pupil: 3.78mm, but actual figure depends on lens aperture
Focal length: 12.5mm	Weight: 136g
Ocular magnification: 20x	
Eyesight adjustment: +/- 3 dioptres	Length: 57mm

21MM, F/2.8 ELMARIT-M

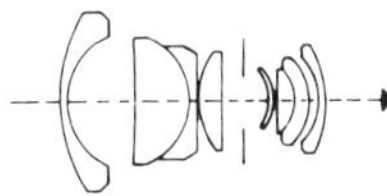

Applications

The relatively high speed for the focal length makes this an excellent lens for snapshots and photo-journalism. Other applications will be architecture, interiors, landscapes, as well as industrial photography, advertising and the photography of scale models. As the widest angle lens in the M-system, it is the choice for any work in confined spaces. Pictorially it can give dramatic perspectives with monumental foregrounds and rapidly receding backgrounds. Moderate stopping down will extend the depth of field from the near foreground to infinity. It needs a special accessory finder [12008] which fits into the camera accessory shoe.

Characteristics

The residual distortion which is inherent in ultra-wide-angle lenses has been reduced to a level which can be ignored for all practical purposes. Detail rendition and contrast are excellent, even at full aperture, but some vignetting is unavoidable and is improved on stopping down. The lens has a long back focus and can be used on the LEICA M5 and CL models with through-lens metering without any adaptation; unlike the old 21mm SUPER-ANGULON which it replaced. The focusing mount is fitted with a lever for easier handling.

Construction: 8 elements in 6 groups
Lens hood: separate, supplied
Filter size: E60
Weight: 290g
Length: 46.5mm

Angle of view: 92°
Smallest aperture: f/22
Closest focusing distance: 70cm, 28in
Smallest object area: 705 x 1058mm, 28 x 42in

Extreme Wide-Angle Group

28MM, F/2.8 ELMARIT-M

New optical design 1993

Applications

Popular with press photographers because it can cover a wide field in confined spaces and the large depth of field means that focusing does not have to be very critical. The wide-angle lens to choose if 35mm does not cover a large enough field but a well balanced perspective is required without too much exaggeration. For architecture, interiors, broad landscapes, townscapes, and for industrial and advertising photography. A special accessory finder [12009] is required for all LEICA M-cameras other than the M6 and M4-P.

Characteristics

Exhibits extremely high definition of detail and contrast over the entire image area, only slightly improved in the corners by stopping down one stop, which also completely removes coma. Barrel distortion, characteristic of wide-angle lenses, is so low it can be ignored. With back-lighting or with point light sources in the picture area, undesirable reflections are virtually non-existent. These image qualities are maintained right into the near focusing range under 2m. A modified retrofocus design. The front element has a concave front surface and the rear element is a dispersing meniscus. The large diameters of these elements means that artificial vignetting is virtually eliminated.

Construction: 8 elements in 7 groups
Lens hood: push-on
Filters: E46
Weight: 260g
Length: 41.5mm

Angle of view: 76°
Smallest aperture: f/22
Closest focusing distance: 70cm, 28in
Smallest object area: 502 x 753mm, 19.8 x 29.7in

35mm, f/1.4 SUMMILUX ASPHERICAL

New lens 1990

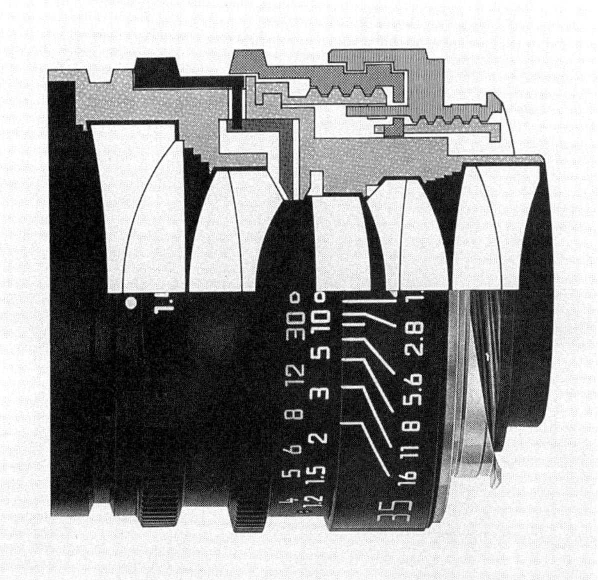

Applications

The most versatile general purpose lens for the LEICA M. It was, of course, primarily designed for available-light work in adverse conditions, and because of this it is ideal for snapshots or photojournalism indoors or outside. However, many photographers find 35mm suits them better than a 50mm as their standard lens and its imaging qualities make it eminently suitable for landscape and townscape work as well, particularly for scenes of intricate detail. The lens focuses down to 70cm with virtually no change in performance, so it is also useful for close-ups of museum exhibits, for example. The special rectangular lens hood has a cut-out to reduce obstruction in the viewfinder to a minimum and a rectangular protective cap so that the hood can remain permanently in position on the lens.

Construction: 9 elements in 5 groups, 2 aspherical surfaces

Lens hood: supplied with lens

Filters: E46

Weight: 275g

Length: 44.5mm

Angle of view: 64°

Smallest aperture: f/16

Closest focusing distance: 70cm, 28in

Smallest object area: 420 x 630mm, 16.5 x 24.8in

35mm, f/1.4 SUMMILUX ASPHERICAL *(continued)*

Characteristics

Two internal aspherical surfaces give the lens its name. Another unique feature is the concave outer surfaces of the front and rear elements. The imaging performance at full aperture is superb among compact 35mm lenses, with brilliant contrast and excellent resolution of fine detail. The lens is almost completely free from coma, has good flatness of field and the very slight barrel distortion, characteristic of this type of lens, is negligible. Image forming performance is enhanced even further by stopping down a little, and maintained throughout the focusing range right to the closest focusing limit. Slight vignetting is removed by stopping down to f/4. The lens hood, an essential part of the design, must be fitted when shooting against the light to prevent ghost images from internal reflections.

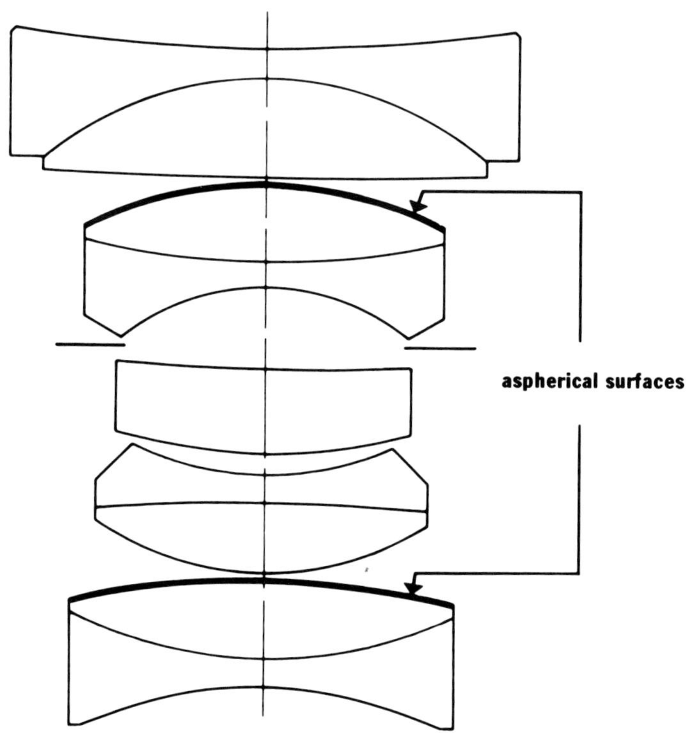

35MM, F/1.4 SUMMILUX-M

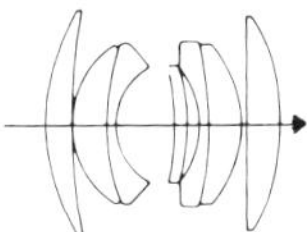

Applications

The less expensive, but well-tried 35mm high speed lens for quick, dynamic photography, snapshots, photo-journalism, etc., in available light. The shorter focal length means that focusing does not have to be quite so critical as with the 50mm Summilux. Very compact, light in weight and very handy. It would make a good companion for the 70mm Summilux for a handy, high-speed outfit, although its performance at maximum aperture does not match that of the 70mm lens. Available in titanium finish to match the Leica M6 Titanium.

Characteristics

This is the oldest Leica lens still in production. It was a remarkable lens in its day, but is now overshadowed by its R namesake and the 35mm, f/1.4 Summilux Aspherical. It keeps its place because it is only half the price of the aspherical lens and is lighter and more compact. It is an excellent lens when stopped down one or two stops, but at maximum aperture its contrast is not up to the standard of more recent Leica high speed lenses and it suffers somewhat from coma.

Construction: 7 elements in 5 groups	Angle of view: 64°
Lens hood: separate, also acts as filter holder	Smallest aperture: f/16
Filters Series 7	Closest focusing distance: 1m, 40in
Weight: 200g	Smallest object area: 630 x 950mm, 25 x 37.7in
Length: 28mm	

Wide-Angle Group

35MM, F/2 SUMMICRON-M

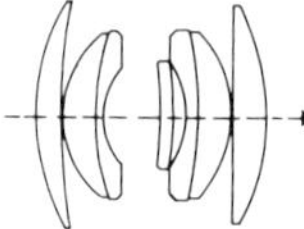

Applications

The lightest-weight M-lens, being 5g lighter than the standard 50mm SUMMICRON. It is an ideal snapshot lens, and is particularly suitable for producing brilliant colour pictures because its outstanding optical qualities fully match those of the 50mm and 90mm SUMMICRON lenses. Many photographers prefer this as their standard lens, perhaps partnered with the 90mm, f/2.8 ELMARIT-M, for a very compact and versatile outfit. A universal wide-angle lens for architecture, landscape, etc., giving a normal perspective. For pictorial work the soft transition from sharp definition to unsharpness gives enhanced relief to the subject whilst retaining modelling in the unsharp areas. Also available in satin chrome.

Characteristics

Its optical quality is equal in every way to that of the 50mm, f/2 SUMMICRON-M. It gives superb definition and contrast over the entire picture area. Stopping down one or two stops will remove the residual aberrations in the extreme corners of the image. Distortion is very low, even in the close-focusing range. Even at full aperture strong light sources in the picture area do not give unpleasant flare. The lens gives its peak overall performance at f/5.6 or f/8 when all these factors, including slight vignetting, are virtually removed. The lens mount is fitted with a lever for focusing.

Construction: 7 elements in 5 groups	Angle of view: 64°
Lens hood: separate, supplied with lens	Smallest aperture: f/16
Filters: E39	Closest focusing distance: 70cm, 28in
Weight: 150g	Smallest object area: 430 x 640mm, 17 x 25in
Length: 26mm	

50MM, F/1 NOCTILUX-M

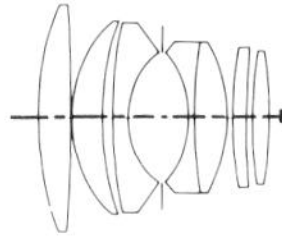

Applications

This is still the fastest standard lens in the world available for normal 35mm photography. It has been corrected to meet the demands of available-light photography, combined with high speed films. Its uses will be in reportage, photo-journalism, candid portraits, any interior or night shots where lighting conditions are very poor and high shutter speeds are demanded. It will secure pictures in the extremes of twilight that are denied with any other lens. It can reveal detail in pictures taken in very poor light that was not apparent to the eye. It is not a general purpose lens and results will not be so good as with a 50mm, f/2 SUMMICRON-M or a 50mm, f/1.4 Summilux-M if it is taken into the bright sunshine.

Characteristics

Designed to produce very high contrast at full aperture. Light sources appearing in the picture area are reproduced without distortion or secondary images and do not reduce the general image contrast. It is thus very good in artificial lighting when lights may appear in the picture. Performance is improved on stopping down. It is considerably bigger and heavier than the SUMMILUX.

Construction: 7 elements in 6 groups	Angle of view: 45°
Lens hood: separate, supplied with lens	Smallest aperture: f/16
Filters: E60	Closest focusing distance: 1m, 40in
Weight: 580g	Smallest object area: 410 x 620mm, 16 x 24.5in
Length: 62mm	

Standard Focal-Length Group

50MM, F/1.4 SUMMILUX-M

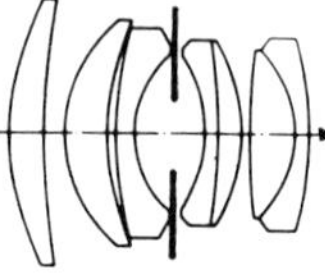

Applications

The high speed standard lens for the Leica M-system that can still be used as a general purpose lens, but its strength lies in available-light photography. It is ideal for reportage, sport, photo-journalism, and candid photography at close quarters in available light, and for all hand-held work in poor light, eg: in museums, galleries, theatres, etc., especially when slow colour film is being used. It can also be used for creative effects by exploiting the wide aperture to limit the depth of field.

Characteristics

Even at full aperture definition and contrast are outstanding. It shows very good neutral colour rendering and accurate colour differentiation. Powerful light sources in the picture area do not produce secondary images, which is a tribute to its lack of internal reflections; neither do they cause loss of detail in the background.

Construction: 7 elements in 5 groups
Lens hood: separate, supplied with lens
Filters: E43
Weight: 255g
Length: 46mm

Angle of view: 45°
Smallest aperture: f/16
Closest focusing distance: 1m, 40in
Smallest object area: 410 x 620mm, 16 x 24.5in

50MM, F/2 SUMMICRON-M

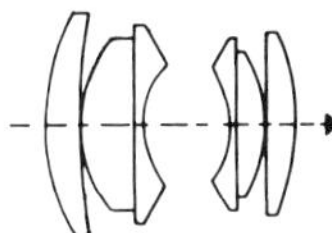

Applications

The universal standard lens for the LEICA M-system, it is small and light in weight. It combines a speed high enough for most purposes with an outstanding optical performance. It is excellent for all subject distances from infinity down to its shortest focusing distance. If you always carry a camera, but don't want to carry additional lenses, then this is the lens that will be most useful – it is also the cheapest lens in the LEICA M-system. It will suit all subjects from landscapes and architecture to animals and people, but avoid head-and-shoulder portraits because the near camera position will exaggerate features, such as the nose or an ear, which are closer to the lens than the rest of the features. Also available in satin chrome.

Characteristics

This lens set the world standard for a fast 50mm lens when first introduced. It has been redesigned several times since and still maintains that position. Even at maximum aperture the definition and optical correction are outstandingly good. Stopping down to f/2.8 or f/4 will enhance contrast and sharpness a little more. At all distances distortion is extremely low.

Construction: 6 elements in 4 groups	Angle of view: 45°
Lens hood: separate, supplied with lens	Smallest aperture: f/16
Filters: E39	Closest focusing distance: 70cm, 28in
Weight: 195g	Smallest object area: 277 x 416mm, 11 x 16.4in
Length: 42mm	

Moderate Long-Focus Group

75MM, F/1.4 SUMMILUX-M

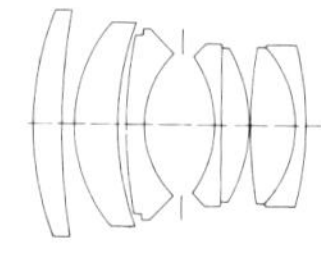

Applications

This short telephoto of very high speed is ideal for sport, theatre, portraiture, photo-journalism, and indeed any action photography in available light. The longer focal length over its 50mm namesake enables the photographer to "stand off" somewhat further and therefore be less obtrusive. The high speed offers two advantages: it permits faster shutter speeds, and the shallow depth of field effectively isolates the subject from the background. The perspective is closer to that of a 90mm lens than a 50mm. Paired with a 35mm Summilux it makes a compact high-speed outfit.

Characteristics

The focal length of 75mm, shorter than its R-counterpart, was chosen so as not to obstruct the viewfinder with the larger front element that would have been inevitable with a longer focal length. Its contrast transfer is excellent at all apertures and performance is improved slightly on stopping down to f/2. It is outstanding in its reproduction of point light sources in the picture area, with practically no sign of coma at full aperture and freedom from internal reflections. Like the R-lens it is noted for the way it reproduces graduated tonal values within the highlights and shadows. The lens performs best at fairly long range; for distances less than 1.5m (5ft) it should be stopped down to a medium aperture if maximum sharpness is important. Vignetting and distortion are virtually undetectable in practice.

Construction: 7 elements in 5 groups	Angle of view: 31°
Lens hood: built-in, extensible	Smallest aperture: f/16
Filters: E60	Closest focusing distance: 75cm, 29.5in
Weight: 625g	Smallest object area: 192 x 288mm, 8 x 11in
Length: 80mm	

90MM, F/2 SUMMICRON-M

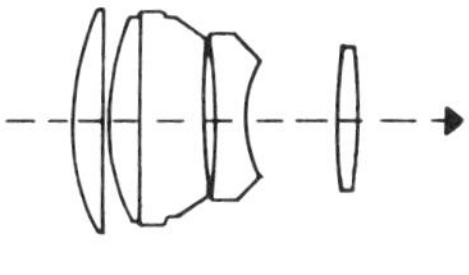

Applications

More compact and lighter in weight than its well-known earlier versions, this lens is a favourite of the photo-journalist. The combination of high speed and medium focal length makes it ideal for snapshots in available light and from a discrete distance, as with shots of children. Other applications include landscapes, architectural detail, and particularly portraits when the large aperture can be used to isolate a portrait head. Available also in satin chrome finish.

Characteristics

It has very high resolution and good contrast when focused at infinity. When focused closer than about 2.5m (8.5ft) the telephoto system results in a slight loss of contrast, which is of benefit in portraiture. For absolute maximum sharpness it should be stopped down to f/5.6 or f/8. At the shortest focusing distance there is a slight pin-cushion distortion. The contrast remains excellent under extreme conditions of backlighting, but if the light source appears in the picture area there may be slight flare at full aperture and at close range, which will be improved by stopping down to f/4.

Construction: 5 elements in 4 groups	Angle of view: 27°
Lens hood: built-in, extensible	Smallest aperture: f/16
Filters: E55	Closest focusing distance: 1m, 40in
Weight: 460g	Smallest object area: 220 x 330mm, 8.7 x 13in
Length: 77mm	

Moderate Long-Focus Group

90mm, f/2.8 ELMARIT-M

New lens 1989

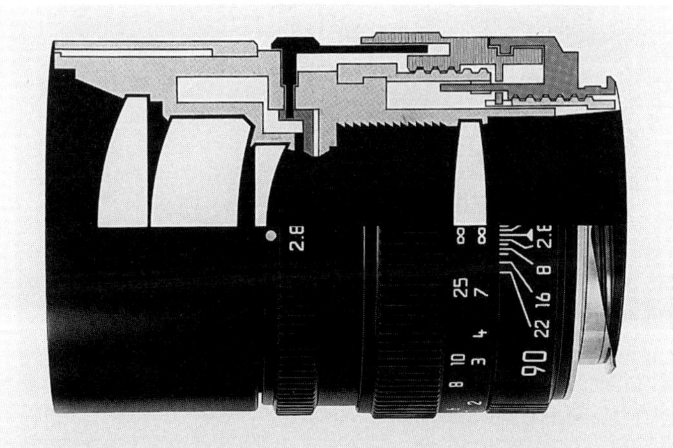

Applications

A light and compact medium lens. It is particularly suitable for selection of detail in broad landscapes, head-and-shoulder portraits and modest close-ups. It is ideal for the traveller; when partnered with the 35mm SUMMICRON it makes a very versatile and compact travelling outfit. It is the choice of the photographer who always carries a camera but prefers a longer lens than the standard for general use.

Characteristics

Optical performance at full aperture is excellent, right into the corners, with high contrast and resolution of fine detail, and flatness of field. It is practically free from vignetting and coma. Stopping down to f/4 produces an even slightly better performance. Performance is maintained into the close focusing range, less than 2m (6.5ft), the very slight vignetting being insignificant. The optical head is detachable.

Construction: 4 individual elements	Angle of view: 27°
Lens hood: built-in, extensible	Smallest aperture: f/22
Filters: E46	Closest focusing distance: 1m, 40in
Weight: 380g	Smallest object area: 220 x 330mm, 8.7 x 13in
Length: 72mm	

135MM, F/2.8 ELMARIT-M

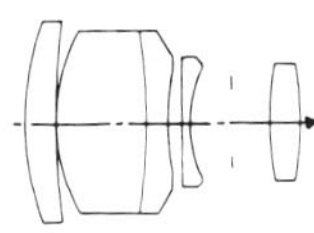

Applications

The lens for photo-journalism in available light: the viewfinder magnifier of 1.5x enlarges the image for easier framing and more accurate focusing. It is equally suitable for all other uses for a lens of this focal length, such as landscape detail, architectural detail, animals and children, and portraits. The large aperture provides more opportunity for limiting the depth of field for creative effects or emphasising the subject. It is somewhat bulky and heavy for the traveller.

Characteristics

A unique feature of this lens is the pair of magnifying oculars which enlarge the viewfinder and rangefinder images, and effectively the rangefinder base, to allow much faster framing and focusing, as well as greater accuracy in focusing – necessary because of the limited depth of field at full aperture. The lens exhibits good flatness of field and high resolution. Optimum performance is reached at f/4 to f/5.6. At the infinity setting the lens is practically free of coma and distortion is not evident. In the closer focusing range the best detail rendering is produced by stopping down to f/5.6 or f/8. It is optically identical to the 135mm, f/2.8 ELMARIT-R.

Construction: 5 elements in 4 groups	Angle of view: 18°
Lens hood: built-in, extensible	Smallest aperture: f/32
Filters: E55	Closest focusing distance: 1.5m, 5ft
Weight: 735g	Smallest object area: 220 x 330mm, 8.7 x 13in
Length: 114mm	

Long-Focus Group

135mm, f/4 TELE-ELMAR-M

Redesigned mount 1993

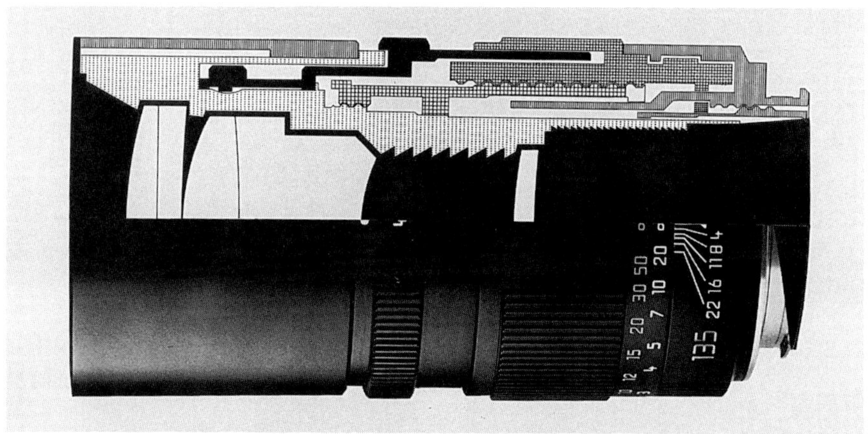

Applications

A very easy to handle, compact and handy lens of the longest focal length available for rangefinder focusing with the LEICA. It has similar applications to its 135mm, f/2.8 companion – landscapes, architectural detail, portraits, children and animals – except that it has only half the speed. However, it is much handier and lighter for the traveller and the rapid focusing movement makes it particularly suitable for sport. This 135mm lens is for the traveller, walker or mountaineer.

Characteristics

This lens is optically identical to the previous 135mm TELE-ELMAR but is in a modern mount more suited to the rapid action required by M6 users. Over its entire focusing range from infinity to 1.5m, the optical performance at full aperture is recognized as one of the best in the entire Leica system. The outstanding resolution and contrast at f/4 are improved only slightly by stopping down, particularly at close range. It is free of coma and light sources in the picture area cause no ghost images or reflections. Vignetting is minimal and distortion so slight it can be ignored.

Construction: 5 elements in 3 groups	Angle of view: 18°
Lens hood: built-in, extensible	Smallest aperture: f/22
Filters: E46	Closest focusing distance: 1.5m, 5ft
Weight: 550g	Smallest object area: 220 x 330mm, 8.7 x 13in
Length: 107mm	

Index of Current Lenses

Page numbers in italics refer to illustrations, tables and diagrams. Lens Directory entry is in ***bold.***

Leica M-Lenses

Leica R-Lenses

General Index

Page numbers in italics refer to illustrations, tables and diagrams.